STUDIES IN GERMAN LITERATURE,
LINGUISTICS, AND CULTURE

VOL. 21

STUDIES IN GERMAN LITERATURE, LINGUISTICS, AND CULTURE

CAMDEN HOUSE
Columbia, South Carolina

Three Viennese Comedies

Nestroy as Titus in *The Talisman*
(Österreichische Nationalbibliothek — Bildarchiv
und Porträtsammlung)

Three Viennese Comedies

by Johann Nepomuk Nestroy

Translated and with an
introduction by

Robert Harrison and Katharina Wilson

CAMDEN HOUSE

All photographs are used by the gracious permission of the
Österreichische Nationalbibliothek,
Bild-Archiv und Porträt-Sammlung

Printed on acid free Glatfelder paper.

Contents

Johann Nepomuk Nestroy
(Austrian National Library)

INTRODUCTION

ALTHOUGH KNOWLEDGEABLE CRITICS have included Nestroy in the august company of Aristophanes, Shakespeare and Molière, his comedies are well known only in Austria, and properly appreciated only in his native city of Vienna. As Martin Esslin has observed, he is "one of those great playwrights whose fame, it seems, is doomed to remain founded on mere hearsay."[1]

Some reasons for this neglect are suggested by the following account, written by a contemporary, of the meeting of Nestroy and the celebrated German tragedian, Friedrich Hebbel:

> Hebbel, who in spite of his ungainliness, loved to play the man of the world, approached the great comedian of the Leopoldstadt and greeted him as a colleague. Nestroy thanked him in his diffident manner. The two never entered into more serious dialogue, for Hebbel's compulsion to communicate fell to the ground before the shy and monosyllabic Nestroy. And indeed how could these fundamentally different natures have struck a common chord, which would have made it possible for them to share their thoughts? Even in external appearance they stood in amazing contrast to one another. Hebbel, an utterly Nordic type: blue-eyed, blonde, his complexion pale as birch bark, his forehead extraordinarily high; in his fashion elegantly dressed, but abrupt and awkward in his gestures; his speech, though always cogent in substance, stilted and pedantic in expression and turn of phrase. Nestroy, a gangling, clumsy-looking man, wore an old-fashioned long coat with a horse-collar and a sagging, flowered waistcoat with deep pockets in which he plunged his hands throughout the conversation; a loud necktie with a bold red thread running through it completed his *petit bourgeois* costume. His markedly ruddy face, deeply ingrained with the ravages of life and the stage; not a handsome feature, but an overall impression of canniness, and beneath fluttering black eyebrows blazed and scintillated a pair of cunning and audacious eyes. Language: the Viennese idiom, which in its effort to approach the written language fell doubly into dialect.[2]

The differences between the two men are both striking and illuminating. Hebbel was famous in large part because he was an artist of his own time. The Nineteenth Century in Austria (as elsewhere) was a time for tragedy, not because its events were any more tragic than those of any other century, but because it still held itself in high enough esteem to entertain the possibility of noble thought and gesture. Nestroy, whose genius was diabolically satirical, would have to await another century and a less exalted view of man.

Yet if Nestroy's pitiless lampooning of his fellow man was not considered suitably elevating for the culture-seekers who frequented the Burgtheater in downtown Vienna, it was just the ticket in the suburban houses where his "popular" comedies played to the ordinary people of the city. To modern playgoers much of his humor seems heavyhanded. And so it is, much in the way that the humor of Aristophanes and Shakespeare and Molière is often heavyhanded. This is hardly surprising: they were all professional playwrights, writing not to make a place in literary history but to make a living, and they knew that in order to do so they had to appeal to a wide range of tastes. "Lucky Shakespeare, Molière, Raimund and Nestroy," wrote Austrian playwright-critic Hans Weigel, "lucky Mozart and Verdi, that you did not know you were Shakespeare, Molière, Raimund, Nestroy, Mozart, and Verdi! The burden of this knowledge might have intimidated you and hindered you from becoming Shakespeare, Molière, Raimund, Nestroy, Mozart, and Verdi."[3]

Actually, it was thanks to the more obvious qualities of his comic genius that Nestroy was able to survive, and even flourish, in the troubled first half of the Nineteenth Century in Austria, in order that his nobler qualities might be discovered by literary critics half a century later. In fact, among his suburban audiences Nestroy was less known as a playwright than as a comic actor. All his plays were tailored to show off his great comedic talent, and during his lifetime no other actor ever played his parts. So closely were his roles associated with his own virtuoso performances that after his death in 1862 it was widely assumed that they—together with his plays—had died with him. And indeed there is little doubt that some of the humor did. Nestroy bore a marked resemblance to the late comedian Marty Feldman, and, according to contemporary accounts of his performances, was a master of innuendo and pantomime. This is how one journalist described him in action:

> On the stage he is from head to foot a living caricature.... He has an odd, unsurpassed talent for suggesting, with a single curl of the lip, a single wink of the eye, the heights of intellectual irony inherent in what would seem the most asinine line.... Suddenly through the agility of his gestures he stands triumphant over everyone and everything on the stage; in the mind's eye people, objects, relationships all lie tangled in confusion at his feet. Tumultuous applause brings him back out, his lanky figure bends double, he smiles—and even then one does not know: is Nestroy really thanking us, or is he satirizing our curtain calls and bravos?[4]

Despite his popularity as a performer, few persons regarded his work as having any intrinsic literary merit, least of all Nestroy himself.[5] The poetaster Leicht in the parody *Weder Lorbeerbaum noch Bettelstab* seems to speak for his creator when he says: "To write comic things and go for the laurel wreath with them, that's a mixture of stupidity and arrogance, that's like making a gingerbread man and claiming to be a rival of Canova."[6]

It was only when the crusading Viennese journalist and self-styled prophet Karl Kraus took up the cudgels for Nestroy that the literary world began to take notice of him. In 1912, on the fiftieth anniversary of Nestroy's death, Kraus rented the largest hall in Vienna and launched his one-man Nestroy appreciation campaign. Before a standing room only crowd he read his encomium of Nestroy, proclaiming him "the deepest satirical thinker the Germans have produced since Lichtenberg."[7] Thanks in large part to the tireless efforts of Kraus, and later the scholars Otto Rommel and Franz B. Mautner, Nestroy was rescued from the ash-heap of literature. His plays began to appear again, first in the suburban theaters where he had performed, then finally in the prestigious Burgtheater itself. Nestroy had finally arrived.

Since then his reputation has been slowly but steadily on the rise. In his lifetime only twelve of his eighty-three plays were published, and only two collections had appeared by the turn of the century. Six more editions saw the light of day prior to World War II; since then seventeen have come out. Nor has his triumph been merely literary. As a driving force behind the revival of the *Volkstheater*, Nestroy has become a national institution, and today there is in Vienna a company dedicated exclusively to the performance of his works.

This rise in Nestroy's stock is, as we have suggested, not altogether due to the efforts of scholars. The very attitudes that made Nestroy suspect in his own day have contributed largely to his success in recent years. Fans of writers such as Max Frisch, Bertold Brecht and Günter Grass, and of painters like Max Ernst and Magritte and Georg Gross, recognize in Nestroy a congenial spirit. His razor-edged wit, his ridicule of a pretentious, tradition-ridden society, his view of man shipwrecked on an indifferent planet—these are themes no longer regarded as dangerously subversive but fashionably modern. Typical of Nestroy's anachronistic cynicism is the attitude he takes toward the Nineteenth Century comedy's favorite *deus ex machina*: a sudden and unanticipated financial windfall. At the close of *Einen Jux will er sich machen*, Weinberl steps momentarily out of the action to criticize his creator with a scorn worthy of Ionesco: "Then it has happened again? My, the way uncles and aunts have to die, just so everything will turn out for the best!"[8]

His comedies are full of the gimmickry so dear to the *Volkstheater*—comic mixups, funny disguises, slapstick, clownish asides (often with sexual overtones), show-stopping comic songs, etc. Still, their essence is satire, brilliant verbal sallies that expose the individual as well as the collective follies of mankind. Most of the characters who people his plays are either rogues or fools (the two classes are not mutually exclusive), forever tricking others and being tricked themselves, but they are always funny, funny because the audience knew that in the end their schemes would be exposed and they would get their just deserts.[9]

In the roles Nestroy wrote for himself he usually played the disillusioned, clear-eyed cynic, whose function it was to puncture with deadly accuracy the imposters of the world, wherever they might be found. Behind this comic façade lurks a Steppenwolf view of mankind: "When two wolves meet by chance, neither is in the least concerned that the other is a wolf; but two men cannot meet in a forest without each thinking: he may be a robber."[10]

Nestroy attacks not only the usual targets of Nineteenth Century social satire—lazy, uppity servants, superstitious peasants, parvenus, social climbers, pompous bureaucrats—but especially the institutions most sacred to Austrian society. Marriage, for example.[11] "Is there a more convenient opportunity to make someone you hate miserable than to marry her?"[12] "Marriages are made in Heaven. —Right you are; and since they're made in Heaven, they call for otherworldly patience."[13] "Love is a dream; marriage a business deal."[14] Even so, he frequently bowed to the convention in his comedies for the sake of his audience, rationalizing through the barber Slippy in *The House of Humors*: "Better to nick others than oneself: better to help someone else get a wife than to take one oneself."[15]

At times his cynicism seemed to approach existential heights. "Men's lots are drawn from the urn of Fate—if I could only get my hands on the lad that drew mine!"[16] Most daring of all, however, was his attack on the holiest of all Austrian bourgeois institutions, *Gemütlichkeit*. Over and over again he laid siege to the smug, comfort-worshipping geniality of the Austrian middle class. While devastatingly accurate in his portrayals, he often went too far even for his easygoing audiences, and many of his finest satirical works were utter failures in their own day. Yet sharp as his wit was, it was never mean-spirited. Nestroy never poked fun at the physical or mental shortcomings of people, except when they were coupled with arrogance and pretension. He was a realist, not a misanthrope.

Nor was his wit all of a piece. His earliest works were *Zauberspiele* in the manner of Ferdinand Raimund (1790-1836). These played heavily on the Romantic susceptibility for fairy tales, while at the same time exploiting the Biedermeier fondness for simplicity and the common man, a trait that would persist throughout his works. (The closest modern equivalent of the *Zauberspiel* is the enduring children's classic, *The Wizard of Oz*.) Even so, the transcendent cynicism of the later Nestroy occasionally shows through the stardust; in one of his *Zauberspiele* King Fate, called upon for help by his nephew Stellaris, responds in the following manner:

FATE I know everything. (*Stepping forward, to himself.*) Actually I don't know anything at all, but I'm far too lazy to listen to this whole business. It's great to be Fate: one does nothing at all and in the end, whatever happens, everybody says it was the work of Fate.

STELLARIS (*to Fate*) Then we may hope?

FATE Sure, sure. Go ahead and hope!... (*Fate sits down again on his cloud and falls asleep.*)[17]

4

It was in his *Possen* (farces) however that Nestroy really hit his stride. His strength never lay in inventing plots (of his fifty major plays only two are not adapations from works by other authors), but in breathing life into characters and in manufacturing verbal fireworks. Nestroy was a master at "naturalizing" plays of foreign origin. Forever in search of good parts for himself and his dumpy sidekick Wenzel Scholz (the two were the Mutt and Jeff of the Viennese *Volkstheater*), he systematically plundered the literatures of Germany, France, and England, borrowing material from vaudeville comedies, farces, pantomimes, operas and operettas, even novels (*Die Anverwandten* is based in part on Dickens' *Martin Chuzzlewit*). It was never a question of plagiarism, however; all he wanted was the plotlines. His versions, generally far more lively than the originals from which he took them, all have a strong local flavor, and his characters are so thoroughly transformed that even theatergoers familiar with his sources often did not recognize them when they saw them in his plays, but took them for authentic Viennese originals. In addition to his many farces, he wrote numerous parodies of dramatic works he regarded as bombastic or fraudulently Romantic. Here his favorite targets were Hebbel, Wagner, Meyerbeer, and Karl von Holtei.

At first glance it might appear that Nestroy's wit knew no limits, but this is not quite true. Though some of his chosen victims were aristocrats, he never took on the *ancien régime* itself. In Nineteenth Century Austria that was something even a Nestroy did not do.

To understand the reason for his reticence, one must know a bit about the political situation at the time. When, after Waterloo, the exhausted and war-weary members of the Holy Alliance sat down at the Congress of Vienna, their principal goal was to restore peace and tranquility to Europe at all costs. To the absolutist Austrian emperor Franz I. and his powerful minister Metternich this meant "stability and legitimacy"—that is, the preservation of the status quo. Following the principle that repression ought to begin at home, Franz practised with an iron hand throughout his empire what Metternich preached at the conference table. The popular assemblies were allowed only *pro forma* sessions and given no power to enact laws; taxes were raised without consultation with representatives of the people; political dissidents were summarily arrested and tortured with Inquisitorial piety, in the hope thereby of purging them of their "criminal spirit of Enlightenment." Count Leopold Sedlnitzki's secret police were everywhere: his paid informers reported what was said at public gatherings and kept controversial public figures under constant surveillance. Letters abroad were intercepted and censored; schools were compelled to instruct only in accordance with state-approved guidelines; and all expression of opinion in print and on the stage was subjected to draconian censorship.

In his terror of the people Franz grew ever more repressive as the years went by, in the end surpassing even Metternich. In his will the aging emperor left his son Ferdinand these words to live by: "Rule, and change nothing." While the spiritless Ferdinand followed his father's advice, the social cauldron continued to simmer. Local assemblies throughout the empire grew openly truculent; nationalist movements began to spring up among the non-German minorities; the works of Heine stirred the souls of the intellectuals, while economic repression moved the masses to sporadic rioting. The year of the revolutions, 1848, was near at hand.

It was the policy of government censorship that best brought out the social critic in Nestroy. While working as an actor in Brünn in 1826, he had his first run-in with the authorities. Harassed by the police for making supposedly subversive comments on stage, he began to resort to pantomime. Faithfully mouthing the lines approved by the censor, he accompanied them with highly suggestive gestures, thereby not only restoring their original intent but actually heightening the effect. The reaction was immediate and predictable: the audience understood what he was up to, but so did the police. Unable to stop this form of improvisation (it is difficult to regulate the movements of an eyebrow), they forced the theater management to terminate his contract. The battle was on. When he returned to Vienna and went to work for Carl Karl at the Theater an der Wien, Nestroy made use of the Viennese dialect as a weapon in his ongoing war with the censor, masking his political and social comments with what Brecht has since called "slave language," in order that they might seem harmlessly "folksy" to the censor, while delivering their pungent message to the audience.[18]

Nestroy celebrated Austria's brief period of freedom from censorship (March-November 1848) with an open assault on the censor. The *raisonneur* in *Freiheit in Krähwinkel*, the journalist Ultra, describes this petty official as "a pencil made man or a man made pencil, an incarnate slash drawn across the creative spirit, a crocodile that lurks on the bank of the stream of ideas and bites off the heads of the *literati* swimming in it." And again, with a double-barreled indictment: "The censor is the younger of two vile sisters; the elder is called Inquisition. The censor is the living acknowledgement of the mighty that although they may be able to tread upon ignorant slaves, they are incapable of ruling a free people."[19]

In light of such comments it is tempting, though inaccurate, to regard Nestroy as a hero of the class struggle.[20] He was no utopian socialist; far from it. Nestroy's muse, like that of Molière, Swift and Voltaire, was quintessentially negative. With the exception of his understandable grudge against the censor, his attacks on society were selected with a view to establishing a rapport with his audience.

But the greatest obstacle to success Nestroy faced—and still faces—is that of language. In a century when much was made over the purity of the mother tongue,[21] one can imagine the reception given his heady brew of literary German and the Viennese dialect, heavily laced with puns, *double entendres*, portmanteau words, foreign phrases, mixed metaphors, neologisms, proverbs taken out of context, virtually unpronounceable tongue-twisters, etc.[22] As Weigel has pointed out, it is all but impossible to translate Nestroy even into German,[23] and even Austrian editions of his plays must gloss many neologisms, as well as expressions familiar only to natives of Vienna.

Yet paradoxically his popularity in modern times is largely owing to his linguistic virtuosity. Many of his one-liners have passed into the public domain as aphorisms. "I believe the worst of every man, even me, and I have seldom disappointed myself."[24] "Actuality is always the best proof of possibility."[25] "One can be forgiven for having acquired wealth, but never fame."[26]

In all Nestroy's comedies the language is tailored to the situation and the social milieu. He aped the elegantly blasé slang of the salon, the finishing school French of Austrian debutantes, the bureaucratic jargon of civil servants. Parvenus routinely attempt High German, while the punch lines of the comic are usually delivered in dialect. This last was of course another instance of Nestroy playing to his audience, and belies the fact that he was himself an educated man. The son of a well-to-do lawyer, he attended Vienna's finest secondary school, the Theresianum, then studied political science and law for several years at the University of Vienna before going on the stage. Now and then in his plays he betrays his academic background, punning in several languages and tossing out references to history, mythology, and classical literature,—but always to get a laugh, never to impress his audience with his learning.

The theater he worked in was hardly the place to parade one's academic credentials, anyway. The *Volkstheater,* whose fare consisted largely of melodramas and raw comedies, was the product of several traditional forms of popular entertainment, grafted onto Viennese folk literature. Although the Jesuit theater and the baroque court opera had some minor part in its genesis, its more immediate ancestor was the Italian *commedia dell'arte*.[27]

In some ways Nestroy's theater also bore a resemblance to the theater of Aristophanes, notably in its use of incidental music. Nestroy's plays were always "*mit Gesang*," and the songs—more than 200 of them—were much like those sung by the chorus of Old Comedy during its parabasis. The singer—more often than not Nestroy himself—would step momentarily out of the action of the play, sometimes even out of character, and address the spectators directly, with wry observations on human foibles, events of the day, even at times the ups and downs in the life of the playwright. Most of these songs had no fixed form, but were constructed in the flexible manner of the folk ballad, with a variable number of stanzas sharing a common punch line, a structure which made it possible for Nestroy to add topical comments at his pleasure. As one might expect, these were enormously popular with the *Volkstheater* audiences, and obviously also dear to Nestroy himself. As a young man he had had ambitions of becoming an opera star, and when he dropped out of school it was to embark on a career as a bass soloist with the Imperial Court Opera. His first theatrical success was in the role of Sarastro in *The Magic Flute,* and as late as 1831, at the age of thirty, he was still singing opera, appearing in Graz as Figaro in *The Barber of Seville.*

THE TALISMAN (1840)

This most popular of all Nestroy's *Possen* was lifted from Dupeuty and de Courey's *Bonaventure,* an indifferent French vaudeville comedy of 1806, whose only claim to fame lies in the fact that it was an early precursor of the operetta.

Here as elsewhere Nestroy displays his rare talent for turning the mediocre works of foreign authors into authentic Viennese masterpieces. In addition to substituting his own jokes and songs, adding new dialogue and scenes and characters (the three opening scenes which establish the milieu are his own, as is the role of the beer distributor Bung), he also created what many critics regard as the strongest role he ever played, that of the redheaded vagabond Titus Feuerfuchs.

Titus is the archetypal *eiron,* Nestroy's intellectualized version of the traditional Hanswurst.[28] The *Vorstadt* audience loved him because of his audacious, irreverent wit, his ability to get himself out of jams by quick thinking and rapid changes of disguise, and his knack for getting the better of his "betters." Titus is the perfect example of upward mobility, going literally from rags to riches in a single day.

For a long time after Nestroy's death *The Talisman* was all but forgotten. When it made its comeback in the Twentieth Century, it was no longer as a lighthearted farce but as a biting social satire. Nowadays it is seen as a brilliant attack on prejudice, though admittedly it is not easy for modern audiences to accept the fact that rural Austrians of the early Nineteenth Century looked on redheads as madcaps and potential arsonists. Seen in this light, Titus is no longer merely a wise-cracking, opportunistic, cracker-barrel philosopher and part-time misanthrope; he is the outsider, isolated from the other characters of the play not only by his appearance but by his trenchant wit, his self-awareness, his nonconformist mind, and his ability to see through deception and hypocrisy—even when they are his own.

Yet in spite of Titus' verbal and intellectual *bravura, The Talisman* never threatens to turn into a one-man show, as did many of Nestroy's lesser efforts. The situation is cleverly conceived and interesting in its own right, the other roles are good ones (even the small part played by the goose-girl Salome is a gem for an *ingénue*), and the theme stands firmly on its own two feet.

JUDITH AND HOLOFERNES (1849)

Judith and Holofernes is a parody of Hebbel's Apocryphal melodrama, *Judith* (1840), a typical example of the German school of rodomontade. Described at the time of its premiere in Vienna as "much attended and talked about," Hebbel's play is remembered today only by literary historians, while Nestroy's version is generally regarded as a masterpiece of its type.[29]

At the heart of Nestroy's parody lies the bombastic, overblown rhetoric of the *Übermensch* Holofernes, which lends itself readily enough to ridicule. Here is a sample:

HEBBEL

HOLOFERNES If only I had a foe, only one, who would dare stand against
me! I would want to kiss him, and when after a heated struggle I
had flung him into the dust, I would want to fall upon him, and die
with him.

NESTROY

HOLOFERNES I am the virgin among generals. I'd like to assault myself
some time, just to see who is stronger, I or myself.

Yet the parody is not limited solely to this Germanic *miles gloriosus*.
The play consists of two separate series of scenes, one laid in the camp
of Holofernes, the other in the beleaguered Jewish town of Bethulia. In
the latter the parody becomes good-natured horseplay, as Nestroy turns
the venial, self-centered Bethulians into caricatures of middle-class
Viennese Jews. But to read *Judith and Holofernes* as anti-semitic
propaganda is both inaccurate and anachronistic. It is the notion that any
group should regard itself as the chosen people, on whatever grounds,
that is Nestroy's target here. For the same reasons Wagner's *Tannhäuser*
and *Lohengrin* were later to meet a similar fate; pomposity of any sort
fairly cries out for a Nestroy. *Judith and Holofernes* is à devastating
satire on the brutality of the oppressor, but it is also a satire on the
cowardice of those who allow themselves to be oppressed. Holofernes,
the epitome of all the Metternichs and Hitlers of the world, is reduced
to a simple bully. Yet even bullies have their uses: it is Holofernes who
exposes the pious frauds of the Assyrian priests, and points out upon
what Nebuchadnezzar's claim to divinity is based. And when Holofernes
beheads his courtiers both for agreeing and disagreeing with him and
fills his tent with headless sycophants, it is difficult to fault him.

Yet when all the macabre humor is done, Nestroy provides the
customary happy ending to this gory tale. Joab, a young Jewish boy
disguised as his beautiful sister Judith (Nestroy), vamps Holofernes
(Scholz) and frees his besieged city. Actually Nestroy had little choice in
this matter—the censor would hardly have approved a comic treatment of
Hebbel's sanguinary conclusion, with its morbid sexual overtones—hence
the substitution of Joab for Judith, and a *papier-maché* head of
Holofernes for the genuine article.

The best way to appreciate Nestroy's skill as a parodist is to observe
him at work. In the following passage Judith describes to Holofernes the
strange events of her wedding night with her late husband Manasses:

HEBBEL

JUDITH Three lamps were burning, he wanted to put them out. "Stay,
stay," I pleaded with him. "Little fool!" said he, and tried to seize
me—whereupon one of the lamps went out. We scarcely noticed it;
he kissed me—and the second went out. He shuddered, as did I, then

laughed and said: "I shall extinguish the third myself." "Quickly, quickly," said I, for I felt a chill run through me; and he did so. The moon shone brightly in the chamber; I crept into bed, and it shone full on my face. Manasses called out: "I can see you as clearly as if it were day," and approached me. Suddenly he froze in his tracks; it was as if the black earth had reached out a hand from below and seized him. I was uneasy; "Come, come!" I cried, and felt no shame at doing so. "I cannot," he replied in a hoarse, toneless voice. "I cannot!" he repeated, and stared in horror at me with bulging eyes, then flung himself to the window and said at least ten times, "I cannot!" He seemed not to be looking at me, but at some strange, loathsome thing.... I began to sob uncontrollably, I felt myself defiled, I hated and loathed myself. He spoke tender words to me, I stretched my arms out to him, but instead of drawing near he began to pray softly....

NESTROY

JUDITH (JOAB) The chamber was lit by the tallowy light
        Of three candles—he hugged me and put out the first;
        My heart pounded so that I feared it would burst;
        Then he gave me a kiss and—what could I do?
        At that moment he snuffed out the second one too.
        My maidenly protests and pleas went unheard;
        He gave a big puff and like out went the third.
        ...
        Now cavorting around and as gay as a lark,
        He said, "Judith, I can see you still, there in the dark."
        Nu, of course he could see me, the moon was so bright,
        It came in at the window and made the room light.
        Unresisting, I let myself sink in a chair;
        Whereupon he sprang back and stood fixedly there,
            Without moving—I trembled—
            So much he resembled
            A man that an evil dybbuk
            Has bound by his feet to a rock.
        What's he up to? What is this, I wonder.
        Still he stood there, as though struck by thunder.
        "Would you scare me? Stop kidding," I cried.
        "Bad Manasses, come here to your bride."
        ...
        With the look of a sheep he stood fixed to the spot
        And repeated ten times in one breath, "I cannot!"
        ...
        Wringing my hands and beginning to weep,
        I suddenly fell—

HOLOFERNES   In his arms!

JUDITH (JOAB)   No, asleep.

THE HOUSE OF HUMORS (1837)

The House of Humors (Das Haus der Temperamente) presents a cross-
section of Biedermeier society as seen through the analysis of the four
traditional personality types, and owes much of its effectiveness to its
experimental *mis-en-scène*. The stage is divided into four apartments,
wherein reside four widowers: the choleric Mr. Boyle, the phlegmatic
Mr. Yawn, the melancholy Mr. Dole, and the sanguine Mr. Blythe.[30]
Each has a son and a daughter of the same humor. Contrary to the
wishes of the father, each daughter is in love with the son of the parent
of the opposite humor (i.e., choleric/phlegmatic, melancholy/ sanguine)
and refuses to marry the man of her father's choice. After many alarms
and excursions, deceptions and intrigues, misunderstandings and
character clashes, the situation is ultimately resolved in the approved
manner of light comedy by revelation, reconciliation, and a quadruple-
ring ceremony.

As the plot develops, the play's didactic purpose soon becomes
evident. Though physically separated, each household experiences, more
or less simultaneously, the identical sequence of events. The result is a
kind of thematic counterpoint that superficially resembles the form of a
fugue. (The adaptation of counterpoint for dramatic purposes seems to
have fascinated Nestroy, for he attempted it in a number of his plays.)
Contrapuntal devices are evident not only in the minor details of action
and the echo-effect produced by the rapid alternation of dialogue from
household to household, but are also imposed on the larger structure of
the play as well. The first act, for instance, consists of twenty-eight
scenes grouped about three main themes to form a complex pattern of
balance, contrast, repetition and variation. Then the themes themselves
are varied, the new sets of variations played off against one another, etc.

This highly stylized structure, coupled with an utterly unremarkable
dramatic situation, would appear to have had little chance of succeeding
on stage. As every detail is repeated, *mutatis mutandis,* in each of the
four households, the characters become little more than marionettes of
Nestroy's contrivance, and the contrapuntal machinery threatens to crush
the life out of the play. And in fact, despite the play's enthusiastic
critical reception, it was not one of Nestroy's greater successes.

That it was not an abject failure is in large part due to the fact that
even while indulging his innovative fancy, Nestroy did not entirely lose
sight of the fact that he was playing to a *Vorstadt* audience. When the
action threatens to become bogged down in the interplay of the four
humors, two quintessentially comic characters, the barber Slippy
(Nestroy) and the clothes cleaner Hutzibutz (Scholz), come on the scene
with their usual repertoire of slapstick, deception, wise-cracks, songs,
etc., and save the day.

1. "Nestroy—Between Hanswurst and Horvath," *Theatre*, XII, 2 (Spring 1981), 62.

2. Ludwig Speidel, "Johann Nestroy," in *Kritische Schriften* (Zurich, 1963), 100f.

3. "Johann Nestroy," *Der Monat*, VII, 39 (December 1951), 303.

4. A. Silberstein, *Österreichische Zeitung*, 46 (1861).

5. A notable exception, Friedrich Schwarzenberg, proclaimed Nestroy a true poet of the people and prophesied that the future would grant him a place of honor among the great dramatists of Germany. More typical of the time was the judgment of Hebbel, who called him "der Genius der Gemeinheit," "The Spirit of Commonness." (*Viennese Letters*, March 1861. In *Werke*, ed. R. W. Werner, Pt. II, 2, 224.)

6. I, 12.

7. "Nestroy und die Nachwelt: zum 50. Todestage," *Die Fackel*, XIV, 349 (May 1912), 1-23. In *Untergang der Welt durch schwarze Magie*, Vienna-Leipzig, 1922, 240-262. Kraus's promotion of Nestroy was not quite so highminded as the above phrase might suggest. Himself an ardent iconoclast, Kraus was always ready to use other authors to gore his favorite oxen. Here is another passage from the same *Festschrift:* "We shall not deny credence to his message because it was in rime ... nor because he wrapped his dynamite in cotton wool and blew up his world only after bringing it around to the conviction that it was the best of worlds, nor because he soaped it up with Gemütlichkeit when it was time to cut off heads, and otherwise didn't want to cause any fuss." (P. 5.)

8. IV, 10.

9. This aspect of his work is well illustrated by a remark in his diary which he later used in *Frühere Verhältnisse:* "Deception is the slender but strong chain that runs through all members of society—to deceive or to be deceived, that is the choice, and whoever believes there is a third deceives himself." "Aus dem literarischen Nachlaß," *Gesammelte Werke*, ed. Otto Rommel (Vienna, 1962), VI, 561, No. 12.

10. Edelschein in *Die Anverwandten*, I, 6.

11. Nestroy's jaundiced view of matrimony was no doubt founded on his own unhappy experience. He married young, divorced his wife when he caught her with another man, and spent the remainder of his life in a series of desultory liaisons with one woman after another, while living with the singer Marie Weiler, whom he, being a Catholic, could not marry.

12. Dickkopf in *Heimliches Geld, Heimliche Liebe*, I, 30.

13. Weinberl in *Einen Jux will er sich machen*, II, 7.

14. "Nachlaß," *op. cit.*, 575, No. 227.

15. I, 5.

16. Rot in *Müller, Kohlenbrenner und Sesselträger*, I, 3.

17. *Die Familien Zwirn, Knieriem und Leim*, I, 5.

18. Cf. Joel Schechter and Jack Zipes, "Slave Language Comes to Krähwinkel: Notes on Nestroy's Political Satire," *Theatre*, XII, 2 (Spring 1981), 72-75.

19. I, 14.

20. Marxist critics have in fact done so. An East German edition of his plays (Paul Reimann, ed., Leipzig, 1962) took this position, which is difficult to justify in light of textual evidence. See, for example: "Oh, when liberty becomes Communism, no—/Then it ceases to be fun" (Heugeig'n in *Lady und Schneider*, II, 17), "The masses are a giant in the cradle who awakens, stands up, staggers about, tramples everything, and in the end falls back down in a worse place even than the cradle" (*Ibid.*, I, 8), "It is a triumph for the slave who cannot pull himself up to his lord to pull his lord down to him" ("Nachlaß," *op. cit.*, 569, No. 142), "The main thing about Progress is that it always looks much better than it really is" (Gottlieb in *Der Schützing*, IV, 10).

21. Mallarmé was not alone in wishing to give "*un sens plus pur aux mots de la tribu.*" There were movements dedicated to this purpose all over Europe. It is hardly surprising that Nestroy should have come under critical fire at a time when even the word for nose (*Nase*) was in disrepute because of its French origin (the approved "echtdeutsch" replacement was *Gesichtsecke*—bay-window-of-the-face!).

22. Cf. Schechter and Zipes, *op. cit.*

23. *Flucht vor der Größe* (Vienna, 1960), 76.

24. Strick in *Die beiden Nachtwandler*, I, 16.

25. Titus in *Der Talisman*, III, 18.

26. "Nachlaß," *op. cit.*, 578, No. 8.

27. The Kärtnertortheater, established by Joseph Anton Stranitzky, was Vienna's first *Volkstheater*. Stranitzky (1676-1726) won fame as the creator of Hanswurst, an Austrian version of the *commedia* clown Arlecchino. While both were outsiders (i.e., rustics from the provinces), Nestroy's version of this character is ordinarily an outsider intellectually rather than physically.

28. At every turn Titus betrays his *Volkstheater* heritage. In the sexual innuendo at the end, for instance. In the Stranitzky comedies Hanswurst winds up getting married and making coyly suggestive remarks about soon hearing the patter of little footsteps about the house, etc. While closely adhering to the tradition, Nestroy turns it to good use as a means of restating his central theme in unequivocal terms and identifying the source of the evil.

29. On 12 January 1849 Hebbel wrote in his diary: "I love a good *Posse*. Just as a living fly is assuredly worth more than a dead eagle baked of marzipane or carved from wood, it assuredly ranks above a mediocre tragedy, and a connoisseur of the arts is sure to prefer a single first-rate Nestroy joke to a million commonplace iambics, no matter how exalted they may be, which only seek vainly to conceal the windy, trivial mind of a so-called poet." (*Werke*, Pt. II, 3, 261.) One wonders if Hebbel felt so charitably toward Nestroy two months later, when *Judith and Holofernes* opened at the Carls Theater.

30. Nestroy borrowed this stage arrangement from *Jonathan Bradford*, an 1833 melodrama by the Englishman Edward Fitzball. The use to which he put it, however, was entirely his own invention.

The Talisman

Farce with Song in Three Acts

DRAMATIS PERSONÆ

TITUS[1] FOXFIRE an unemployed journeyman barber

LADY CYPRESSBURG a widow

EMMA her daughter

CONSTANCE her lady's maid, also a widow

FLORA PRUNINGSHEARS head gardener, also a widow

PUMPKINSEED assistant gardener

M. MARQUIS hairdresser

BUNG beer-seller

CHRISTOPH ⎫
HANS ⎬ country boys
SEPPEL ⎭

HANNA a country girl

A GARDENER ⎫
GEORGE ⎬ servants of Lady Cypressburg
CONRAD ⎭

MR. FLATT

NOTARY FALK

SALOME GOBBLER goose-girl

GENTLEMEN, LADIES, COUNTRY BOYS, COUNTRY GIRLS, SERVANTS, GARDENERS

The action takes place on the estate of Lady Cypressburg, near a large city.

ACT I

The scene is a village square. Upstage center, a well flanked by two stone benches; to the left, a garden wall with a little gate standing ajar which opens into the manor garden.

Scene 1

COUNTRY GIRLS, *among them* HANNA, *enter from upstage left during the ritournelle of the following chorus.* COUNTRY BOYS, *among them* CHRISTOPH, SEPPEL *and* HANS.

CHORUS

GIRLS The dancing starts early on the day of church-fair,
Now here come the boys who'll be taking us there.

BOYS (*entering stage right*)
What's keeping them? No one's in sight, that's just grand!
On the dance floor they've already struck up the band.

GIRLS We *are* ready, though.

BOYS It's about time; let's go!

ALL Let's each choose a partner, it's easily done;
The music is playing, today there'll be fun!

CHRISTOPH (*to a* COUNTRY GIRL) We two will dance together!

HANS (*to another*) The two of us have been partners at ten church-fairs now.

HANNA (*to a* BOY) I'll dance with no one in the world but you.

CHRISTOPH (*looking upstage left*) Look! Here comes Salome.

HANNA With the bass-fiddle-colored hair![2]

CHRISTOPH What does *she* want at the church-fair?

HANNA To set your hearts on fire, that's what!

Scene 2

SALOME (*In poor country clothing, with red hair, enters downstage left.*) There's a lot of fun going on here; has the dance already started?

CHRISTOPH (*coolly*) Possibly.

SALOME You won't mind if I come along?

HANS Well—why not? Anybody can come.

CHRISTOPH (*with reference to her hair*) But think of the fire hazard!

HANS (*likewise*) The constable will be there—

CHRISTOPH (*as before*) And he has grave suspicions about you. You drove your geese by a barn, and the day before yesterday it burned down.

HANNA And it is believed you set it on fire with your hair-do.

SALOME That's really mean, the way you always pick on me. But of course I'm the only girl in the village with hair like this. You won't admit I'm the prettiest, so you'll have me the ugliest.

GIRLS Ah, that's priceless! She think's she's pretty!

CHRISTOPH (*to* SALOME) Look to it that you find a partner.

SEPPEL (*a very ugly boy*) I'll dance with you; what have I got to lose?

CHRISTOPH What's gotten into you? A fellow like you surely can find another partner.

SEPPEL That's true. I mustn't throw myself away.

HANS Onwards! No more dawdling around!

ALL To the dance floor! Hurrah! To the dance!

(ALL *exit upstage right.*)

Scene 3

SALOME Well, I'm left behind again. And why? Because I am the red-headed Salome. And yet red is certainly a pretty color—the prettiest flowers are roses, and roses are red. The prettiest thing in nature is the morning, and it announces itself with the most brilliant red.

Clouds are of course not a very pretty invention, and yet even the clouds are pretty when they stand there fiery red in the evening sun. That's why I say whoever has anything against the color red, doesn't know what pretty is. But what good does that do me? I don't have anyone to take me to the church-fair!—I could go there alone, but the girls would make fun of me, laugh and gaggle. I'll go back to my geese. They don't gaggle out of meanness when they see me, and when I bring them feed, they look at my hands and not at my head.

(*Exits downstage right.*)

Scene 4

FLORA *and* PUMPKINSEED *enter upstage left.* PUMPKINSEED *carries a heavily laden bag.*

FLORA (*annoyed*) Now this is really maddening! An hour and a quarter to come the little way out from the city. That post-chaise ought to be ashamed of itself.

PUMPKINSEED How so? That's why it's called a post-chaise, because it never leaves the post.

FLORA It's a pity, slow as you are, that you didn't become a post-chaise.

PUMPKINSEED I'm not clever enough for that. A post-chaise is the cleverest thing in the world, because it lets everyone sit, regardless of standing.

FLORA I believe you're having one of your witty days; you are even more unbearable than usual.

PUMPKINSEED Stop fussing, don't take your spite out on me. It won't be much longer.

FLORA Perhaps you want to leave her ladyship's service? That would be clever.

PUMPKINSEED Oh no, you're sure to marry soon; then a new field will be open for your nagging and I'll no longer be the playground for your spleen.

FLORA Stupid creature! I'll never marry again, but remain true to my dear departed.

PUMPKINSEED Maybe he believes that, now that he is dead; when he was alive he never did.

19

FLORA If I were her ladyship, I would have run you off long ago.

PUMPKINSEED (*pointedly*) If *I* were her ladyship, I'd have made some changes around the place too.

FLORA Who knows, you may be about to be sacked! I've been given permission to take on a bright, able young fellow.

PUMPKINSEED That's fine, then the work won't be quite so hard. I'll water the radishes, that's all the influence I need.

FLORA Now go to Uncle Polz; he's to recommend a man for me.

PUMPKINSEED Good. Perhaps some day your man will become your master.

FLORA Not on your life! I'll leave them all holding the bag.

PUMPKINSEED Unfortunately I feel you're right. But now you'll have to take it back if I'm to go see Uncle. (*Hands her the bag.*)

FLORA Look lively now, you lazybones! (*Exits through garden gate.*)

PUMPKINSEED (*alone*) H'm, h'm! The garden isn't all that run down, yet how she carries on about getting a bright, able gardener—h'm, h'm. (*Exits right.*)

Scene 5

TITUS FOXFIRE *enters in a fury downstage right during the ritournelle of the following song.*

1

He wasn't looking, the clown;
I almost knocked him down.
Yet even so, I swear
He was making fun of my hair!
Whose business is that, anyway?
I hope at least that I may
Be permitted to have my own hair.
It's more than a body can bear!
Should red hair be a sign of a nature untrue?
Judging one by one's hair, what a dumb thing to do!
There are plenty of rounders with raven-black locks,
And whoever believes them will go on the rocks.
And many a blond lad is languid and mute
All day long—why? All night he's been out on a toot.

And those wise-looking gents with their hair of steel gray,
Why, they're often more hairbrained than young folks today.
   Yet they all have to go by the hair,
   Then afterwards catch it for fair.

2

(looking menacingly in the direction from which he has come)

   I shall never forget it—
   He'll live to regret it!
He'll be in for a hard time, I swear,
When he finds he's got *me* in his hair!
   He'll lose his forelock
   When I run amok
And yank it all out by the root;
Then he'll go around bald as a coot.
They say red-headed girls lead men on, and it's true,
But how silly! That's something all shades of girls do.
Brunettes, it is said, are hot-blooded, I know,
And enticing, yet some are as dull as a froe.
Blondes are cuddly, you say? Oh, a blonde's a delight!
Yet I know of a blonde who will nag day and night.
But the gray-headed ones will be true, you suggest?
No, they give themselves rinses and no one else rest.—
   Yet they always must go by the hair,
   Then afterwards catch it for fair.

So wrongheadedly the world judges heads, and even if one were to
stand on his, it would do no good. Prejudice is a brick wall, and
those that run against it rebound with bloodied heads. I have taken
the wide world for my home, and the wide world is much closer
than you think. From the thorn bush of bitter experience I have
carved myself a walking stick; I've put on my Seven League Boots,
waved my traveling cap quietly, and with one step I've entered the
wide world. "Enjoy and understand seldom go hand in hand." What
I'd like now is to come across a really stupid fellow; I'd look on that
as a good omen.

Scene 6

PUMPKINSEED Another wasted trip!— *(catching sight of* TITUS*)* But ho! A
stranger takes shape before my eyes!

TITUS *(to himself)* Fortune, I think you were listening.

PUMPKINSEED *(sizing up* TITUS*)* According to the description Mister Polz
gave me, this could be the very man he was expecting. Big frame,

21

big mouth, very big eyes, ears in proportion—but that hair!— (*to* TITUS) It the gentleman seeking his daily bread?

TITUS I'm seeking money; I'll figure out how to get the bread afterwards.

PUMPKINSEED (*to himself*) He seeks money—and so suspicious looking— (*aloud*) Are you perhaps a treasure-seeker then?

TITUS If the gentleman will show me where one is buried, I'll take lessons from a mole.

PUMPKINSEED Or a robber?

TITUS Not up to now, my talent is still in a developmental phase.

PUMPKINSEED Do you know anything about gardening?

TITUS I am qualified in all things.

PUMPKINSEED (*to himself*) He's the one! (*to* TITUS) Then you'd like to become our pretty young gardener-widow's helper?

TITUS A widow's helper?—As I said, I'm qualified in all things.

PUMPKINSEED She'd be helped by such a helper too—but she'd run me off if I brought her a Florian-noodle.[3]

TITUS (*furiously*) Sir, that remark outrages me to the depth of my being.

PUMPKINSEED Then I suppose you'll be moving on, carrot-top? (*Exits disdainfully through the garden gate.*)

Scene 7

TITUS *alone, looking after* PUMPKINSEED *in silent fury.*

TITUS I am disarmed! The man is so decisive in his rudeness that it leaves one at a loss for words. People certainly are friendly, one might even say neighborly, when they meet me! But within me too misanthropy is already taking form—yes—I hate you, inhuman humanity, I'd like to flee you; let the wilderness receive me, give me complete solitude. Whoa there, bold spirit; such resolutions are appropriate to a full stomach; a hungry man can not carry them out. No, humanity, you won't lose me. Appetite is the tender bond linking me to what reminds me three or four times a day that I cannot get along without society. (*looking to the right*) Here comes an individual driving other individuals into a pen. Geese they are—geese!—Oh goose-girl, why don't you drive these geese before you roasted, I'd like to expropriate one.

Scene 8

SALOME, *not observing* TITUS, *enters from the right with a half loaf of bread and a knife in her hands.*

SALOME I need a drink of water; something's pressing on my stomach. (*Goes to the well and drinks.*)

TITUS (*to himself*) Oh, if only I could share that blessed feeling!

SALOME (*catching sight of him, to herself*) A young stranger—and such beautiful hair, just like mine!

TITUS (*to himself*) Wonder if *she's* going to say "carrot-top?" (*aloud*) Hail, elective affinity![4]

SALOME Your most obedient servant, fine sir!

TITUS (*half to himself*) She thinks me fine; she's the first of all—

SALOME Oh stop it, I'm the last of all here in the village; I'm only the goose-girl, the poor Salome.

TITUS Poor? I feel sorry for you, devoted governess of young geese! Your colleagues in the city are much better off, and yet they frequently spend years giving their charges only an imperfect upbringing. You, on the other hand, turn yours over to mankind every Martinmas[5] well crammed for their fine career.

SALOME I don't understand you, but you talk so nicely—who is your father?

TITUS He is at present a deceased schoolmaster.

SALOME That's nice. And your mother?

TITUS Was before her death the long-time connubial consort of her lawfully-wedded spouse.

SALOME Ah, that's nice!

TITUS (*to himself*) She finds everything nice, no matter what kind of nonsense I talk.

SALOME And may one know your name—at least your given name?

TITUS I'm called Titus.

SALOME That's a nice name.

TITUS One fitting only for a man with a head on his shoulders.

SALOME But what an odd name it is!

TITUS Yes, and I hear it will soon be extinct altogether. Parents all fear they will be embarrassed in the future if they let their children be baptised Titus.

SALOME And have you no living relatives?

TITUS Oh yes! Aside from the aforementioned deceased there are definite traces on my family tree of a cousin—but he does nothing for me.

SALOME Perhaps he has nothing.

TITUS Don't be silly, child, he is a beer-distributor, they all have means. They're industrious fellows; not only do they turn beer into silver, they gild their own accounts as well.

SALOME Did you perhaps do something to him to make him dislike you?

TITUS Very much. I touched him on his tenderest spot. The eye is a person's most sensitive part, and I offend his eye every time he looks at me, for he can't abide red hair.

SALOME The horrid thing!

TITUS He concludes from my hair that I have a false, malicious character, and in light of this conclusion has closed his heart, and his bank account, to me.

SALOME That's hateful.

TITUS More stupid than hateful. Nature gives us here a gentle hint. If we take a look at the animal kingdom, we find that cattle hate the color red, and among them bulls manifest the most violent antipathy—in which gross defect man also indulges, in seeing red when he sees red!

SALOME Oh, how cleverly you speak! One would never guess it to look at you.

TITUS Flatterer! Let me tell you a bit more about my destiny. Rejection by my cousin was not the only bitter pill I had to swallow. I sought happiness also in the sanctuary of Love, but the Graces declared me in poor taste. I looked in at the Temple of Friendship, but my friends were all so clever, witticisms rained about my head until I retired permanently from that field as well. Without money, without love, without friendship, my situation became intolerable; therefore I cast off all human relationships, as one casts off a quilted jacket in hot weather, and here I stand before you in the shirtsleeves of liberty.

SALOME And are you happy now?

TITUS If only I had a mantle of provisions to protect me from the storm of famine...

SALOME Oh, then it's a question of bread? Well, if you're looking for work, that's easily solved. My brother is apprenticed to the baker here; he has a big business and is in need of a helper.

TITUS What? I become a flunky? I who have been a journeyman barber?

SALOME A barber? We had one of those here, but he came to a bad end.

TITUS How so?

SALOME Because he was barbarous, the judge said.

TITUS Oh, that cannot be. But to get back to your brother— (*pointing to the loaf of bread that* SALOME *carries*) did he create this bread?

SALOME Well, he was there when the loaf — as apprentice, of course—

TITUS I'd like to see how far your brother has progressed in his breadological studies.

SALOME Here, taste it! But it won't agree with you. (*She cuts off a very small slice of bread and gives it to him.*)

TITUS (*eating*) H'm — it is—

SALOME My geese like it, of course; animals have no sense.

TITUS (*to himself*) Oh, that smarts; I like it too.

SALOME Well, what do you say? It's awful, isn't it?

TITUS H'm. I don't want to condemn your brother prematurely; to judge a work, one must delve into it deeply. (*Takes the loaf of bread and cuts off a very large piece.*) I will give the matter careful con-

25

sideration and notify you of my findings in due time. (*Puts the piece of bread in his pocket.*)

SALOME So you'll be staying with us for a while? That's good; one must set aside pride when one has nothing. And you'll do just fine if the baker takes you on.

TITUS All my hopes rest on the patronage of his apprentice.

SALOME Everything will be all right. (*looking upstage left, horrified*) Look! Look there!

TITUS (*looking*) The carriage?—The horse is running straight for the water—the devil, all is lost! (*Exits, running, upstage left.*)

Scene 9

SALOME He's not going to—? He's running that way—oh don't let anything happen to him—he's grabbing the horse—it's pulling him down! (*screaming*) Ah! The horse has stopped—he stopped it—what a daredevil! A gentleman is getting out of the carriage—he's coming this way with him. I must tell the baker right away! When he hears about this, he's sure to hire him. (*Exits right.*)

Scene 10

MARQUIS Ah! I'm still trembling in every limb!

TITUS Would it please your honor to sit down for a little while?

MARQUIS (*Sits down on a bench.*) That damned jade, in all its life it has never run away!

TITUS Would it please your honor perhaps to have a sprain?

MARQUIS No, my friend.

TITUS Or perhaps to have broken an arm?

MARQUIS No, thank God!

TITUS Or, if your honor pleases, to have suffered a little skull fracture?

MARQUIS Not in the least. I am completely recovered now, and nothing remains but, as proof of my gratitude—

TITUS Oh, I beg of you—!

MARQUIS Three young men who know me were standing right there, screaming at the top of their voices, "Monsieur Marquis, Monsieur Marquis: the carriage is going into the water!"

TITUS What? I have saved a marquis? That's really something!

MARQUIS (*continuing his discourse*) But not one of them lifted a hand to help me! Then you flew to my rescue—

TITUS An ordinary humanitarian duty.

MARQUIS And just in the nick of time—

TITUS An extraordinary coincidence.

MARQUIS (*rising*) Your nobility of character places me in an awkward position. I don't know how to express my gratitude. One cannot reward such a deed with mere money.

TITUS Well, I must say, money is a thing that—

MARQUIS Can only insult a man of such high principle.

TITUS Well, you see—that is—

MARQUIS And it would only cheapen the value of your deed if one were to try to measure it in terms of money.

TITUS Well, that depends—

MARQUIS On *who* performs such a deed. Exactly! There was once a man—I don't know his name—who saved another's life—a prince it was—I don't know his name either. Anyway, he wanted to reward him with diamonds, but the rescuer replied: "Virtue is its own reward." I am certain you think no less nobly than what's-his-name.

TITUS And yet there are circumstances in which nobility of character—

MARQUIS Is offended by too many words, you say? Quite right. Words are inadequate to express true gratitude; therefore, nothing more will be said about the affair.

TITUS (*to himself*) The marquis has delicate sensibilities—if he were a scoundrel, I'd have come off just the same.

MARQUIS (*looking intently at* TITUS' *hair*) But friend, I notice something here—h'm, h'm—that could prove a liability to you in many ways.

27

TITUS It seems to me your honor takes exception to my head—it's the only one I have, I can buy no other for myself.

MARQUIS Perhaps you can—I will—you must accept a small token of my—wait just a moment! (*Exits running upstage left.*)

Scene 11

TITUS (*alone*) He came within an ace of saying "carrot-top" out of pure gratitude. What a fine marquis!—But what's he doing? (*looking offstage*) He's running to the carriage—he's looking for something—"a token," he said—maybe he'll give me an expensive present after all! What's that? He has taken out a hatbox—he's running this way with it. He's not going to reward me for saving his young life by giving me an old hat?

Scene 12

MARQUIS (*with a hat box*) So, friend, take this, you will need it! A pleasing exterior can do much—almost anything—it won't let you down. Here is a talisman (*giving him the box*); I shall rejoice if I become the author of your good fortune. Adieu, friend! Adieu! (*Exits hurriedly downstage left.*)

Scene 13

TITUS (*alone, holding the box in some bewilderment*) Author of my good fortune?—Talisman?—I wonder what's in it? (*Opens the box and takes out a black wig.*) A wig!—Nothing but a coal-black wig! I think he was making fun of me! (*calling after him*) Wait, you human wig-stand! I'm fed up with always being the butt of jokes!—But wait! Isn't this what I have always wanted? Haven't I always been thwarted by the unattainable fifty gulden that these deceiving wigs cost?—Talisman, he said—he is right! When I put on this wig, Adonis will dwindle to a gipsy lad and Narcissus will be deleted from the books of mythology. My career goes forth, Fortune's gate yawns— (*noticing the garden gate standing ajar*) Why, the gate *is* standing open; who knows—? I'll risk it! Nothing can stand in the way of a good-looking fellow! (*Exits through garden gate.*)

Scene 14

SALOME (*entering downstage right*) Oh, my dearest Master Titus, what a misfortune!

TITUS (*looking around*) Salome—! What has happened?

SALOME The baker won't take you on. I can't help you; it makes me want to cry.

TITUS And it makes me want to laugh. Is it then so hard to get a job as a servant around here?

SALOME The baker said that on the one hand, he hasn't seen your credentials, and on the other, he gets so many recommendations that he is obliged to observe a certain protocol in allocating this position—

TITUS Too bad he is not holding competitive examinations! My dear Salome, other opportunities have opened up for me. I have been summoned to the manor house.

SALOME The manor house? That can't be. Oh, when her ladyship sees you, she'll chase you off right away. (*with reference to her hair*) I am not even permitted to come into her sight!

TITUS Her ladyship's antipathies are immaterial, now that I have changed materially. I go to meet my destiny with bold confidence.

SALOME Well, I wish your luck luck. It isn't right of me, but it hurts nonetheless, to think another hope of mine has been dashed.

TITUS What kind of hope?

SALOME Were you to stay here, looking like me, they'd have said, "There goes redheaded Titus and redheaded Salome, the wildest pair in the village!" And no girl would have looked twice at Titus, just as no boy ever looks at Salome.

TITUS And then Titus, reduced to a single object, would have had to succumb, like it or not, to an inevitable passion.

SALOME We would have had a very close friendship, of course—

TITUS And the road from friendship to love is a path strewn with flowers, eh?

SALOME Oh, I hadn't thought that far ahead.

TITUS Why not? Thoughts are tax-free.

SALOME Oh, no; there are thoughts which tax the peace of one's heart. My plans never work out.

TITUS Ah, yes, man proposes, and— (*aside*) the wig disposes, that's what I say. Adieu then, Salome. (*Starts to leave.*)

SALOME Don't be so proud, Master Titus; you could show a little friendship and take me by the hand and say in a friendly way, "God be with you, dear Salome!"

TITUS All right. (*Shakes her hand.*) We part the best of friends.

SALOME (*shaking her head*) Farewell! Perhaps I'll see you again soon.

TITUS That is most unlikely.

SALOME Who knows? You go in through the gate so proudly that I can't help thinking I'll see you thrown out through the same gate.

TITUS You are prophesying a convenient catastrophe.

SALOME (*indicating the stone bench*) I'll sit here every day and watch the gate—

TITUS And wait until I'm thrown into your arms. Fine, enjoy your private fantasies. Goodbye! My destiny calls: "Please come in!" I'll follow its summons, and bring myself along in the bargain. (*Exits through garden gate.*)

Scene 15

SALOME (*alone*) There he goes, and I don't know—I have never had any luck at all, and now it seems as though he has taken even some of that away. If only I could get him off my mind! But how? By what means? If I were a man, I would know what to do—but as it is ... Oh, men really have it over us in all sorts of ways.

Song

1

When a man doesn't know right away that we care,
What's a person to do? It's not easy, I swear!
For a man it is simple, he chases her so,
In two weeks, if not sooner, she can't help but know.
Then he plays the despondent, bangs his head on the wall,
With his hand in between, so there's no pain at all,
And the girl must give in, lest he damage the wood—
Ah yes, men have it good, have it good, have it good!

2

If somebody hurts us, we have no reply
Save to go to our bedroom and have a good cry.
If we hurt a man, though, it's almost a joke!
He goes to a tavern, sits down, has a smoke,
And while we think he's moping, he's eating a cheese,
Drinking wine, having fun with the waitress. If he sees,
On his way home, another as pretty, he would—
Ah yes, men have it good, have it good, have it good!

3

Let a girl have a second or third love affair,
It's all over, she's tarnished. But if we compare
How a man fares in matters like this, he's a king.
Though he ruin fifty girls, it's a trivial thing.
Girls in fact are attracted to such a Don Juan,
And if not out of love, out of envy they're drawn
To compete for his favor with all womanhood—
Ah yes, men have it good, have it good, have it good!

(*Exits.*)

Change of scene: *a room in the head gardener's quarters with a door in the center, a door to the right, and a window to the left.*

Scene 16

FLORA (*entering alone*) The weeds of gall and discontent grow all too thick in my garden patch; I can no longer uproot them alone. My dearly departed told me, shortly before his departure, that I should remain a widow—how could a late lamented have such a lamentable idea? The servants do not fear me, they show me no respect; I must have a husband to be their master. My dearly departed is going to shake his head in the clouds, if indeed he doesn't come back as a ghost. In the night, when I hear a knock at the door— (*There is a knock at the door; she screams in terror.*) —Agh! (*Tottering, she clutches at the table for support.*)

Scene 17

TITUS (*Wearing the black hairpiece, rushes in through the center door.*) Has there been an accident? Or do you always shriek like that instead of saying "Come in?"

FLORA (*collecting herself with difficulty*) No, I was terrified!

TITUS (*to himself*) Strange creature! She is terrified when someone knocks at the door. Usually women find it terrifying when no one knocks at the door any more.

FLORA The gentleman must wonder at my weak nerves.

TITUS Wonder at the commonplace? Oh no! Nerves of gossamer, hearts of wax, and heads of iron—the very blueprint of feminine architecture.

FLORA (*aside*) A most pleasant person—and such raven-black hair!—However, I must— (*aloud, in a rather forced manner*) Who are you, sir, and what do you want?

TITUS Oh, please, the honor is altogether mine! I am your most obedient servant.

FLORA (*Surprised, nods a cursory adieu to him, under the impression he is taking his leave. When he remains standing before her, she says, after a pause.*) Well? ... That phrase is ordinarily spoken when one wants to leave.

TITUS I said it, however, because I want to stay. You are in need of a servant, and as such I am at your service.

FLORA What? The gentleman is a servant?

TITUS Available for gardening.

FLORA As an assistant?

TITUS Whether you call me assistant or gardener or—it's all the same to me. Even if—and I am only speaking hypothetically—as gardener I were to succeed in planting some feelings in your heart—speaking hypothetically, of course—and you were to grant me sole possession of that dear plantation—only hypothetically—even then, I should always remain your servant.

FLORA (*aside*) The man is well bred, but— (*aloud*) Your language is somewhat bold, somewhat forward, sir!

TITUS May I humbly point out that when one says, "I am speaking only hypothetically," then one may say anything.

FLORA Then you are—?

TITUS An exotic species, not indigenous to this soil, but uprooted by circumstance and transplanted by chance in the amiable parterre of your home, where, warmed in the sun of your graciousness, the tender plant hopes to find nourishment.

FLORA The question is, first of all, do you know anything about gardening?

TITUS I know the ways of men, consequently also the ways of plants.

FLORA How does that follow?

TITUS Quite naturally. Whoever knows men also knows vegetables, because very few men live, while many, untold numbers, vegetate. He who gets up early, goes to the office, then goes to eat, then goes to play cards, and then goes to bed, vegetates. He who goes to the shop early and then goes to the tax office and then goes to eat and then goes back to the shop, vegetates. He who gets up early, then studies a part, then goes to rehearsal, then goes to eat, then goes to a coffeehouse, then goes to perform a comedy, and continues to do so day in and day out, vegetates. In order to live one needs, at a modest estimate, a cool million, and even that is not all. Intellectual verve is also required, and the combination is most rare. At least, judging by what I know of millionaires, almost all of them, in their passion for profit, lead such a boring, dry, businessman's existence that it scarcely merits the flowery name of vegetation.

FLORA (*aside*) The man must have studied advanced gardening! (*aloud*) The interior of your head seems as bright as its exterior is dark.

TITUS Perhaps you find dark hair objectionable.

FLORA Objectionable? You rascal, you know only too well that a head of dark curls sets a man off best.

TITUS (*to himself*) The wig is working!

FLORA So you wish to work here? Very well, you are hired. But not as a laborer! You are a man of experience and quality; you present a favorable appearance—

TITUS (*to himself*) Wig-power is winning out!

FLORA You shall supervise the garden personnel. You are to give the orders to the others; after me, you shall be the first in the garden.

TITUS (*aside*) The wig has won! (*aloud*) I am as ignorant of how to thank you as of how I came to be so fortunate.

FLORA (*studying his hair*) My, how dark, quite Italian!

TITUS Yes, it borders on the Sicilian. My mother was a southern gardener.

FLORA You know, though, you are really a vain man. I'll bet you use a curling iron. (*Tries to touch his locks.*)

TITUS (*leaping back*) Oh, please don't touch! My head is extremely ticklish.

FLORA Silly man! Oh, by the way, I can't possibly present you to her ladyship in that suit.

TITUS So you believe the saying, "Clothes make the man," the saying which makes us stoop before the tailor, and which is nevertheless so untrue! For many fine fellows go around in ragged coats.

FLORA But the suit is nothing like what a gardener—

TITUS Oh, the suit is altogether too gardenerish! It is oversown in patches, and it has come out at the elbows and elsewhere. It gets watered often, since I have no raincoat, and when it was in its bloom I frequently got a loan on it.

FLORA What nonsense! (*pointing to the right hand door*) Go through that room into the bedroom. In the chest the pocket watch is on you'll find my late husband's wedding suit.

TITUS I am to put on the wedding clothes of your dear departed? Listen— (*Runs his fingers engagingly through his hair.*) I cannot help it if certain feelings have been awakened which— (*Gives her a meaningful look and exits through the right hand door.*)

Scene 18

FLORA (*alone*) My, what a charming person!—Well, one never knows what might happen. Wouldn't it be fun if I were to remarry before her ladyship's maid, who always looks down her nose at me because she has a hairdresser for a beau. But he's taking his own sweet time marrying her. Things might go faster with me—what a triumph that would be!—First of all, though, I must call the help together. (*Goes to the window.*) Oh Pumpkinseed! (*calling*) Summon the help, a new gardener has been hired; in the future he will be giving the orders instead of me.

PUMPKINSEED (*from without*) That makes sense!

FLORA But who is this?—her ladyship's maid! (*greeting her through the window*) Your obedient servant! (*moving away from the window*) She is coming to see me; what can this mean? Another complaint, no doubt. The help have made a mess of something, and I'll have to clean it up.

Scene 19

CONSTANCE (*entering by center door*) Mrs. Pruningshears—

FLORA (*with a curtsey*) At your service, ma'am. What is it you wish?

CONSTANCE Her ladyship is expecting company from the city this afternoon and desires that no spoiled fruit be sent up to the manor house, as it was last time.

FLORA I have some of the most beautiful—

CONSTANCE Her ladyship is also most dissatisfied with the entire operation of the garden.

FLORA It's not my fault. The help—but all that is going to change now. Her ladyship has given me leave to hire an able man, and as it happened, a very able man—

CONSTANCE Good. I shall inform her ladyship of the news.

FLORA I will take the liberty myself of presenting him to her ladyship.

CONSTANCE What are you thinking of? Present him to her ladyship—a common lout?

FLORA Oh, but I pray you, madam, you mustn't confuse this person with a common garden laborer; he is—it is even possible—almost certain, in fact, that I shall marry him.

CONSTANCE So? This betrothal will be of as little interest to her ladyship as the man himself. As I have said, I find it entirely inappropriate that he should be presented to her ladyship.

Scene 20

TITUS (*Enters through the right hand door, wearing a somewhat old-fashioned gardener's suit and carrying a bundle in his hand. He does not at first see* CONSTANCE.) Well, here we are; I've bundled up my things here.

FLORA You could have left them in there.

35

TITUS Wearing this suit have I succeeded in conjuring up the faded picture in your soul?

CONSTANCE (*to herself*) I don't know when I've seen such a handsome black head of curls.

TITUS (*to* FLORA, *pointing to the bundle*) And these things—where shall we put them?

FLORA (*pointing to a chest to the left*) As far as I am concerned, you may leave them there in the chest.

TITUS (*turning away*) Good. (*catching sight of* CONSTANCE) Oh! I wouldn't bleed a drop, not even if you severed an artery! (*bowing deeply before* CONSTANCE) I humbly beseech you— (*to* FLORA) Why didn't you tell me—? (*to* CONSTANCE *with a deep bow*) —please do not be angry with me— (*to* FLORA) —that her ladyship was here— (*to* CONSTANCE *with a deep bow*) — for not immediately showing the respect due your ladyship—! (*to* FLORA) Oh, it's terrible, the situation you've put me in!

CONSTANCE But I am not her ladyship.

FLORA (*to* TITUS) What has gotten into you?

CONSTANCE I am only—

TITUS No, your ladyship only wishes to spare me the embarrassment.

FLORA She is her ladyship's maid.

TITUS Oh, go on!—This lofty carriage of forehead; this haughty batting of eye; this autocratic swing of elbow—

CONSTANCE (*flattered*) H'm ... Nevertheless I am still only Lady Cypressburg's maid.

TITUS Can it be?—I believe it only because I hear it from your own lips. Her ladyship's maid, then! My mother too was a lady's maid.

FLORA But you said your mother was a gardener!

TITUS She was a gardener first, then later she became a lady's maid.

CONSTANCE (*aside*) Really, what an interesting, cultivated person!

FLORA (*to* TITUS, *who is gazing fixedly at* CONSTANCE) Just put your things in there!

TITUS (*still staring at* CONSTANCE) Destiny really does not know what it is doing, placing such a one in the antechamber.

FLORA Weren't you listening? There, in the chest!

TITUS Yes, right away— (*gazing in admiration at* CONSTANCE) A figure of classic salon elegance! (*He goes, still looking at* CONSTANCE, *to the chest standing by the door.*)

FLORA (*to herself*) How she leads him on, the brazen hussy!

Scene 21

PUMPKINSEED (*entering by the center door*) The help will be here right away.

TITUS (*Noticing* PUMPKINSEED, *turns away quickly.*) Damnation! If he should recognize me!— (*Turns to* CONSTANCE *in order to keep his back to* PUMPKINSEED.)

PUMPKINSEED (*to* FLORA) So this is the new gardener! I must pay my respects to him. (*Steps between* TITUS *and* CONSTANCE.)

TITUS (*Turns to* FLORA *in order to keep his back to* PUMPKINSEED.) Send the fellow away! I am no friend to such ceremony.

FLORA Don't be so shy.

PUMPKINSEED (*trying to get around in front of* TITUS) Sir, as the most deserving member of the staff—

TITUS (*Much at a loss, dives into his pocket.*) Oh!—I must get a handkerchief in front of my face— (*Instead of a handkerchief, he draws from his pocket a gray wig with a pigtail and buries his face in it.*)

PUMPKINSEED That's a strange handkerchief you have there.

TITUS But what's this?

FLORA (*laughing*) That's my late husband's wig.

TITUS It does look somewhat *passé*. (*Puts the wig in the bundle which he still holds in his hand.*)

PUMPKINSEED What the devil! This gardener looks strangely familiar!— (*to* TITUS) Don't you have a brother with red hair?

CONSTANCE What has gotten into him?

TITUS I don't have a brother.

PUMPKINSEED Oh? I guess he must have been somebody else's brother.

FLORA What is the blockhead talking about?

PUMPKINSEED Well, I saw this redheaded fellow ... There's nothing wrong with that....

Scene 22

(*A pair of* GARDEN LABORERS *enter through the center door, each carrying two baskets of fruit.*)

FIRST LABORER Here's the fruit!

FLORA That should have been taken directly up to the manor house.

CONSTANCE It would have been a fine how-do-you-do, sending up the fruit by the servants just like that.

FLORA It has always been done that way.

CONSTANCE (*pointing to* TITUS) The gardener will deliver the fruit. That will offer the most appropriate occasion to present him to her ladyship.

FLORA (*to* CONSTANCE) Present him? Why do you suddenly find it necessary to present him to her ladyship? You just said it was unseemly to bring such a lout into her ladyship's presence.

CONSTANCE (*nonplussed*) That was—that it to say—

TITUS Lout?

FLORA (*in malicious exultation over* CONSTANCE'S *embarrassment*) Yes, yes!

TITUS That is really too much—

CONSTANCE (*very nonplussed*) I have—

TITUS That is outrageous!

FLORA Well, I think so—

TITUS Incomprehensible (*to* FLORA) that you could use the word "lout" to refer to me.

FLORA Those were Madame Constance's very words!

TITUS (*to* FLORA) If you will permit me, there are plenty of louts around beside me, and I am not such an egotist as to take everything personally.

CONSTANCE (*recovering from her embarrassment*) I only wanted—

TITUS (*indicating* CONSTANCE) If this lady actually let her lips form the word "lout," she no doubt had reference to a servant, perhaps one of these gentlemen here (*pointing to the two* LABORERS), because she did not even know me at the time, and still knows far too little of me to pass judgment on my loutishness. (*to* CONSTANCE) Am I not right?

CONSTANCE Entirely!

FLORA (*very upset and annoyed*) So I am to be made a liar?

TITUS No, merely a slanderer.

CONSTANCE (*to* TITUS) Come along now.

FLORA He is to go to the manor house? Why all the hurry? Her ladyship is out riding.

CONSTANCE Well, would it not be more seemly for the gardener to wait on her ladyship than for her to wait on him?

TITUS Clearly. (*to* CONSTANCE) She knows nothing of etiquette. At any rate, the most seemly thing is for me to wait with you until the appropriate moment arrives.

FLORA (*very annoyed, aside*) I could tear her limb from limb, that person, that—!

TITUS As gardener, however, I must observe the proper decorum—aha! Just what I need! (*Rushes to the window and tears the flowers from the pots.*)

FLORA What's this? My flowers!

TITUS They'll have to do for a bouquet. But we'll need a ribbon, too. (*hurrying to the table*) Ah, here's one. (*Takes a wide satin band and wraps it around the flowers.*)

FLORA Here now, what do you think you're doing? The new ribbon I just bought in the city—

TITUS For such a festive occasion even one's best is not good enough. (*to* CONSTANCE, *indicating* FLORA) The good soul, she knows nothing of etiquette.

Scene 23

Several LABORERS (*entering center stage*) We are here to pay our respects.

TITUS Ah, my subordinates! You shall carry the fruit and follow me.

LABORERS At your service.

CONSTANCE (*to* TITUS) You must avail yourself of this opportunity to win the respect of the staff by showing your generosity—at least I think that it would not be out of place for you to do so.

TITUS I too think it my place—however— (*exploring his waistcoat pocket*) —in another place I seem to find nothing.

CONSTANCE It would give me pleasure if you would accept this— (*Proffers him a purse.*)

FLORA (*preventing her*) If you don't mind, this is my affair. (*to* TITUS) Here, sir, take this! (*Tries to give him money.*)

CONSTANCE (*preventing* FLORA) Stop! I shall not tolerate this. This is a matter that touches the honor of the house, and consequently I must represent her ladyship.

FLORA I can hand her ladyship the bill, too; but it is *my*—

TITUS Permit me. This matter can be resolved without anyone getting hit over the head. If I may— (*taking the money from* CONSTANCE) Give me that! (*taking the money from* FLORA) There! The important thing in such matters is that no one should be slighted. (*to the* LABORERS) I'm treating everyone today.

LABORERS Hurrah!

TITUS Now onward, to the manor house!

Chorus

The new gardener is off to a promising start;
Drink his health, he's a real man after our heart!

(TITUS *comes forward with* CONSTANCE, *the* LABORERS *follow with the fruit baskets,* FLORA *looks after them furiously,* PUMPKINSEED *observes her with a meaningful smile; amid the general jubilation of the* GARDEN STAFF, *the curtain falls.*)

---

1. The "Titus-head" was a fashionable Nineteenth Century French hair style, modelled on the bust of the Roman emperor.

2. A coppery red, the traditional color for this instrument.

3. The guardian of church buildings (he died trying to put out a church fire), St. Florian became in time the patron of buildings in general. In Austrian farmyards, an image of the saint often appeared as a talisman to ward off fires.

4. An obvious play on Goethe's *Wahlverwandtschaften* (Elective Affinities).

5. November 11, feastday of St. Martin, whose iconography almost always includes a goose. A goose is the traditional main course of a Martinmas dinner.

ACT II

The scene depicts a part of the manor garden. Downstage right, the head gardener's quarters, with a usable entry. Downstage left, a table with several lawn chairs. In the background right one can see a wing of the manor house, with a window which can be opened.

Scene 1

PUMPKINSEED *and several* GARDEN LABORERS *sit around the table drinking.*

CHORUS

You'd never believe one could drink
A whole tankard of wine in a wink!
Though while working one loses one's temper,
While drinking there's nary a whimper,
For there'll never be too much for one,
Nor does one ever long to be done.
Ah yes, drinking's a real delight
—To be continued tonight.

PUMPKINSEED The work isn't pressing today; we've still got more than half the money left, and it's got to be drunk up; all this means we'll knock off early today!

FIRST LABORER Nobody ever comes late for something like this.

PUMPKINSEED Just remember, a gardener is the noblest of all plants and must be irrigated regularly, or else he'll dry up.

FIRST LABORER But this new gardener is an unusual man, really a fine fellow.

ALL That's right.

PUMPKINSEED Oh shortsighted folk! He is a lazy rascal, believe me, I know! He won't get us out of any work, on the contrary, we'll have to wait on him, this stray mongrel. He'll stick his hands in his pockets and try to play His Lordship, the puffed-up deadbeat!

LABORERS Wouldn't that be something!

FIRST LABORER Well, if he does he'll—

PUMPKINSEED Easy now— We'll have plenty of time this evening for

42

such charges, and more like them. Then we can also make plans as to how to get rid of him.

ALL Yes, we can do that.

PUMPKINSEED So take it easy, everything in its own good time!

Scene 2

FLORA (*Enters from her house with a basketful of crockery and silver.*) Now I shall have to ask you to make an end of it. Take your tankards and go. I need this table now.

LABORERS We were just going anyway.

PUMPKINSEED All this is in honor of the new gardener.

FLORA (*to the* LABORERS) Get back to work!

LABORERS (*leaving*) All right! (*Exit upstage left.*)

Scene 3

PUMPKINSEED I don't see how you can have the heart to disturb these good people in their innocent pleasure.

FLORA (*Takes the tablecloth from her basket and spreads it over the table.*) Shut your mouth and help me set the table.

PUMPKINSEED Right away! I never have to be told a second time to do this job. (*Takes crockery and silver from the basket.*) But this is only for two people!

FLORA Of course! I don't know why there should be more.

PUMPKINSEED Then the new gardener is going to eat in the manor house with her ladyship's maid?

FLORA Idiot! He is eating here with me.

PUMPKINSEED He, you, and I—but that makes three.

FLORA You have eaten at my table because I found it boring to eat alone; now you have become superfluous. You have your food allowance; you may leave as soon as you have served us.

PUMPKINSEED (*piqued*) There was a time when I never left.

FLORA Stop whining and go fetch the soup.

PUMPKINSEED (*maliciouly*) So soon? It might get cold! Who knows when he'll be coming?

FLORA (*looking impatiently toward the manor house*) He will be here any minute now. (*half to herself*) Anyway, I can't understand what's keeping him so long.

PUMPKINSEED Aha! I'm beginning to understand.

FLORA Be quiet and do what you are told!

PUMPKINSEED (*leaving, as if talking to himself, but so that* FLORA *cannot help but hear*) He must have made other arrangements in the manor house; otherwise I can't explain this long delay. (*Exits into the gardener's quarters.*)

Scene 4

FLORA (*alone*) That's the last time he'll go up there. The way that Madame Constance forces herself on men, it simply defies description!

TITUS (*Appears at the manor house window with a napkin about his neck and the drumstick of a pheasant in his hand.*) Ah, Mrs. Pruningshears, how good to see you....

FLORA Where have you been? I am waiting with the meal.

TITUS Not I! I have already eaten.

FLORA In the manor house?

TITUS In the anteroom with her ladyship's maid. And very well, I might add. This was the first pheasant to whom I have done the last honors; with this drumstick his earthly shell is gathered into mine.

FLORA But it is not proper for you to sponge up there! I forbid it.

TITUS You can forbid *yourself* whatever you wish, but you can't forbid *me* anything! I no longer live beneath your tyranny, I have assumed a far, far better state.

FLORA (*greatly taken aback*) How's that?

TITUS Wait a second! I want to give you something. (*Withdraws.*)

FLORA (*alone*) Madame Constance, I know you, this is your work! A widow who already has a beau of her own filches another's from her—that is a piece of widow's work without parallel!

Scene 5

PUMPKINSEED (*carrying the soup tureen*) Here's the soup.

TITUS (*reappearing in the manor house window*) And here are the old clothes that I no longer require. My compliments! (*Hurls down the bundle of clothing so that it lands on* PUMPKINSEED'S *head, then withdraws.*)

PUMPKINSEED Bullseye! What's going on?

FLORA (*to* PUMPKINSEED) Go to the devil!

PUMPKINSEED Then you're not going to eat?

FLORA No, I tell you. (*to herself*) Whoever wouldn't lose his appetite at this has none to lose.

PUMPKINSEED (*pointedly*) Am I to understand the dinner engagement is broken, for which I was superfluous?

FLORA Out of my sight! (*to herself, leaving*) What a malicious rascal he is! (*Exits to her quarters.*)

PUMPKINSEED (*alone*) So he's not eating here, she's not eating at all, and I, the uninvited, will eat for the both of them! Oh, inscrutable Fortune! I wouldn't have thought you capable of such poetic justice. (*Exits into the gardener's quarters.*)

Change of scene: *The hall at the manor house, with a center door and two side doors.*

Scene 6

TITUS (*Alone, enters through the center door; he is dressed in an elegant forester's uniform.*) She has done just what the other one did: offered me the late wardrobe of her former husband and wants me to become a forester. Well, if her ladyship demands no more of a forester than opening her little carriage door and hopping onto the footboard, that much forestry-science I can take care of. Oh, wig! I have much to thank you for! The food here is delectable, the drink exquisite—I really don't know whether it is my change of fortune or the Tokay that is making my head swim so.

Scene 7

CONSTANCE (*entering from the left*) Ah, I like that! That gardener's suit was so boorish; your exterior was made for the noble livery of the forester.

TITUS If only my exterior will elicit an equally ladylike response from her ladyship! I fear greatly that one unkind look from her may wrest the deer rifle from my hand and put back the shovel and hoe.

CONSTANCE You credit me with little influence in this house. My late husband was forester here, and my mistress will certainly not expect me to remain a widow forever.

TITUS Certainly not! Such features were not shaped to wear a lifelong veil.

CONSTANCE Assuming I were to remarry, can you doubt that her ladyship would find a place in her service for my husband?

TITUS To doubt would be blasphemy—

CONSTANCE I do not say this, of course, with any designs on you—

TITUS Of course not, it never occured to you—

CONSTANCE I say this only that there be no misunderstanding, merely to show you it is within my power to secure anyone a position at the manor house.

TITUS (*aside*) Oh raven-black crest, you work sky-blue wonders!

CONSTANCE My sainted husband—

TITUS Stop! Do not call that man sainted whom the conjurer Death has transported from your arms into the Great Beyond! No, sainted is rather he who in life still enjoys those embraces! Oh Constance!— We pay a very poor compliment indeed to wedlock when we call "sainted" only the dead, who have passed beyond it.

CONSTANCE Then you are of the opinion that at my side one could—?

TITUS Gaze proudly into the unknown and think to oneself: "Things can be good anywhere, but here they are best."

CONSTANCE Flatterer!

TITUS (*aside*) Such are the new metaphysical gallantries that we've taken up lately. (*aloud*) I think I hear someone in the anteroom.

Scene 8

SALOME (*Enters timidly through the center door.*) With your permission—

TITUS (*startled, to himself*) Oh Lord, it's Salome! (*Throws himself carelessly into a chair so that his face is turned away from her.*)

CONSTANCE How did you get in?

SALOME There was no one outside, and I thought this must be the anteroom, but now I see— Oh, I beg you, Madame, please come outside for a moment; I am speechless in the presence of so much elegance.

CONSTANCE Stop beating around the bush. What do you want? Quickly now!

SALOME I am looking for someone, I have already looked for him at Mrs. Pruningshears', but I didn't find him there, so I came here.

CONSTANCE (*her suspicions aroused*) Who are you looking for?

SALOME Well—that is—I'm looking for a man with red hair.

CONSTANCE (*relieved*) Well, you should be able to find him easily; he'll beam you a signal from a hundred paces.

TITUS (*to himself*) Oh rare new joke, how often have you delighted me!

CONSTANCE You are wasting your efforts in the manor house, for neither her ladyship nor I would tolerate such a one here; we both have an antipathy for red hair.

SALOME Still, if he should happen to come here, would you please tell him some people from the city were looking for him? They were asking me about him ever so suspiciously—

TITUS (*Forgetting himself, leaps up startled.*) And what did you tell these people?

SALOME (*recoiling*) What's that—?! (*recognizing Titus*) Oh! (*Sways and falls into* CONSTANCE'S *arms.*)

CONSTANCE What's wrong with the creature? (*to* TITUS) Well, bring a chair over here. I can't just stand here holding her.

TITUS (*bringing a chair*) Put her here.

CONSTANCE (*lowering* SALOME *into the chair*) She's not moving, she's utterly motionless. (*to* TITUS) This is very odd. The sight of you had this effect on her.

TITUS (*nonplussed*) I don't see how that can be. I'm not ugly enough to make one faint, and as far as my good looks are concerned, they are not so great as to bowl one over, either.

CONSTANCE But you can see for yourself, she isn't moving at all.

TITUS (*very nonplussed*) Yes, I can see that.

CONSTANCE But now it seems to me—yes, she's moving!

TITUS Yes. I can see that, too. I'll go fetch some fresh water. (*Makes to leave.*)

CONSTANCE None of that; that will not be necessary. Or do you perhaps have a special reason for sneaking away?

TITUS I wouldn't know why!—I don't know this person.

CONSTANCE Then you needn't be afraid of her waking up.

TITUS Not at all! Who says I am afraid?

SALOME (*regaining consciousness*) Ah, Madame—I'm better now—

CONSTANCE What came over you?

SALOME The gentleman—

CONSTANCE Then you know him?

SALOME No, I don't know him, certainly not! (*standing up*) But he spoke to me so sharply—

CONSTANCE Was that the reason you—?

SALOME It's a pity, isn't it—such city nerves in a country girl? (*to* TITUS, *who stands by astonished*) Don't be angry, sir, and if you happen to see the man with the red hair, please tell him I meant well, I only wanted to warn him; and tell him, too, please, I'll never stand in the way of his good fortune! (*holding back her tears*) Tell him that, when you see the man with the red hair. (*to* CONSTANCE) Again, I beg you to forgive me for having fainted in these rooms that are not for the likes of me, and God bless both of you and— (*Breaks into tears.*) —now I am going to start crying—that is not the proper thing to do—I mean no harm—I am such a silly thing! (*Exits by center door, crying.*)

Scene 9

CONSTANCE (*looking after her in wonder*) H'm, —this creature—I must confess the whole thing strikes me as highly suspicious.

TITUS (*only gradually recovering his composure*) What?

CONSTANCE She was so upset, so moved—

TITUS About a red-headed man, you heard her.

CONSTANCE She did speak of such a one, but it was *you* that she seemed so violently to—

TITUS Now stop that! What has gotten into you?

CONSTANCE You're not going to try to tell me she wasn't greatly moved?

TITUS What is that to me? First you accused me because she was motionless, now you take me to task because she was moved. I really don't understand—

CONSTANCE There's no need to lose your temper; I could be completely wrong—that you would have any connection with such a common person—that would be unthinkable.

TITUS I should say so! I am a young man with a career to make! (*with emphasis*) My aspirations soar to the heights....

CONSTANCE (*coquettishly*) Really? It was fortunate that this unpleasant scene took place in her ladyship's absence.... Her ladyship has an uncommon hatred of commoness; she interests herself only in intellectual pursuits, as do I.... She is herself an author.

TITUS An author?

CONSTANCE Should the conversation turn to letters—are you acquainted with such things?

TITUS No.

CONSTANCE That's too bad.

TITUS Mere child's play! Though I may know nothing about writing, I know all the more about authors. I only need find her things divine, and she is bound to say: "Ah, this man understands ... deep insight ... solid background!"

CONSTANCE You are a sly dog! (*to herself*) How unlike my hairdresser he is!

Scene 10

MARQUIS (*entering by center door*) Most lovely Constance....

TITUS (*to himself*) It's the illustrious wig dispenser—if only he won't blab—! (*Draws to one side.*)

MARQUIS I was very nearly deprived forever of the pleasure of pressing this charming hand to my lips. (*Kisses her hand.*)

TITUS (*to himself, shocked*) Such condescension! —A marquis kissing her hand, the hand of an anteroom person— What a thing!

CONSTANCE It is so late, I thought you were not coming today.

MARQUIS As you must know, only an extraordinary incident—but what's this? (*Catches sight of* TITUS, *who seizes an antimacassar from a nearby chair and begins to dust the furniture furiously.*) Has a new forester been taken on?

CONSTANCE This very day. A man of many parts.

MARQUIS How can you judge the parts of a forester? Did he make a hit? And anyway, why a forester in the household of a lady?

CONSTANCE As you can see, he is very industrious, and makes himself useful in all sorts of ways.

MARQUIS (*Tries to catch a glimpse of* TITUS' *face, while the latter avoids him with comic bustle.*) Yes, yes, I can see that.

TITUS (*to himself*) I mustn't show him my face at all costs.

CONSTANCE But you are quite forgetting to tell me about the incident.

MARQUIS (*glancing frequently toward* TITUS) It was really more an accident, one that might easily have ended in a neck-breaking water fall, had not chance sent a man at the very moment that beastly animal, my fiery Fox—

TITUS (*taken aback*) I thought he was about to call me by name.

CONSTANCE Fox? I thought you still had that ugly sorrel.

TITUS (*to himself*) Yet another veiled compliment!

MARQUIS I traded him off because his appearance offended you so. At any rate, this man— (*looking intently at* TITUS) my rescuer— (*whirling* TITUS *around*) I was not mistaken!— This is he!

TITUS (*bowing deeply*) Please, your honor, the marquis has taken me for another! (*Makes to leave by center door.*)

MARQUIS (*restraining him*) Why deny it, noble sir? It is you,—that carriage, that voice, that hair color—

TITUS (*to himself, in alarmed embarrassment*) Uh-oh, now he's coming to the hair!

CONSTANCE Truly, whoever has seen this head of hair once, will never forget it. Such locks are indeed worthy of admiration.

MARQUIS (*feeling himself to have been complimented*) Oh, please, you are too kind!

TITUS (*to* CONSTANCE) The marquis thanks you on my behalf for the compliment; thus in my humility nothing remains to be done save to—

CONSTANCE (*to* MARQUIS) You understand these things: have you ever seen such lustre, such waves—? (*Gestures toward* TITUS' *head, as if about to run her fingers through his hair.*)

TITUS (*leaping back*) Oh, don't touch! I am so ticklish there—

MARQUIS (*piqued, sotto voce to* CONSTANCE) Incidentally, you seem to be taking a particular interest in the new domestic.

CONSTANCE (*somewhat embarrassed*) I—? H'm—there is a kind of camaraderie, which—

MARQUIS (*as above*) Which in my opinion does not exist between a forester and a lady's maid.

CONSTANCE (*to* MARQUIS, *sotto voce*) Monsieur Marquis, I thank you for the explanation, but I am quite capable of judging what is proper and what is not.

MARQUIS (*to himself*) Now I've offended her. (*to* CONSTANCE *in a soft tone*) Forgive me, most lovely Constance, I only wanted to—

CONSTANCE You only wanted to comb out her ladyship's little blonde wig; you will find it in the dressing room (*pointing to the right*), in the big wardrobe. Now go about your business!

TITUS (*astonished*) What's this? A hairdresser! (*to* MARQUIS) I thought you were a marquis, a mixture of baron, duke, and knight of the realm.

MARQUIS No, my name in Marquis, and I am a wig-maker.

TITUS That's a horse of a different color. The vacant room of respect is now furnished with barbers' kits, and we can become friends without embarrassment. (*Extends his hand.*)

MARQUIS (*Also extends his hand.*) I owe you a debt of thanks. (*softly*) But you also owe me one, and it will be very much in your best interest to see that we remain friends.

TITUS Friends to the death!

CONSTANCE (*to herself*) Monsieur Titus must not learn of my relationship with Marquis; the hairdresser's jealous behavior could easily—I had better leave. (*aloud*) Gentlemen, important duties ... I must leave you two friends alone now. (*Exits center door.*)

TITUS (*calling after her*) Adieu, dear lady of the chamber!

Scene 11

MARQUIS Sir, why this gallantry? I tell you straight out, I forbid it! Madame Constance is my fiancée, and woe be unto you if you dare—

TITUS What? Are you threatening me?

MARQUIS Yes, my dear sir, at least I am warning you. Do not forget that your fate hangs by a hair, and—

TITUS And you could be so ungrateful as to divulge the wig-connection.

MARQUIS And that I could be so clever as to get rid of a rival that way.

TITUS What? Thus speaks *this* man? This very man, to the man without whom this man would have been a dead man? Without which man this man would now be carp food?

MARQUIS I owe you a debt of gratitude, but under no circumstances the relinquishment of my fiancée.

TITUS Who says she is to be relinquished? I am no rival for her love, only for her patronage.

MARQUIS Ah, now you are talking sense! If this is so, you may count on my gratitude and, above all, on my keeping the hair-secret. Be careful, though, to give me no cause for displeasure, or else— (*threateningly*) Just keep in mind that your head is in my hands! (*Exits to the right.*)

Scene 12

TITUS What a damnable affair! Everything has come down about my head today! If only there weren't so much in it! But the Tokay vapors—and the fact that the lady's maid is also the hairdresser's fiancée, that too— (*pointing to his head*) makes it spin. (*Flings himself into an armchair.*) It really ought to be an affair of the heart, but the heart is silly and at the same time indiscreet. Every time a ticklish situation comes along, right away it's turned head over heels, even if it sees the head already has its hands full. I am so tired. (*Yawns.*) It could be another half hour before her ladyship returns— (*Lets his head sink into his hands.*) I could— (*yawning*) take a little nap—not really go to sleep—only a little nap—a little—nap— (*Falls asleep.*)

Scene 13

MARQUIS (*Enters from the right after a short pause.*) There is a broken window in there. I can't stand draughts, so I closed the shutters. But now it is so dark in there that without light I can't possibly—the forester ought to—but where is he? Can he have sneaked away to my Constance after all? If so, he will— (*Starts to run out the center door, then sees the sleeping* TITUS *in the armchair.*) On, no, I have wronged him—this jealousy—a foolish thing—I must get over it. How peacefully he lies there—no man in love sleeps like that, he surely has no thought for her....

TITUS (*mumbling in his sleep*) Con-sta-sta-stance—

MARQUIS The devil! What was that? (*Tiptoes nearer.*)

TITUS (*as above*) Char-ming—figure—Con-Constance—

MARQUIS He is dreaming of her! The scoundrel has the nerve to dream of her!

TITUS (*as above*) Only—another—kiss-kiss—

MARQUIS Hell and damnation! I'll not tolerate such dreams! (*Starts to seize him by the shirtfront, then reconsiders.*) Wait!—it is better so. Let's see whether she'll give a redhead a kiss-kiss! (*Approaches the chair from the back and very carefully grasps the wig.*)

TITUS (*as above*) Let go—Stan-stance—I'm ticklish—on my head—

MARQUIS (*Takes the wig away.*) Now try your luck, you redheaded Adonis! Never again shall you have the talisman! (*Puts the wig in his pocket and hurries out through the center door.*)

Scene 14

TITUS (*talking in his sleep*) Oh—delicate—little hand!— (*One hears from without the sound of a carriage entering the courtyard, shortly thereafter a loud ring at the door.* TITUS *wakes with a start.*) What was that? I believe— (*Runs to the center door.*) A servant is dashing out—her ladyship is coming home—now I shall be presented. (*Straightens his suit.*) My suit is all rumpled—my tie wrinkled—quick, where's a mirror? (*Runs to a mirror which hangs on the left-hand wall, looks into it, then leaps back.*) Good heavens, the wig is gone!—It must have fallen off while I was asleep— (*Runs to the armchair and searches for it.*) No, it's gone, lost, stolen! Who could be so malicious? There is jealousy at play here! Othello of a hairdresser! Pomaded monster! This is your work! You have committed this foul wignapping! Now, at my most critical, auspicious moment, I stand here like a windlantern[1] on the bier of my budding career! But wait!—He's in there combing out her ladyship's wig—he'll not get away from me! You shall give my wig back or tremble for your life, Knight of the Combs! I'll shake your hair-powder soul till there's not a grain left in your body! (*Rushes out enraged through the side door.*)

Scene 15

LADY CYPRESSBURG I must say, I find it most high-handed, almost impertinent of Constance, that she should take it upon herself to hire domestics in my absence without my authorizaton.

EMMA Don't upset yourself over it, mother dear; after all, she took on a forester, and it has long been my wish that we should have a forester. He will look so much better than our two bowlegged footmen in their old Franconian[2] livery.

LADY CYPRESSBURG But why should ladies have need of a forester?

EMMA And he is supposed to be quite a soldierly-looking, dark-haired fellow, according to Constance, though he doesn't have a moustache; you must get him to grow one, mama, and also fine black sideburns, so that one can't see anything of his face except for two black, glowing eyes! Such a thing would look marvelous on the back of the carriage.

LADY CYPRESSBURG (*not paying much attention to Emma's last speech*) Hush! I shall send the person away, and that's that! But where is he? Didn't she say his name was Titus? Hallo! Titus!

Scene 16

TITUS (*Enters from the right, wearing a blonde wig.*) Here I am; I grovel in the dust before your highness, whom I am to serve in the future.

EMMA (*astonished, aside*) What's this! He is no brunette!

LADY CYPRESSBURG (*to herself, though loudly*) What a well-behaved towhead!

TITUS (*having heard the last word, to himself*) What? Did she say "towhead?"

LADY CYPRESSBURG (*to* TITUS) My maid offered you the post of forester, and I have no objections— (*turning to* EMMA) Emma—! (*Begins to speak with* EMMA *in dumb show.*)

TITUS (*to himself*) Towhead, she said! But I have— (*Looks around in confusion and catches sight of himself in a mirror hanging on the right hand wall, in great surprise.*) By my soul, I *am* blonde! I must have picked up a blonde wig there in the dark. If only her ladyship's maid doesn't come in now!

LADY CYPRESSBURG (*continuing her conversation with* EMMA) And tell Constance—

TITUS (*alarmed, to himself*) Uh-oh, she is sending for her now!

LADY CYPRESSBURG (*continuing*) She is to get my dress ready for the soirée this evening.

TITUS (*with a sigh of relief, to himself*) Thank God! That'll keep her busy for a while.

EMMA At once! (*to herself, leaving*) That silly Constance was putting me on! Pretending a blonde is a brunette! (*Exits by center door.*)

Scene 17

TITUS (*to himself*) Now I stand before an author. Everyday words won't do; every speech must be clothed in one's Sunday best.

LADY CYPRESSBURG And now to you, my friend.

TITUS (*making a deep bow*) This is the moment I have longed for and feared in equal degree, the moment which I contemplate with timorous valor and courageous trembling, so to speak.

LADY CYPRESSBURG You have no cause for alarm. You have a good carriage, an agreeable manner, and if you behave yourself ... Where have you served previously?

TITUS Nowhere; it is the first fruit of my forestry that I lay at your ladyship's feet, and the livery which I now inhabit encloses an individuality which, though dedicated to service, has up to now never been in it.

LADY CYPRESSBURG Is your father also a forester?

TITUS No, he plies a quiet, retiring trade, whose only stock is that of peace. Though bound to a Higher Authority, he is nevertheless quite independent, and free to mold himself—in short, he's dead.

LADY CYPRESSBURG (*to herself*) How prodigally he uses twenty elevated words to express what one could say in a syllable! The person obviously has an aptitude for literature. (*aloud*) What then was your father?

TITUS He was a master of scholars; book, slate, and ferrule were the elements of his existence.

LADY CYPRESSBURG And what sort of literary training did he give you?

TITUS A kind of pedagogical potpourri. I have had a smattering of geography, a glimmering of history, a notion of philosophy, a hint of law, an inkling of surgery, and a foretaste of medicine.

LADY CYPRESSBURG How charming! You have studied much, but nothing thoroughly! That way lies genius.

TITUS (*to himself*) That's the first time I ever heard that! Now I see why there are so many geniuses about.

LADY CYPRESSBURG Your blonde curls indicate an Apollonian temper.

Was it your father or your mother who was blonde?

TITUS Neither of them. It is by sheer accident that I am blonde.

LADY CYPRESSBURG The more I observe you, the longer I listen to you speak, the more I am convinced that livery is not suitable for you. Under no circumstances shall you be my domestic servant.

TITUS Then am I to be rejected, broken, crushed?

LADY CYPRESSBURG By no means. As an author, I require someone—not an ordinary copyist, more a consultant or a secretary—to stand at my side during my intellectual endeavors; it is to this position that I intend to appoint you.

TITUS (*happily surprised*) Me?—Your ladyship believes me capable of serving as an intellectual sidekick?

LADY CYPRESSBURG No doubt of it. I am also pleased to say that the position is at present vacant. I have just dismissed a man who was recommended to me, a man of great scholarship and learning. But he had red hair, and that to me is an abomination. I told him right off, "No, no, my friend, it's no use, adieu!" And I was glad to see him leave.

TITUS (*to himself*) I must really be on my guard, or else my career will fly right out the door.

LADY CYPRESSBURG Now get out of that livery at once; I am expecting company in an hour, to whom I wish to present you as my new secretary.

TITUS My lady, even if I set aside this forester's livery, my other suit is also a livery of sorts, that is to say, the livery of poverty: a coat of patches with ragged lapels.

LADY CYPRESSBURG That is easily remedied. Go in there (*pointing to the right*), through the billiard room into the corner closet; there you will find my late husband's wardrobe. He was just your size. Choose what you like and come directly back here.

TITUS (*to himself*) Yet another suit from a late lamented. (*bowing*) I'm off! (*to himself, leaving*) I'll have had a whole lamentable flea market on my back before the day is out.

Scene 18

LADY CYPRESSBURG (*alone*) The heights to which I have raised the young man have made his head swim! How will he feel when I lead him into otherworldly regions through the recitation of my verse?

CONSTANCE (*Excited, enters by center door.*) Mean, that's what I call mean.

LADY CYPRESSBURG What's the matter?

CONSTANCE I really must complain about Miss Emma's behavior. I find it very mean to carry a joke to such extremes. She scolded me for having lied about the forester's hair. At first I thought she was joking, but she wound up calling me a silly goose.

LADY CYPRESSBURG I shall reprimand her for that. By the way, the man is no longer a forester. I have made him my secretary, and as such he will be shown the respect due his position.

CONSTANCE Secretary? I am delighted that he has met with your approval. The black secretarial suit will go nicely with his black hair.

LADY CYPRESSBURG What did you say?

CONSTANCE His black hair, I said.

LADY CYPRESSBURG You must be mad. I have never seen a more beautiful golden head of hair.

CONSTANCE Your ladyship is jesting!

LADY CYPRESSBURG It seldom occurs to me to jest with my subordinates.

CONSTANCE But my lady, with my own eyes I have seen—

LADY CYPRESSBURG My eyes are no less my own than yours are yours.

CONSTANCE (*very puzzled*) And your ladyship calls that blonde?

LADY CYPRESSBURG What else?

CONSTANCE If your ladyship will forgive me, that would require a very singular pair of eyes! I would call it the blackest black that ever existed.

LADY CYPRESSBURG Laughable creature, make your little jokes with someone else.

CONSTANCE Oh, this is enough to drive one mad!

LADY CYPRESSBURG (*looking to the right*) Here he comes now—well? Is that blonde hair or not?

Scene 19

TITUS (*Enters from the right, wearing a black tail coat, knee breeches, silk stockings and shoes.*) Here I am, most gracious mistress! (*startled at the sight of* CONSTANCE, *to himself*) Uh-oh, it's Constance!

CONSTANCE (*much surprised*) What's this?

LADY CYPRESSBURG (*to* CONSTANCE) In the future I shall not tolerate this sort of—

CONSTANCE But my lady, I have—

LADY CYPRESSBURG Not another word!

TITUS (*to* LADY CYPRESSBURG) Your ladyship seems upset. What is it?—

LADY CYPRESSBURG Can you imagine, this fool here insists that you have black hair.

TITUS That is a black lie!

CONSTANCE I am going to lose my mind!

LADY CYPRESSBURG A trifling loss—more importantly, I am liable to lose my patience! Go now and prepare my toilet!

CONSTANCE Again, I can only assure you—

LADY CYPRESSBURG (*angrily*) And for the last time I am telling you to go.

CONSTANCE (*regaining her composure with great difficulty and leaving*) This is beyond all comprehension! (*Exits by center door.*)

Scene 20

LADY CYPRESSBURG What an insolent person!

TITUS (*to himself*) My position here in this house is like the timber of a shipwrecked sailor; I must push the others under or go under myself.

(*aloud*) Oh, my lady, there is more to this female than meets the eye.

LADY CYPRESSBURG Has she perhaps been discourteous to you?

TITUS Oh, no, not that, she has been only too courteous! It may seem strange that I should discuss such a matter, but I find it offensive. This person constantly makes eyes at me, as if—and talks incessantly, as though—and invariably acts, as it were—and I simply don't care for it.

LADY CYPRESSBURG She shall go this very day!

TITUS Then too there is the behavior of your ladyship's hairdresser. He is carrying on shamelessly with your ladyship's maid, which naturally touches the honor of the house—

LADY CYPRESSBURG I'll tell him goodbye, too.

TITUS All this flirting, these amorous liaisons, trouble me, I don't like to stand by and see this sort of thing going on— (*aside*) I'd much rather be doing it myself.

LADY CYPRESSBURG What delicate, noble sentiments! (*aloud*) Marquis has done my hair for the last time.

TITUS And then there is the head gardener—No, I'll not say anything more—

LADY CYPRESSBURG Speak up, I demand it!

TITUS She halfway proposed marriage to me.

LADY CYPRESSBURG The impertinence!

TITUS A formal halfway proposal of marriage it was.

LADY CYPRESSBURG She must leave my house this day!

TITUS (*to himself*) Once they're all gone, I'll remain the fairhaired boy! (*aloud*) I am sorry if I—

LADY CYPRESSBURG Write letters of dismissal to all three of them immediately.

TITUS No, that I cannot do. My first act as secretary must not be such a cruel one.

LADY CYPRESSBURG My, what a noble heart the young man has!

Scene 21

EMMA (*Enters from the left side door.*) Mama, I have come to complain about Constance. Because of the way she behaved, she forced me to call her a silly goose.

TITUS (*aside*) They always have to peck away at one another!

LADY CYPRESSBURG You shall dismiss her forthwith, Constance orally, and Mrs. Pruningshears and the hairdresser in writing.

EMMA All right, mama dear!

TITUS (*feigning amazement*) Mama?

LADY CYPRESSBURG Yes, this is my daughter.

TITUS Ah!—No!—No!—Go on!—No, it cannot be!

LADY CYPRESSBURG Why not?

TITUS The years do not add up.

LADY CYPRESSBURG (*Feels herself very flattered.*) Oh but they do, my friend.

TITUS Such a young lady—and this grown-up daughter? No, you may deceive someone else, but— She must be a younger sister, or perhaps a very distant relative of the house. If I am to believe your ladyship has a daughter, then she could at most, at the very most, be only *so* big— (*Indicates the height of a newborn infant.*)

LADY CYPRESSBURG Yet it is as I have said. One has conserved oneself well.

TITUS Oh, I know what conservation can do, but no conservatory could have achieved this!

LADY CYPRESSBURG (*smiling benignly*) Silly man ... But now I must make my toilet, or my guests will take me by surprise! You, Emma, come with me!— (*to* TITUS) I shall see you by and by.

TITUS (*as though overcome by feeling*) Oh, let it be soon! (*Pretending to be shocked at his own words, collects himself, makes a very deep bow, and adds in an obsequious tone.*) Oh let there be soon some way for me to prove my eagerness to serve you!

LADY CYPRESSBURG (*leaving*) Adieu! (*Exits with* EMMA *by left side door.*)

Scene 22

TITUS Gracious lady! Gracious lady! For the time being that's all I'll say: Gracious lady! It's impossible to say how much fun it is when one has been despised, suddenly to become charming. When I think of this morning and then now, that's quite a change in the space of four or five hours. Yes, Time is the longsuffering tailor's apprentice who does the alterations in the workshop of eternity. Sometimes the work goes swiftly, sometimes slowly, but it always gets done, there's no denying it. Time changes all!

Song

1

This iron man would go dancing and work up a steam,
Then sit down in a draught with a bowl of ice cream;
At a gallop from mistress to mistress he sped,
Drank and played cards all night, never thinking of bed.
Ten years later he's hectic, his stomach's awry,
He must wear flannel nightshirts in the month of July,
And a warm quilted nightcap, *la grippe* to forestall—
Yes, time changes all.

2

This one spends the whole day with the girl he's to wed,
Leaving only when the servants are ready for bed,
Then sighs up at her window on high from below
And freezes his nose, standing there in the snow.
Six months after the wedding he's nowhere in sight,
Coming home, if at all, in the dead of the night.
When she's in Brühl,[3] he's in Naples, having a ball—
Yes, time changes all.

3

A singer once sang like the heavenly spheres,
When she belched, faery melodies rang in one's ears.
Her delivery was flawless, her tone so unique,
That the nightingales fled from their nests in sheer pique.
Silver bells were old dishpans compared with this crooner.
Six years later her voice was as cracked as a schooner.
Now she frets through a play in a theatrical squall—
Yes, time changes all.

4

What a well-behaved fellow, such a fine little man,
So handsome and modest, so spick and so span,
Though soft-spoken, he answers enquiries one makes him,
And redounds to one's honor wherever one takes him.
Men and women alike fawn over the boy.
Ten years later the lad's a great hobbledehoy,
A fool who butts in with remarks off the wall—
Yes, time changes all.

5

This great beauty turned down thirteen offers of marriage,
Eight of which were from owners of house, horse, and carriage.
Two strung themselves up at the door of the gal,
Three others were found in the Schanzel canal.[4]
In the Third Coffeehouse[5] four more shot themselves dead.
That was years ago. Now she would not turn a head,
If she stood on her own. What a terrible fall!
Yes, time changes all.

6

Once if someone said something of one one held dear,
Then pow! One received a good clout on one's ear!
The boxing of ears led of course to a duel;
All year long bloody feuds such as this were the rule.
Lovers now at such forwardness take no offense,
But themselves make bad jokes at their sweethearts' expense,
Make their girls laughingstocks at the local beer hall—
Yes, time changes all.

(*Exits through right door.*)

Scene 23

(MR. FLATT, *several* GENTLEMEN *and* LADIES *enter during the ritournelle of the following chorus.*)

CHORUS

Nowhere else in the world is a party so nice
As this house, where one plays neither card games nor dice.
For when dear Lady Cypressburg holds a soirée,
One pays homage to naught but the Muse and the tea.

(*During the chorus,* SERVANTS *bring in a large table spread for tea and place chairs about it.*)

Scene 24

LADY CYPRESSBURG Welcome, ladies and gentlemen!

GUESTS We took the liberty—

LADY CYPRESSBURG You are all well, I trust?

GENTLEMEN Yes, thank you kindly.

LADIES (*among themselves*) Migraine, headaches, rheumatism—

LADY CYPRESSBURG If you please— (ALL *sit down to tea.*)

TITUS (*entering from the right side door*) Perhaps I come at an inopportune—?

LADY CYPRESSBURG Not at all! (*presenting him to the company*) My new secretary.

ALL How do you do?

LADY CYPRESSBURG (*to* TITUS) Be seated. (TITUS *sits.*) This gentleman will read you my latest memoirs at our next soirée.

ALL How charming!

MR. FLATT It's a pity your ladyship does not write for the theater.

LADY CYPRESSBURG Who knows what may happen? Perhaps I shall try my hand at it soon.

TITUS I understand it's fantastically easy to do, that it goes slick as a whistle.

MR. FLATT I myself have long had a passion to write a farce.

TITUS (*to* FLATT) Then why don't you?

MR. FLATT My wit in not so composed as to compose anything comical.

TITUS Then write a sad farce. In a gloomy story even the dullest joke will stand out by contrast, just as the dullest needlework shows to good effect on black velvet.

MR. FLATT But one cannot call something that is sad a farce!

TITUS No. If there are three jokes in a play and other than that nothing but death, dying, corpses, graves, and gravediggers, nowadays that is called a slice of life.

MR. FLATT I didn't know that.

TITUS It is quite a new invention, and belongs to the school of House and Garden Poetry.

LADY CYPRESSBURG Are you then no lover of sentiment?

TITUS Oh yes, but only in a worthy cause, and one is not found very often. That is why a noble soul can make do for a long time with one handkerchief, while the common, good little garden-variety souls need a dozen hankies for a single comedy.

LADY CYPRESSBURG (*to her neighbor*) What do you think of my secretary?

Scene 25

FLORA (*Enters crying through center door.*) My lady, please forgive me—

ALL (*surprised*) The head gardener!

TITUS (*dismayed, aside*) Damnation!

FLORA (*to* LADY CYPRESSBURG) I can't believe you have turned me out of service, I've done nothing!

LADY CYPRESSBURG I owe you no explanation for the grounds which led to my decision. By the way—

FLORA (*catching sight of* TITUS, *astonished*) What's this? He has blonde hair!

LADY CYPRESSBURG What is the hair of my secretary to you? Out!

Scene 26

CONSTANCE (*Enters, weeping, with* EMMA *through center door.*) No, it cannot be!

EMMA I've only told you what mama told me to.

CONSTANCE I've been dismissed?

ALL (*surprised, turning to* LADY CYPRESSBURG) Really?

CONSTANCE My lady, I would never have thought it of you! Without cause—

MR. FLATT What has she done?

CONSTANCE It's all because of the secretary's hair.

LADY CYPRESSBURG How ridiculous! That is not the reason at all. (*to the* COMPANY) By the way, what do you think of this fool? She insists he has black hair! Now I ask you: is he blonde or not?

CONSTANCE He is black-haired!

FLORA That's what I say, too; he's a brunette!

Scene 27

MARQUIS (*entering by center door*) And I say he is neither!

ALL What is he then, M. Marquis?

MARQUIS He's redheaded!

ALL (*astonished*) Red?

TITUS (*to himself*) That does it! (*Stands up and throws the blonde wig to the floor in the center of the stage.*) Yes, I am redheaded!

ALL (*astonished, rising*) What's that?

LADY CYPRESSBURG Fie!

CONSTANCE (*to* TITUS) How revolting you look!

FLORA (*to* TITUS) And this carrot-top wanted to marry me?

LADY CYPRESSBURG (*to* TITUS) You are a deceiver, and have maligned the most faithful members of my staff. Go, out with you, or my servants will—

TITUS (*to* LADY CYPRESSBURG) No need of that. You are overcome with anger—I'm leaving—

ALL Out!

TITUS Such was Ottocar's rise and fall![6] (*Exits slowly with bowed head through center door.*)

CHORUS

Now that was really too much!
Who ever heard of such?

(LADY CYPRESSBURG *pretends to faint, and the curtain falls amid general consternation.*)

---

1. A candle protected by a glass lens, usually reddish in color, against the wind. Wind lanterns were a part of the paraphernalia of funeral cortèges.

2. Old fashioned, unstylish, and stiff.

3. An inexpensive vacation community just outside Vienna in the Vienna Woods.

4. A tributary of the Danube in Vienna, noted for its fruit market.

5. One of the more infamous coffeehouses in the Prater, Vienna's amusement park.

6. Here Nestroy is playing on Franz Grillparzer's popular tragedy, *König Ottokars Glück und Ende,* which treats of the medieval Bohemian monarch's meteoric rise and equally spectacular downfall.

ACT III

The scene is the same as at the beginning of Act II: part of the garden with the gardener's quarters.

Scene 1

TITUS (*Alone, enters in a melancholy mood from behind the wing of the manor house.*) The proud edifice of my hopes has burned down uninsured; my fortune's stock has fallen by a hundred per cent, and that brings my net worth to a good round sum, namely zero. Now I may call out boldly: "World, close your forests about me; Forests, set your robbers upon me; whoever now can make me a kreuzer poorer, him will I revere as a higher being!"— But wait! I did make a profit in this affair: destiny left me an excellent suit of clothes, though perhaps only as a mocking souvenir of a career thwarted and fallen on its face. Nonetheless, a boon—this black tail coat—

Scene 2

GEORGE (*Who has quickly entered during* TITUS' *last words, now interrupts him.*) —Is to be returned to the manor house, together with the vest and stockings.

TITUS Oh, dear envoy, do you know what an unpleasant mission you—?

GEORGE Don't make any fuss, now!

TITUS Have you considered, dear envoy, that I might already have skedaddled?

GEORGE Oh, our constable catches every vagrant.

TITUS Or have you reflected, dear envoy, that I might ignore the rights of man and knock you down and run away? Then what would you—?

GEORGE Help! Help!

TITUS Why are you yelling so? I was merely inquiring; surely questions are permitted?

GEORGE (*calling toward the gardener's quarters*) Pumpkinseed!

PUMPKINSEED (*from within*) What's up?

GEORGE (*opening the door and speaking inside*) He is to put on his old rags and leave the respectable clothing here.

PUMPKINSEED (*from within*) Fine!

TITUS (*to* GEORGE) You are too good.

GEORGE No more of your compliments! In a quarter of an hour the clothes must be here and you must be God knows where! Understood? (*Exits behind the manor house.*)

Scene 3

TITUS (*alone*) Oh yes, I understand everything. Misfortune has visited me; I wanted to receive the visit in a black tail coat, but Misfortune said: "Don't go to any trouble for me, I'm an old friend, just put an any old rag—"

PUMPKINSEED (*from within*) Well, what's keeping you?

TITUS Coming, coming! (*Exits into the gardener's quarters.*)

Scene 4

(SALOME *and* BUNG *enter from the left.*)

SALOME Then you really mean him no harm?

BUNG I keep telling you, no! I'm only doing what the brewmaster told me to. He is the only man who has any spiritual influence over me.

SALOME And what did he tell you?

BUNG He said: "You had it coming, because you didn't look out for him when he was a boy! Now he has run away and may make your family a laughingstock in the world." That's why I have come after him.

SALOME And do you want to have him jailed?

BUNG Who, me? I'd give my life to! But the brewmaster said that that too would be a disgrace to the family.

SALOME Oh, go on, how can you be so cross with your own nephew—?

BUNG Even a nephew can be a thorn in one's side when he has red hair.

SALOME Is that then a crime?

BUNG Red hair aways indicates a foxy, scheming dispositon— besides, he brings disgrace on the whole family. Of course they're all dead now except for me, but while they were in the family, we all had brown hair, all dark brown heads, not a fair head to be found in the whole family, and then this boy had the effrontery to come into the world redheaded!

SALOME Still, that's no reason to let a relative go to ruin when one has means oneself.

BUNG What I have I owe entirely to my own wits.

SALOME And are you really a man of means?

BUNG I should hope so! My parents didn't leave me a kreuzer. I was confined entirely to my own wits, and that's a pretty narrow confinement, I'll tell you!

SALOME I can believe that, but—

BUNG Then shortly afterwards a godmother died and left me ten thousand gulden. I thought to myself, if only a couple more relatives die, I may be able to make ends meet. And right away, four weeks later, an uncle died and left me thirty thousand gulden. The next summer another uncle came down with malaria and I got twenty thousand gulden; the following winter an aunt caught the fever and turned in her dinner pail, leaving me forty thousand gulden. A couple of years later another aunt, then another godmother—all just as I had planned! —Then too I won eighteen thousand gulden in the lottery.

SALOME That too?

BUNG Yes, one can't count on inheritances for everything; one must diversify. In short, I can say that all I have I owe to my wits.

SALOME Well, Master Titus must be just as clever, since he'll inherit from you when you die.

BUNG A wise man once told me I could not die—he didn't say why—he was probably only flattering me, but if I do, I will find myself some people to my taste to leave my money to. I can't have that redhead disgrace me by doing me the last honors.

SALOME Then you aren't going to do anything for poor Master Titus, either now or after your death?

BUNG I'll do what the brewmaster told me to. I'll buy him a shop in the city; that much I owe the dead relatives. Then I'll give him a couple of thousand gulden to set himself up as a respectable man; then I'll toss off a few well-chosen remarks about his red hair, and afterwards he is never to come into my sight again.

SALOME (*joyfully*) So you're going to make him rich and happy after all?

BUNG I'm going to do what the brewmaster told me to.

SALOME (*sadly, to herself*) I'm glad to hear it, though when he's no longer poor, he'll be quite lost to me. (*sighing*) Oh well, he didn't want me anyway.

BUNG What is he doing at the manor house?

SALOME I don't know, but he is trimmed from head to toe with gold braid.

BUNG He's in livery! Oh, blot on the family honor! The nephew of a beer distributor covered with gold braid! I'll bet the whole family have turned over in their graves! Oh unheard-of scandal! Quick, take me up there, I'll shake him out of that livery—hurry! I'll not rest until the stain is expunged and my family lie at peace in their graves again.

SALOME But let me tell you—

BUNG (*highly agitated*) Onward, I say! Lead on, torch bearer! (*Drives her before him out behind the wing of the manor house.*)

Scene 5

FLORA (*Enters from the left.*) Hi! Pumpkinseed! Pumpkinseed!

PUMPKINSEED (*Enters from the gardener's quarters.*) What do you want?

FLORA That person has gone, I trust?

PUMPKINSEED No, he's not quite ready.

FLORA Tell him to hurry up!

PUMPKINSEED (*maliciously*) Perhaps you would like a little farewell supper for two, at which I would be superfluous?

FLORA Idiot!

PUMPKINSEED I just thought you might like to, since you were so eager at lunchtime; now would be the perfect opportunity, her ladyship's maid won't snatch him away from you now.

FLORA Shut up and send him away!

PUMPKINSEED (*calling into the gardener's quarters*) Get a move on, sir!

TITUS (*from within*) Right away!

Scene 6

TITUS (*In the shabby suit of clothes he wore at the beginning of the play, enters from the gardener's quarters.*) Here I am.

FLORA Hardly the thing for a person who ought to have been gone by now.

TITUS Oh, good Mrs. Pruningshears, who also found a hair in my hair! Would you perhaps care to give me something for the road?

FLORA *Give* you something? For the impertinent hoax which you played on me? I'd better make sure you haven't *taken* anything. (*Looking him up and down contemptuously, exits into her quarters.*)

TITUS (*outraged*) What?

PUMPKINSEED Well, one never knows. (*Also looks him up and down contemptuously.*) Hairy snake in the grass! (*Exits into gardener's quarters.*)

Scene 7

TITUS (*alone*) Impertinent folk! People certainly treat one kindly when one is down on his luck. Though actually, I had it coming. I didn't behave very generously when I was on top, either—but so much for that. Evening is coming on, evening in every sense of the word. The sun of my good fortune and the real sun have both set in the west—where turn now, where find shelter for the night without a kreuzer to my name?—that's the real Western Question.[1] (*Looks toward the manor house and the gardener's quarters.*) There are plenty of rooms there, but I seem to be a diet that these rooms cannot stomach.

GEORGE (*Enters from behind the manor house and approaches* TITUS *with great circumspection.*) Master Titus?

TITUS (*annoyed by his servility*) I beg you, don't take me for a fool!

GEORGE I know perfectly well what to take you for— (*aside*) though I am not allowed to say it. (*aloud*) Would you be so good as to come up to the manor house?

TITUS (*astonished*) I?

GEORGE To her ladyship's maid.

TITUS I? To Madame Constance?

GEORGE And then perhaps to her ladyship. But not right away, in about half an hour. In the meantime you might like to take a turn about the garden.

TITUS (*to himself*) Incredible!—but I'll do it. (*to* GEORGE) I shall wait here and then come as ordered. Would you be so kind as to tell the garden help over there (*pointing to the left*) that I am strolling here by her ladyship's leave. In light of the proverb, "Ingratitude is the world's reward,"[2] I have reason to suspect they may wish to show their gratitude to me for the way I treated them today by trying to toss me out on my ear.

GEORGE Certainly, Master Titus. We shall see to the matter at once. (*Making a courteous bow, exits.*)

Scene 8

TITUS This is what I make of it: her ladyship, in a fit of graciousness, must have realized she has treated me, poor devil that I am, too harshly, and in the end is coming forth with something for the road. Wait! (*struck by an idea*) Just to be doubly sure of success, I'll pay her a delicate compliment— (*reaching into his pocket*) I still have—since she can't abide red hair—I still have the late gardener's gray wig here in my pocket, (*pulls it out*) in which I'll make my farewell visit; she'll be bound to spring for something! I'll try my luck now with the gray. Black and blonde hair turn color all too soon—in my case both enjoyed but a brief moment of glory. Gray hair, on the other hand, never changes; perhaps my luck will hold with the gray. (*Exits downstage left.*)

Scene 9

FLORA (*from within*) Didn't I tell you something like this would happen? (*Enters angrily from her quarters.*) Oh, I know people! (*to* PUMPKINSEED) Run after him!

PUMPKINSEED It's not worth the effort.

FLORA But he stole my late husband's wig; it is invaluable to me when I want it.

PUMPKINSEED Oh, go on, it's full of moths.

FLORA Run after him and recover his loot!

PUMPKINSEED He won't get two groschen for it.

FLORA Run after him, I say. Hurry!

PUMPKINSEED (*slowly making his way out behind the gardener's house*) I'll see if I can catch him—but I don't think I will. (*Exits.*)

Scene 10

FLORA (*very angrily*) What a pity it's already evening! The constable will be drunk by now, otherwise I'd have him arrested, that saucy rascal—I'd give him something to remember me by!

GEORGE (*Enters downstage left.*) What's the matter, Mrs. Pruningshears? Why so angry?

FLORA Oh, it's that good-for-nothing tramp!

GEORGE Shh! Honor to whom honor is due! I too called him a vagabond earlier, but it seems he has a filthy rich uncle who has come to take care of him; he's going to buy him the best barbershop in the city, for he is a trained barber, and then he is going to give him thousands and thousands of gulden.

FLORA (*extremely surprised and taken aback*) Oh, go on—!

GEORGE It is as I say. I was just sent to ask Master Titus to come up to the manor house. He is not supposed to know anything yet, but I did call him "Master," because, as I said, honor to whom honor is due. (*Exits behind the manor house.*)

Scene 11

FLORA (*alone*) This news is enough to give one a headache—and to think of the rough way I treated him! Now everything must be altered and tailored to becoming the wife of a barber! It is a disaster only in the country, in the city one can make do with a redheaded husband. Here he comes now! (*looking to the left*) I'll pretend to regret what I did. What pretend? I'm out of my mind with regret!

QUODLIBET TRIO

FLORA

> Titus! Titus!

TITUS (*Enters from upstage left.*)
> Can the gardener be calling to *me?*

FLORA

> Master Titus, please listen to me!

TITUS

> Can the gardener be calling to *me?*

FLORA

> Master Titus, please listen to me!
> I've lost all the peace I once knew.

TITUS

> Have your say, then; I'm listening to you.

FLORA

> It is never too early to rue!

TITUS

> Your farewell was unworthy of you.

FLORA

> I've lost all the peace I once knew!

TITUS

> Have your say, then; I'm listening to you.

together

FLORA

It is never too early to rue!

} together

TITUS

Your farewell was unworthy of you.

FLORA

It is never, no, never too early to rue!

} together

TITUS

Your farewell, though, was really unworthy of you!

FLORA

Don't turn your back on me, I pray,
Nor look vindictively my way,
I cannot bear it!

TITUS

Well, what is it?

FLORA

I am perishing—!

TITUS

Sure you are!

FLORA

Woe is me!

TITUS

It never fails to smart,
It cuts one to the heart,
To be an object of disdain.
Far distant from your native weald
Shall other bonds of love be sealed;
In Switzerland, by cow-maid healed,
A man may seek surcease from pain.

FLORA

If I seemed somewhat vexed when we parted,
Please forgive my ungovernable passion.
When avenging themselves, the greathearted
Always do so in greathearted fashion.

TITUS

I am engulfed in a storm of vengeance
Called forth by Honor and Love—

FLORA

Does that mean you're still going to leave?

TITUS

Yes. I set forth, joyful and free,
Never thy temple to see.

FLORA

Oh, you cannot conceive of the yearning,
Of the torments within this breast churning,
Of the fires of remorse ever burning,
In a heart that is bleeding and torn!
Yes, I call you my reason for living,
The one, ardent goal of my striving!
How *can* you be so unforgiving
As to answer my tears with scorn?

TITUS

Something's wrong here, unless I mistake her.
To think I'd so quickly awake her
To passion. But so what? From the baker
You can buy kaiser rolls, but not me!
It's no use, you see,
I'm off for a year.
You'll never have me,
We'll not be a pair.
It's all for naught, you'll get nowhere.
It's all for naught, you'll get nowhere.

SALOME (*entering*)

There's really no reason, I vow,
For my face to be smiling and gay.
Yet my mouth opens up even now
And breaks out in a laugh anyway.
It's so funny the way the fat man
Is behaving up there in the house;
Down here he plays the great Khan;
Up there he's as still as a mouse. —Hahaha!

FLORA

What is *she* doing here?

TITUS

It's Salome the goose-girl!
Shall she see me here as a churl?

77

SALOME (*catching sight of* TITUS)
        But what's this?—Now with *her?*
        Yet another *malheur,*
    That I happened upon them this way.
    But I've made up my mind not to say
        Another word more,
        Nor to think heretofore
    Of that which is never to be, ah no,
    Of that which is never to be.

FLORA

        Titus! Don't be a boor!
        We're alone here no more.
    I shall try a soft-spoken refrain;
    Thus I'm certainly sure to regain
        The one I have lost,
        The one I have lost,
    The one who is all things to me, ah yes,
    The one who is all men to me.

TITUS

        I'll at least seem to be
        Full of sweet charity,
    But don't let a soft-spoken refrain
    Have you jumping for joy all in vain,
        For I'm not won with ease,
        And observe my words, please—
        I only said "seem to be."

all
three
together

TITUS

        Oh, to see her caught in the net—
        I confess with a touch of regret—
    Were the work of a moment, and yet
    I cannot, I cannot, I cannot!
    For I'm not deedidledeedum
    In love deedidledeedum
    With her dumdiddledeedum
        At all, not at all!
        Ah, to see her in the net—
        I confess with regret—
        Were so easy, and yet
        I cannot! Her yearning
        I mustn't be burning
    To think of returning, oh no!

ALL THREE

        In airy hopes we often trust,
        And all we hope for turns to dust.

FLORA

      Mine shan't be turned to dust, never fear;
      Luck holds us widows far too dear.

TITUS, SALOME

      Ours shall be turned to dust, we fear;
      Luck favors us but with a sneer.

} together

ALL THREE

      When one has luck beneath one's roof,
            And thinks it's there to stay,
      It slips right out the window, poof!
            And softly steals away.
      In airy hopes we often trust,
      And all we hope for turns to dust.

FLORA

      Mine shan't be turned to dust, never fear;
      Luck holds me far too dear.

TITUS, SALOME

      Ours shall be turned to dust, we fear;
      Fate mocks us with a sneer.

} together

SALOME

      My brother the 'prentice sings thus:
      "With the lasses it is really, really, really
            Always such a lot of fun;
      Although in public they act silly, silly, silly,
            They're not deceiving anyone.
      And I am such a handsome fool, fool, fool,
      As straight and slender as a rule, rule, rule,
      Among all men the very jewel, jewel, jewel,
            That's something no one can deny.
      I've lots of gumption in my head, head, head;
      I'm proud to say I've never plead, plead, plead,
      For very long with a girl who said, said, said,
            She'd not get in the wagon bed, bed, bed,
            She'd not get into the wagon bed."

ALL THREE

      Soon everything will change,
      Take courage on the road
      That leads us to our goal;
      March on till things look up.
            Fortune's round,
      O'er the earth it doth merrily bound;
            Without ground,
      Underneath it one often is found.

FLORA, SALOME

At any rate—

TITUS

We know our state—we're nothing great—
We're pawns of Fate—

FLORA, SALOME

We're pawns of Fate, mere pawns of Fate.

FLORA

Though one may hate—

SALOME

To think of Fate—

TITUS

And have one's back to the wall—

ALL THREE

That's no reason to mope,
With a glimmer of hope,
We'll be able to cope after all.

FLORA, SALOME

Of this there's no question:
With a healthy digestion,

TITUS

With a healthy digestion—

ALL THREE

One can stomach most anything,
One can stomach everything.

(FLORA *exits right,* TITUS *behind the manor house,* SALOME *downstage left.*)

Change of Scene: *salon in the manor house with an arch and french windows in the background, opening onto a moonlit terrace and garden; side doors right and left, table lamps on either side of the room.*

Scene 12

CONSTANCE (*Enters from the right, alone.*) Who would have thought it of the hairdresser! With a careless "Adieu, madame," he breaks off with me forever! Such a thing could cause an ordinary widow to lose her composure, but for me, thank God, it's only a moment before another suitor, Monsieur Titus, lies at my feet. If only her ladyship, who so kindly has made this affair her concern, can get the old walrus to make Titus his heir!

Scene 13

LADY CYPRESSBURG (*entering from the left*) Constance—

CONSTANCE (*hurrying to her*) My lady—?

LADY CYPRESSBURG It's no use.

CONSTANCE Is that possible?

LADY CYPRESSBURG I have agonized over the man for the last half hour, but his waterproof leather soul is impervious to the dew of eloquence. He will set him up in business, nothing more—there is no hope for an inheritance.

CONSTANCE H'mph! That would be fatal. And I thought it would be so easy; I even sent for the notary Falk, who has a summerhouse in the neighborhood.[3] Let's try once more, my lady. Let us both set upon him together.

LADY CYPRESSBURG If you like. Today in my haste I treated you very unjustly, and I wish to make amends through true motherly solicitude.

CONSTANCE (*kissing her hand*) You are so very kind—

LADY CYPRESSBURG (*exiting with* CONSTANCE *by the left door*) I have very little hope, however; perhaps the sight of his nephew—

CONSTANCE He should be here any moment now. (*Both exit left.*)

Scene 14

(CONRAD *escorts* TITUS *in through the french windows which open on the terrace.* TITUS *is wearing the gray wig.*)

TITUS (*entering*) But at least tell me—

CONRAD I am not authorized to say anything. (*ogling him in surprise*) What, what's that? You're wearing a gray wig.

TITUS Is that your affair? I have been summoned here; announce me, and have done with it!

CONRAD All right, all right! (*Exits left.*)

Scene 15

TITUS (*alone, pointing to his heart*) I admit it'll give me a bit of a pang here when I see Constance again. Just think how she said: "Oh, how revolting he looks!" Such a recollection is the universal remedy for chronic heartaches. She can remain a lady's chambermaid wherever she likes; but never again will she enter the chambers of my heart. Those rooms I shall let to a bachelor, whose name in Misogyny.

(*Enter* CONRAD.)

TITUS (*to him*) Well, have you announced me?

CONRAD Not yet; her ladyship is in conversation, and is not to be interrupted.

TITUS But I am—

CONRAD Don't be impatient! Wait here, or (*pointing to the right*) in that room. In time I shall see whether it is time to announce you. (*Exits right.*)

Scene 16

TITUS Off with you, you uniformed order-executing machine! He too is one of a uniform edition. Life is a collection of such editions that may be of great value, because they prompt even the most dissatisfied of us to make the sated remark, "I've had more than my fill!"

Song

1

Someone comes to your room; "Yes, what is it?" you say.
"Please help me, I beg you, I'm in a bad way.
I've been looking for work, but times are so hard,
And I've just spent ten weeks in a hospital ward!"
Yet it's not even noon, and he reeks like a still;
I've had more than my fill, oh yes, more than my fill!

2

"This affair is outrageous!" the husband cries out.
"You don't know," purrs the wife, "what you're talking about.
If to tender addresses the man seems inclined,
It is only because he's in awe of my mind.
What you take for love's ardor is merely good will—"
I've had more than my fill, oh yes, more than my fill!

3

In a cloak with red tassels the maiden is dressed,
And I'll bet she has cambric at home in her chest,
Her smoke-colored gown is the *crème de la crème;*
When she comes to a puddle, she lifts up her hem
And reveals just the merest suggestion of frill—
I've had more than my fill, oh yes, more than my fill!

4

I'm in love with a girl who is modest and bland,
So I go to her parents and ask for her hand.
"She is yours, you may marry tomorrow," they say,
"Though you'll have to look after us too, by the way,
And take in her ten brothers and sisters, if you will—"
I've had more than my fill, oh yes, more than my fill!

5

Two fräuleins are chatting on a neighboring bench,
I hear "oui" and "peut-être"—they are talking real French.
"Allez-vous aujourd'hui au théâtre, Marie?"
"Nous allons," says her friend, "au quatrième galerie,
Je vais toujours avec Maman au théâtre en ville—"
I've had more than my fill, oh yes, more than my fill!

6

"I shall go on the stage!" someone told me, inspired.
"What rôle would you like to play first?" I inquired.
"Well, Hamlet's not bad for a great virtuoso;
Then my Don Carlos will make all the others seem so-so.
There'll be no one like me on the whole Burg playbill—"[4]
I've had more than my fill, oh yes, more than my fill!

(Exits through left side door.)

Scene 17

LADY CYPRESSBURG What can be taking him so long?

CONSTANCE George told me that—

TITUS (*entering from the right*) Does your ladyship have reference to me?

LADY CYPRESSBURG Ah, there you are.—You are in for a surprise!

CONSTANCE (*gazing in wonder at* TITUS' *gray wig and calling* LADY CYPRESSBURG'S *attention to it*) My lady! Just look—

LADY CYPRESSBURG What's that?

TITUS (*pointing to his wig*) This old wig was the only thing I could lay hands on. I used it to conceal the color which is so injurious to your nervous system.

LADY CYPRESSBURG H'm, it's not all that bad. Sometimes I am a bit childish.

TITUS Childish? Not even the most perceptive student of human behavior would find that quality in you.

CONSTANCE Actually, red hair is not all that terrible on you.

TITUS (*astonished*) You say that, you who—?

LADY CYPRESSBURG Now you must take off that wig at once, there is someone who—

CONSTANCE (*Catches sight of* BUNG, *who has entered from the left.*) Too late, he's already here!

LADY CYPRESSBURG (*to* BUNG) Here is your nephew, Mr. Bung. (*Exits through left door.*)

CONSTANCE (*to herself*) Now it is up to him to come to terms with him! (*Follows* LADY CYPRESSBURG *out.*)

Scene 18

TITUS (*astonished*) Uncle? How did you get here?

BUNG In a more respectable way than you did! Running off is not my way of doing things.

TITUS Yes, of course, for one of your dimensions running cannot be very easy.

BUNG You blot on the family, you! (*Comes nearer and notices with surprise the gray hair.*) But what's this? Gray hair?

TITUS (*to himself, startled*) Uh-oh!

BUNG But you are redheaded!

TITUS (*quickly regaining his composure*) I used to be.

BUNG And now?

TITUS Now I am gray.

BUNG But that's impossible!

TITUS Actuality is always the best proof of possibility.

BUNG But you are only twenty-six years old!

TITUS So I was yesterday! But the anguish, the pain of being deserted by my own, my only uncle, and cast out into the world a helpless runaway, aged me a millenium. And I turned gray overnight.

BUNG (*amazed*) Overnight?

TITUS It was seven on the dot when I left home; three quarters of an hour later I looked at myself in the mirror of unfortunates—that is, a puddle of water—and at that time it seemed to me my hair had been lightly dusted. Ascribing it to the poor light, I chose the Linigraben[5] as my mattress, wrapped myself in the night mists, and fell asleep. On the stroke of midnight I was awakened by two frogs in disputation on my necktie. This brought on an attack of desperation which in turn gave me the brilliant idea to pull out a few handfuls of my hair. They were gray! I attributed this to the sickle moon's silvery reflection and fell asleep again. Then, all of a sudden, an ear-splitting chatter of milkmaids awoke me from deepest Linigraben slumber—it was broad daylight, and at my side a gypsy sat making his toilette. He looked at himself in a piece of broken glass that had once perhaps been a mirror; I followed suit, and an iron gray head stared back at me which I recognized as my own only because it was attached to my face.

BUNG This is unheard of!

TITUS Not at all. History offers us numerous examples: there was, for instance, a certain Belisarius;[6] no doubt you have heard of him?

85

BUNG Belisarius? Was he a beer distributor?

TITUS No, a Roman general. His wife got the senate to have his eyes gouged out.

BUNG Wives usually take care of that sort of thing themselves.

TITUS This one however did it with the help of the Justinian Code. Her husband took the matter much to heart and in three day's time was totally gray. Just think, Uncle, what took a Roman general three days, I accomplished overnight. And you, Uncle, are the cause of this historical phenomenon.

BUNG (*deeply moved*) Titus, my boy, my kinsman—I don't know what's coming over me—I the uncle of a historical phenomenon! (*sobbing*) I haven't cried in nineteen years, this is all so unexpected. (*Dries his eyes.*)

TITUS It's good to let the old beer out.

BUNG (*opening his arms*) Come here, my silver-haired boy! (*Embraces him.*)

TITUS (*returning his embrace*) Uncle Bung! (*Leaps back suddenly from his arms.*)

BUNG (*astonished*) Why do you spring back like a wooden hoop?

TITUS (*to himself*) He came within a hair of grabbing my pigtail! (*aloud*) You bruised me; it must have been your ring.

BUNG Don't be so sensitive! Here, into your uncle's arms! (*Embraces him vigorously.*)

TITUS (*Holds the pigtail up with his right hand during the embrace, in order to keep it out of the grasp of Bung.*)

BUNG (*releasing him*) There!—By the way, so as not to bruise you with my ring any more— (*With some difficulty removes the heavy signet ring from his finger.*)

TITUS (*in the meantime, aside*) If he sees the pigtail, that's it; I'll never be able to convince him I grew a pigtail in my grief.

BUNG (*giving him the ring*) There you are! I want you to know I'm here to take you back to the city and make you a successful man—I'm going to buy you a fine barbershop—I—

TITUS (*joyfully*) Uncle!

BUNG But the way you look, that coat—I must present you to her ladyship as a relative of mine, and then there is someone else in there too—

TITUS (*taken aback*) The hairdresser, perhaps?

BUNG Hairdresser! (*Laughs with clumsy roguishness.*) You young scamp, you can't put me on! I may have weak eyes, but I could see very well what that person had in mind. If it weren't for that coat—

(CONRAD *enters through right door and starts to leave through center door.*)

BUNG (*to* CONRAD) Hi, you—if you would—do you have a brush?

CONRAD A brush? Yes, I think so. (*searching his pockets*) Right, I have one here in my pocket. (*Hands* BUNG *the brush.*)

BUNG Good. Give it here! You can go now. (CONRAD *exits through center door.*)

BUNG (*to* TITUS) Now come here so I can clean you up a bit.

TITUS (*worriedly*) What are you going to do?

BUNG Turn around—!

TITUS (*anxiously*) But an uncle can't serve as his nephew's clothes-cleaner!

BUNG I'm not serving a nephew, I am brushing the coat of a natural wonder. I am removing dust from a world event, and that is no dishonor even to a beer distributor! Turn around.

TITUS (*in great anxiety, to himself*) Oh Lord! When he sees the pigtail—! (*aloud*) Start with the front!

BUNG All right. (*Begins to brush* TITUS' *clothing.*)

TITUS (*in great anxiety, to himself*) Fate, if you don't give me a pair of scissors, I'll run myself through with a knife!

BUNG (*brushing more vigorously*) It's awful how messy the boy is!

TITUS (*to himself*) Is there no escape? Then let lightning strike! (*As he stands looking toward the left door, it opens and* CONSTANCE'S *hand appears with a pair of scissors.*) Aha! A flash of cold steel strikes my eyes! An angel with a pair of English scissors![7]

BUNG Turn around, I say!

TITUS Let's go stand over there! (*Without turning his back to* BUNG *moves to the left side of the stage until he is standing near the door with his back to it.*) The light is much better here! (*Reaches back and takes the scissors from* CONSTANCE'S *hand.*)

BUNG Now turn around!

TITUS No, you can see there's still a lot more dust here on the front. (*While* BUNG *continues to brush his lapels, he quickly snips off the pigtail.*)

BUNG No, there's not! Come on, turn around! (*Whirls him around.*)

TITUS (*as* BUNG *turns him around, carries the pigtail forward over his head with his left hand, so that* BUNG, *who now begins to brush the back of the coat, has seen nothing. To himself*) Thanks to you, Fate, the amputation was a success!

BUNG (*as he stops brushing*) Now see here, Titus, you're a good lad, you came to grief because of a hard-hearted uncle. And why was I hard-hearted? Because you had red hair! But now you don't any more, so there's no reason why—I have no choice, my heart must soften. You are my only relative, you are—in a word, you are as good as a son to me, you shall be my sole heir!

TITUS (*astonished*) What?

Scene 19

(LADY CYPRESSBURG, CONSTANCE *and the* NOTARY *enter.*)

LADY CYPRESSBURG "Sole heir," those are the words we've been waiting to hear come from your heart!

CONSTANCE We never doubted you for a moment; luckily the notary is right here, and he always has the proper forms at hand.

BUNG Give them here!

(*The* NOTARY *takes out a sheet of paper and explains its salient points to* BUNG *in dumb-show.*)

TITUS (*to himself, with reference to Constance*) She's falling all over herself; she's going after my inheritance much more eagerly than I ever did myself.

LADY CYPRESSBURG (*to* TITUS) See how this good soul (*indicating* CONSTANCE) is looking out for your welfare? I know all about you two, and am pleased to give my consent to this union which love has sealed and which gratitude can only strengthen.

(TITUS *bows without replying.*)

BUNG (*to the* NOTARY) Good, everything's in perfect order! (BUNG *is led to the table on which lie writing materials, sits down to sign.*)

TITUS (*to himself*) I can let him buy me a barbershop; after all, he is a blood relation. But to become his sole heir through a trick, I can't have that! (*aloud to* BUNG, *who is about to sign the document*) Wait, uncle! If you will permit me—

BUNG What? Aren't you satisified yet?

Scene 20

FLORA (*entering by center door*) My lady, I have come—

LADY CYPRESSBURG At an inopportune moment!

FLORA To settle accounts—

LADY CYPRESSBURG Did I not tell you that you may stay on?

FLORA Yes, but—of course nothing's definite, but it may be that I'll marry in the city.... But why should I keep it a secret? Master Titus—

LADY CYPRESSBURG What?

CONSTANCE (*simultaneously*) The effrontery!

BUNG How many did you promise to marry out of desperation?

TITUS Promise? None.

BUNG Not that it matters; marry whoever you wish, you're still my sole heir!

Scene 21

SALOME (*hurrying in through center door*) Master Titus! Master Titus! (*Startled at the sight of the company, without however noticing* FLORA, *she remains standing in the doorway.*)

LADY CYPRESSBURG, NOTARY *and* CONSTANCE What's this?

SALOME (*shyly*) I beg your pardon—

LADY CYPRESSBURG What can this person want here?

SALOME Master Titus! Mrs. Pruningshears has ordered—

LADY CYPRESSBURG But she's right here.

SALOME (*noticing* FLORA) Right! Then she can say it herself.

LADY CYPRESSBURG Say what?

SALOME Nothing! She's making signs for me not to say anything.

LADY CYPRESSBURG Out with it, now!

SALOME I can't while the gardener over there keeps making signs at me.

LADY CYPRESSBURG (*to* FLORA) Stop that! I won't have it! (*to* SALOME) Now what is it?

SALOME (*embarrassed*) Mrs. Pruningshears told Pumpkinseed, and Pumpkinseed told me to—

LADY CYPRESSBURG (*impatiently*) What?

SALOME Master Titus is to give back the wig.

(LADY CYPRESSBURG *and* CONSTANCE *in confusion*)

BUNG What wig?

TITUS (*taking off the gray wig*) This one!

BUNG (*infuriated, as he becomes aware of the deception*) What's that? You young whelp, you—

CONSTANCE (*to herself*) Damnation! Now all is lost!

LADY CYPRESSBURG (*softly to* CONSTANCE) Stay calm! (*aloud to* TITUS) You have played a rather silly joke on your worthy uncle. But

90

surely you cannot believe he really let himself be taken in. He would have to be the most stupid man under the sun not to have seen through your clumsy deception at once. But as a man of intelligence and understanding—

TITUS He saw through it right away, and let *me* be the butt of the joke.

LADY CYPRESSBURG (*to* BUNG) Is that not so?

BUNG (*utterly dumbfounded*) Oh yes, sure, sure, I saw through the whole thing!

LADY CYPRESSBURG (*to* TITUS) That this sensible man is not going to deprive you of your inheritance just because of your hair is something you can hope for with confidence. (*to* BUNG) Isn't that so?

BUNG (*as above*) Oh, sure, sure.

TITUS (*to* CONSTANCE *and* FLORA) But that I should freely renounce the inheritance, that is *not* something you hope for. My good uncle is going to buy me a shop—I can't ask for more than that. And for that I will be eternally grateful to him. I need no inheritance, I only wish he may live another three hundred years.

BUNG (*touched*) Ah, no beer distributor has ever lived that long! You're a good lad, in spite of your red hair.

TITUS (*with reference to Flora and Constance*) It is clear I cannot marry either of these ladies without an inheritance, for they find red hair pardonable only in a sole heir. Therefore I shall marry someone who cannot hold my red hair against me, someone who already has taken a bit of a fancy for a poor redheaded devil—as I believe is the case with this one! (*Takes the astonished* SALOME *in his arms.*)

SALOME What—? Master Titus—?

TITUS Will be yours!

LADY CYPRESSBURG (*who has been speaking softly with* CONSTANCE, *aloud*) Adieu! (*Exits haughtily through left door, followed by the* NOTARY.)

CONSTANCE Her ladyship washes her hands of the whole affair. (*Follows her.*)

FLORA (*to* TITUS, *sarcastically*) I congratulate you on your excellent choice. As they say, "Birds of a feather flock together." (*Exits center.*)

BUNG (*to* TITUS) You're acting as if I had no say in the matter at all!

TITUS (*with reference to Salome*) I know you don't like red hair, Uncle; most people don't. But why is that? Because it is an unfamiliar sight; if there were many redheads around, it would become popular, and you may rest assured, Uncle, that we'll make our contribution to the multiplication of our species. (*Embraces* SALOME.)

(*As the orchestra strikes a few chords, the curtain falls.*)

---

1. A wordplay on the Eastern Question, one of the most compelling issues in Europe in the 1820s and 1830s. The Eastern Question had ostensibly to do with recognition of the Greeks in their struggle to win independence from the Ottoman empire. Its moral effect was far more wide-ranging, however; liberals all over Europe saw in the Greek rebels the champions of their own causes, and Philhellenism became a thinly-veiled metaphor for resistance to established authority all over the continent. By throwing his support to the sultan, Metternich reaffirmed Austria's reputation as the bastion of reactionary politics and thereby succeeded in isolating Austria from the other major European powers, all of whom were in open sympathy with the Greeks.

2. A German proverb often used in the context of "misunderstood genius" and "unappreciated good deeds."

3. See *The House of Humors*, 120n.

4. The Vienna Burgtheater, the most illustrious (hence most coveted by actors) of Austrian stages, usually performed "serious" dramas by established authors.

5. The Linigraben, a moat enclosing Vienna's twenty-three suburbs, was dug in 1703 and later converted into an avenue. In Nestroy's time it was a dumping ground and haven for indigents.

6. Belisarius, a general of the Byzantine emperor Justinian I, was well known to Nestroy's audience through Donizetti's opera which bears his name.

7. Nestroy is here punning on the two meanings of *englisch:* English and angelic.

Judith and Holofernes

Travesty with Song in One Act

DRAMATIS PERSONÆ

HOLOFERNES field marshal of the Assyrians

IDUN

CHALKOL } captains of the Assyrians

ZEPHO

ACHIOR Holofernes' chamberlain

HERALD

MESOPOTAMIAN EMISSARY

HIGH PRIEST OF BAAL

PRIEST OF BAAL

JOACIM high priest of Bethulia

JOAB his son, volunteer in the Hebrew army

JUDITH his daughter, a widow

MIRZA maid in the house of Joacim

ASSAD

DANIEL a blind mute, brother of Assad

AMMON shoemaker

HOSEA

NABAL

BEN } citizens of Bethulia

NAZAEL

HEMAN tailor

NATHAN

RACHEL wife of Assad

SARA wife of Ammon

PRIEST OF BAAL, ASSYRIAN CAPTAINS, SOLDIERS, *and* SLAVES, MESOPOTAMIAN RETINUE, HEBREW SOLDIERS *and* CIVILIANS

The action takes place in the camp of Holofernes and in Bethulia.

Holofernes's camp, to the right his tent

Scene 1

(HIGH PRIEST *and two* PRIESTS *of Baal;* IDUN, CHALKOL, ZEPHO, *and several* WARRIORS, *all assembled before Holofernes' tent.*)

CHORUS
> Holofernes he is called;
> All mankind stands appalled
> Before this hero's power;
> All earthly creatures cower.

He is the terror of the foe, foe, foe,
Because they know he'll lay them low, low, low,
His fury splits the air asunder, -sunder, -sunder,
His mighty voice rings out like thunder, thunder, thunder.
> Let us sing his great renown,
> For if we don't he'll cut us down!

(*At the conclusion of the chorus,* HOLOFERNES *enters from his tent.*)

Scene 2

(*As above;* HOLOFERNES)

ALL Hail, Holofernes!

HOLOFERNES Here I am. We can start now!

IDUN What do you mean?

CHALKOL The attack?

ZEPHO The battle?

HOLOFERNES No, the offerings to the gods! Whose turn is it today, anyway?

HIGH PRIEST Baal has gone longest without an offering.

HOLOFERNES Swell, Baal is a sweetheart of a god. A few rabbits will keep him happy.

HIGH PRIEST Baal will also give you victories in the field.

HOLOFERNES Sure he will, as long as I keep winning them.

HIGH PRIEST Were it not for his protection—!

HOLOFERNES All right, all right; I won't quibble over a couple of calves. (*aside*) I'm on to their game; I know who eats those sacrificial animals.

HIGH PRIEST Enlightened Holofernes, the ignorant masses—

HOLOFERNES Have got to believe in the appetite of the gods for sacrifices, I know. But if you ever try to peddle *me* god X for reason Y, I may just give your gods the day off and have *you* sacrificed.

HIGH PRIEST My lord—!

HOLOFERNES Shut up!

HIGH PRIEST (*to* CAPTAINS) He is out of sorts today.

IDUN (*softly*) His chamberlain told me that he got up on the wrong side of the bed.

CHALKOL (*softly*) On such days one must fear his right hand.

ZEPHO (*softly*) Some job this is, serving in his retinue!

(*Exit all save* HOLOFERNES.)

Scene 3

(HOLOFERNES *alone*)

HOLOFERNES I am the paragon of nature; I have never lost a battle. I am the virgin among generals. I'd like to assault myself some time, just to see who is stronger, I or myself. (*looking upstage*) Who comes there in Assyrian livery? Ah, a long-winded messenger from my dull lord and master.

Scene 4

(HOLOFERNES; HERALD)

HERALD Nebuchadnezzar, who rules from Orient to Occident, from continent to—

HOLOFERNES Fundament and damn all! What does Nebuchadnezzar want now?

HERALD Nebuchadnezzar desires that in the future no other gods be worshipped save himself.

HOLOFERNES (*to himself*) See how puffed up these kings get when they have Holoferneses to conquer the world for them?

HERALD Nebuchadnezzar desires sacrifices to be made to him every day at sunrise.

HOLOFERNES Only at sunrise? (*aside*) The man is letting us off cheap. We're his subjects, therefore his victims at all hours of the day.

HERALD Such is the will of the King of Kings.

HOLOFERNES Fine. Give him my regards.

(*Exit* HERALD.)

Scene 5

(HOLOFERNES *alone*)

HOLOFERNES Not a bad egg, this King of Kings, but it's lucky for this egg that it's stuffed with Nebuchadnezzar! Hey! Are there any false priests around?

Scene 6

(HIGH PRIEST; *two* PRIESTS; HOLOFERNES)

HIGH PRIEST What is your command, Holofernes?

HOLOFERNES From today on Nebuchadnezzar is a god; that is, from today on he is saying out loud what he has long imagined in private.

HIGH PRIEST My lord, I do not understand!

HOLOFERNES No matter, as long as you make the People understand.

HIGH PRIEST As you wish. (*Exits.*)

PRIEST I'll think up some new rituals.

HOLOFERNES Twelve Assyrian gold louis will be your reward.

(*Exit priests.*)

Scene 7

(HOLOFERNES *alone*)

HOLOFERNES Well, well, so Nebuchadnezzar is now a god. And who made him one? My hanger, by the bastinadoes it has dealt his enemies. (*Slaps his sword.*) Here's the god-factory! What in modern times will be done with the bayonet, we gray prehistoricals accomplish with the sword.

Scene 8

(ACHIOR; HOLOFERNES)

ACHIOR There are emissaries from a king outside; they'd like to have a little audience.

HOLOFERNES From which king?

ACHIOR The devil himself couldn't remember all those names.

HOLOFERNES That's true; such a slew of kings have surrendered to me, it's enough to make one's head swim. One of these days I'll absentmindedly lay a country waste and burn a dozen or so cities to the ground, and only later will it occur to me that it belonged to a friendly subject king. (*to* ACHIOR) Show the emissaries in.

(ACHIOR *signals; the Mesopotamian* EMISSARY *enters with his retinue, along with* IDUN, CHALKOL, *and* ZEPHO.)

Scene 9

(*As above;* EMISSARY, RETINUE, IDUN, CHALKOL, ZEPHO.)

EMISSARY Great Holofernes—!

HOLOFERNES What is the name of your principal?

EMISSARY With your lordship's permission, he takes the liberty of being the king of Mesopotamia.

HOLOFERNES That remains to be seen, whether I shall give my permission or not. You are a funny messenger anyhow; Mesopotamian, you say?

EMISSARY At your service.

HOLOFERNES That's as it should be. Peoples must shut up, emissaries be at my service, and kings surrender up their crowns. I'd like to have all mankind strung up, so that only I would be left to tread the earth as I would step on a bug. I'm quite a guy.

EMISSARY Mesopotamia surrenders unconditionally, at your pleasure or displeasure; even your displeasure is our pleasure.

HOLOFERNES Why so late? You are as slow as molasses! Is Mesopotamia so far from here? Why didn't you make up a special train?

EMISSARY I take the liberty in the name of my king to tremble before your wrath.

HOLOFERNES I swore the nation that surrendered last would be burnt out like cockroaches.

EMISSARY But we are only the next to last, and we pray your mercy ever so nicely, while the obstinate Hebrews still hold out. They entrench themselves in their city and slam their insolent gates in the heroic face of Holofernes.

HOLOFERNES Who are these Hebrews?

EMISSARY The Hebrews are a memorable people.

HOLOFERNES I'll give them something to remember. Who is their king?

EMISSARY Their god is also their king.

HOLOFERNES And somewhere else the king is also god—it all boils down to the same thing.

EMISSARY They love art and science, and hate manual labor and agriculture.

HOLOFERNES No agriculture? What do they live on, then?

EMISSARY On capital gains. Their nourishment consists of fourths, eighths, and sixteenths. They skim all kinds of percentages.

HOLOFERNES Is the Hebrew army strong?

EMISSARY That depends. In battle they are weak, but when Heaven is working miracles for them, you wouldn't believe how they triumph over their enemies.

HOLOFERNES Is that all? Go to their high priest and tell him he is to report to his god that Holofernes is here. Never before has he had such a hero to deal with; there is no one in all Vienna—I mean Assyria—who can hold a candle to me. (*Exit* EMISSARY.) And you, my faithful vassals, follow me into battle! Saddle me up the most humpbacked of my camels, and onward to—to—what was the name of that dump?

IDUN Bethulia.

HOLOFERNES Onward then, to Beggarthulia.

(*Martial music, general movement in the camp.* HOLOFERNES *is given a camel with two enormous humps; he mounts so that he sits between these and rides around the stage amid exultant battle cries.*)

Change of scene: *a street in Bethulia*

Scene 10

(AMMON; HOSEA)

AMMON What do you say, Hosea my friend?

HOSEA What's to say? They are still standing outside the gates.

AMMON But are they going to stay out there? No, they are going to enter by force.

HOSEA So we'll close the gates against them.

AMMON Then they will besiege us.

HOSEA Besiege, what's that?

AMMON Besieging is a maneuver where rolls go up a guilder, where milk will bring its weight in gold, and beef is so scarce people could slaughter one another.

HOSEA What a business we could make! Let's unite.

AMMON Unite? Against Holofernes and his host?

HOSEA What Holofernes? We'll pool our cash and buy up everything edible in town; comes the famine, we'll clear three hundred percent.

AMMON Yes, and starve rich.

Scene 11

(*As above;* ASSAD)

ASSAD Why are you standing around without weapons? What's going on?

HOSEA Weapons, why weapons?

ASSAD Every man must arm himself. All the citizens of Bethulia are to be divided into two ranks: in the first comes possessions, in the second intelligence. I have been signed on as a corporal, now I am going to buy me a sabre.

AMMON Assad, you are throwing away your life. Leave off with the fighting!

ASSAD Who says I'm going to fight? The sabre is for drill.

HOSEA Drill and miss the exchange? Such terrible times—and I had to live to see them.

ASSAD Without exception, every man must drill—otherwise everyone will be running around in all directions. But this way, when the famine comes, one of the columns can starve half-left, the other half-right.

AMMON I'm beginning to feel a little nervous.

HOSEA Me too. I think I'll sprinkle some ashes over my head and get into a sackcloth.

ASSAD What for? To drill is still the best.

HOSEA Here comes the high priest Joacim.

AMMON Surely he will have some words of solace for a pious Hebrew.

Scene 12

(*As above;* JOACIM)

JOACIM (*entering from the side*) Vey, vey! Three times vey!

AMMON This is all the solace the priesthood has to offer us?

JOACIM When you all perish by the sword of the foe, remember you brought it upon yourselves with your sins.

HOSEA How about this man? Off our taxes he lives, he's the one we must tithe to.

JOACIM And in case you should feel guiltless, just remember this: the Lord visits the iniquities of the fathers upon the children and grandchildren unto the tenth generation.

ASSAD Enough *bons mots* about eternal justice! (*to the other two*) Come, let's go drill, it's still the best thing to do.

(*Exits with* AMMON *and* HOSEA *to the left.*)

Scene 13

(*The high priest* JOACIM, *alone*)

JOACIM The wrath of Heaven will fall upon the heads of the godless like as a rain of fire. Yet as the physician pours balm upon a wound, even so may my words give comfort to the soul in anguish. Vey, vey! Three times vey! (*Exits right.*)

Scene 14

(JOAB *enters from left side during the ritournelle of the following song.*)

JOAB

1

Since war has broken out on every side, it's come to pass
That the army of the Hebrews is taking leave *en masse.*
This man has got a wife at home, five kiddies in the crib,
Another hasn't either yet, but he's willing to ad lib.
In brief, each hurries home, and folks who cannot understand
Make fun of us for going round with weapons in our hand.
Our arms are not, as some would have it, merely there for show,
We must have something, after all, to offer to the foe.
          Our people are
          Too wise by far
          To take delight in waging war.

2

When among the peoples of the earth the choice was up to God,
Without a great amount of thought he gave the Jews the nod.
His passion we, and thus it is that we forever win,
Without the bore of having to endure the battle's din.
But just in case the Lord has bet on us to be defeated,
There's little call for our men—or the foe's—to be mistreated.
We've miracles aplenty in our past to brag about,
The miracle of bravery we can get along without.
                  Our people are
                  Too wise by far
                  To take delight in waging war.

(*after the song*) Moses, Moses, now there was a general! On the whole, all the greatest generals are found in Biblical history. Even Adam made a brilliant withdrawal from Paradise; came the angel with the flaming sword, right away he took charge: "Right face, Eve! To the left flank, march!" And what an admiral was that Noah—hero of the Flood, Columbus and Nelson of the Deluge, all in one! And Joshua—what a commander! "Halt!" he yelled, and the sun stood still and saluted him with its rays. Try that nowadays and see how far you get. And how about that colossal siege of Jericho! Tataratatata, and the towers lay in the moat—and they didn't even have valve-trumpets in those days. But most of all Moses! Under his command the Red Sea fell into ranks in spite of the Hanoverian guard;[1] and during his forty years of reconnaissance in the desert it rained quail and snowed Presburg zwieback. Now that's what I call first-class strategy. (*looking to the right*) But what's this? What do I see? Papa—!

Scene 15

(JOACIM; JOAB)

JOACIM Joab, my son, let me embrace you. My son Joab, my brave cadet! (*Embraces him.*)

JOAB Papa!

JOACIM Joab, what a terrible period you had to be born into! Horror and devastation in Israel; upheavals in the business world, the strongest houses crashing down, stars falling everywhere in the commercial firmament.

JOAB Tell me, Papa, how stands it with the Babylonian pound and the Mesopotamian franc?

JOACIM Joab my son, at such a time who can think of the market? Assyrian blue chips are going up hour by hour, the odds for our survival are quoted barely at fifty-fifty, and Holofernes is about to come in as a mortgage broker and write us off completely.

JOAB You say we have inflation and famine ahead of us? In that case it's best to stick with government bonds. —Somebody ought to take that Holofernes to court. After all, he is only a general, and look how he treats kings! This is subordination?

JOACIM All the kings of the earth pay tribute to him.

JOAB What tribute? Is he their landlord? Do they board with him? By the way, Papa, our brave troops are saying he is a cannibal. They say he devours three virgins for dinner, two as doves in a pastry, and dunks the third in his coffee.

JOACIM Joab my son, people tend to exaggerate. Who know what he eats, the great Holofernes? Oy vey!

JOAB But he is strong on killing.

JOACIM On the contrary! The great man has only two weaknesses: good wine and a pretty face.

JOAB My God! What a pity our Judith isn't here. She could have become Israel's salvation already!

JOACIM What are you saying about your sister Judith? She lives out in the mountains and mourns her Manasses.

JOAB Nevertheless, our Judith is a beauty—and isn't it true, Papa, that I look very much like her?

JOACIM You were created her spitting image.

JOAB The nurse always said that if Judith hadn't been born a year earlier, we would have been twins. (*struck by a sudden inspiration*) Aha! Illumination from on high—! Prophetic influence from below—! Enthusiasm from all sides—! Googoo eyes—lullabies—anaesthetize—uprise—saberize!

JOACIM (*terrified*) Joab my son, you are possessed!
(*Mumbles a Talmudic formula over him.*)

JOAB It has passed now, but—where is the key to Judith's room?

JOACIM Judith's room?

JOAB Papa, you're going to be amazed when you see what Joab, your handsome cadet, will bring to pass! (*insistently*) Where's the key to Judith's room?

JOACIM On my hassock you will find the book of Genesis, next to it is the key to Judith's room. But what do you have in mind? Why can't you let your papa in on your plans?

JOAB Why? Because if Heaven wants to work a miracle through me, I say let Heaven have its fun.

JOACIM Joab, take care of yourself! (*looking to the left*) Here come the people of Bethulia; I must not neglect my high vocation. (*exiting*) Vey! Vey! Three times vey! (*Exits downstage left.*)

JOAB (*alone*) My plan is a miracle from Heaven—if it works. Yes, if Heaven wants to work wonders nowadays, it has to come up with something really special, because what people used to call a miracle is now looked on as commonplace.

Song

1

In Babylon they wanted to erect a tower so high,
They could look in through the windows of the Lord and catch His eye;
They'd barely reached the clock, though, when they found to their un-
ease,
That one was speaking Spanish, while the other spoke Chinese.
    And everyone agreed
    It was a miracle indeed.
Though many people nowadays build castles in the air,
Their plans go up in smoke before they've gotten halfway there,
For brawls break out no sooner then the cornerstone is laid
That put the Babylonian fiasco in the shade.
We moderns find such things as this in no way wondrous, though,
But really rather commonplace, no cause for cocks to crow.

2

Our ancestors were nincompoops, face down upon the sod
They threw themselves and took a golden calf to be their god;
For this wanton lapse of common sense they dearly had to pay,
And led a life of misery more years than I can say.
    And everyone agreed
    It was a miracle indeed.
How many men among us now—I'll wager quite a few—
Would make a goddess of a goose, if she were well-to-do.

But Fortune sees that each of these in fullest measure pays,
By being tied to apron strings for all his wretched days.
We moderns find such things as this in no way wondrous, though,
But really rather commonplace, no cause for cocks to crow.

3

When Jonah plopped into the sea, you know what came to pass?
A whale came by and swallowed him, but it must have gotten gas—
Apparently the creature had a weak digestive tract—
And three days later brought the Prophet up again, intact.
    And everyone agreed
    It was a miracle indeed.
Our politicians nowadays are such prophetic sages,
Whatever happens, they proclaim they've known of it for ages.
Though no one swallows this, they sicken everyone in town:
Men often have to stomach what a whale could not keep down.
We moderns find such things as this in no way wondrous, though,
But really rather commonplace, no cause for cocks to crow.

4

Egyptian Joseph languished in a penitentiary,
Until the Pharaoh had a dream that changed his destiny;
Whereupon he had him taken from the dungeon dark and sinister,
And elevated on the spot to Egypt's Interior Minister.
    And everyone agreed
    It was a miracle indeed.
Now, too, such swift vicissitudes of fortune may be found,
Though most men feel they tend to come the other way around.
At first they look upon themselves as Nature's nonpareil,
Till someone shakes them from their dream, and they wake up in a cell.
We moderns find such things as this in no way wondrous, though,
But really rather commonplace, no cause for cocks to crow.

5

The Proverbs of King Solomon are known throughout creation,
Because of them he's called The Wise by men of every nation;
But later through idolatry he tarnished his good name;
Some say it was his herd of wives who brought him to this shame.
    And yet one must concede
    It was a miracle indeed.
How many men are in our midst who both in speech and letter
Without the shadow of a doubt go Solomon one better!
Though looked upon as men of note and objects of respect,
They soon grow old and lose their wits and come to be henpecked.
We moderns find such things as this in no way wondrous, though,
But really rather commonplace, no cause for cocks to crow.

(*Exits upstage left.*)

Scene 16

(JOACIM; CITIZENS *of Bethulia, among them* BEN, NAZAEL, DANIEL, RACHEL, SARA, *enter left downstage;* RACHEL *leads the blind mute* DANIEL.)

SARA This is too much. The famine is on the increase, and when it increases it thrives.

RACHEL (*to* JOACIM) Man of God, what is to be done for the general welfare?

JOACIM Vey! Vey!

RACHEL That we are feeling already. A pair chickens costs ninety-six guilders.

SARA A three-story house you have to give for a pound of veal—

RACHEL (*indicating* DANIEL) My blind brother-in-law only let his hand fall on this Jonathan, and had to pay two ducats for it.

(DANIEL *makes violent gestures to signify his indignation, then wolfs down the apple.*)

BEN (*to* RACHEL) Why didn't he tell them he was blind?

RACHEL Because he is also dumb, more's the pity.

SARA (*pointing to the right*) Look there, Rachel; here come our husbands.

RACHEL I really believe—by Moses's staff! They are drilling! What has gotten into the peaceful citizens of Bethulia?

SARA They are drilling—!

Scene 17

(*As above;* ASSAD, AMMON, HOSEA, *and* NABAL *march about with drawn sabres.*)

ASSAD (*as corporal commanding the other three*) Hup! Harew! Hup! Harew! Hup! Harew! Halt!

RACHEL Oh how nicely they do that!

HOSEA This being ordered around is beginning to get me down.

NABAL Is he any better than we are?

AMMON Isn't one Jew the same as another?

ASSAD (*giving orders*) March!

HOSEA Where to?

ASSAD Who questions my orders?

HOSEA Why don't you sharop, you're one of the common people too.

ASSAD Insubordination! 'Tenshun!

AMMON To what I'd like to know.

ASSAD Eyes left!

HOSEA Why? There's nothing to the left. Why should we look left? What is there to see?

ASSAD May Polish lightning strike—!

JOACIM Vey! Vey!

(HOSEA, AMMON, and NABAL *sheathe their sabres.*)

AMMON I resign.

HOSEA *and* NABAL So do we.

HOSEA Drilling only whets the appetite, just what we need in a time of famine.

ASSAD You should become humpbacked and lame—!

CITIZENS (*to* JOACIM) Help! Bring us help, high priest!

JOACIM Heaven cannot help you; you have tied its hands with your sins.

ASSAD We must have miracles, miracles and portents, otherwise—

HOSEA My neighbor the locksmith said if no help on high comes by Saturday, he'll have his apprentices roasted.

ASSAD All resistance is stupid. Instead we should show a little servility and open the gates to Holofernes, make him a nice deep bow and say: "Your Excellency is the benefactor of all Israel."

DANIEL (*suddenly gaining the power of speech*) Stone him! Stone him!

ALL (*in amazement*) What was that? Did the mute speak?

RACHEL This happens only on special occasions.

ASSAD Ordinarily he is mute.

JOACIM He is divinely inspired; mark his words!

HOSEA If we do, his brother Assad should be stoned to death.

RACHEL I wouldn't like that—my husband—

ASSAD (*to* JOACIM) You must understand—he is blind and can't see what he is saying.

JOACIM (*to* ASSAD) You may go free, but sacrifices must be made to appease the wrath of the Lord. The lips of the mute will mark them.

Scene 18

(*As above;* NATHAN)

ALL Here comes Nathan—!

AMMON He looks very upset—!

NATHAN (*rushing in breathlessly from upstage left*) Have I got news! I have just received a dispatch, and when I make it public, every stock is going to fall fifty percent.

ALL Horrors!

RACHEL Speak, Mr. Nathan!

HOSEA No, don't speak, Mr. Nathan!

NATHAN (*to* HOSEA) I can't remain silent—

DANIEL (*in intense excitement*) Stone him! Stone him!

SEVERAL CITIZENS (*seizing* NATHAN) Away with him! To the place of execution!

(*They drag* NATHAN *away to the right.*)

HOSEA (*following them*) But just let me tell you—

JOACIM He shall be the atonement for the sins of the people!

AMMON (*to* JOACIM) That spiteful dummy only said what he did because he has speculated on a bull market, and was afraid to let the dispatch be made public.

SARA Shah! What if he should hear you? (*Points fearfully at Daniel.*)

JOACIM (*to* AMMON) He is divinely inspired, do not mock him!

Scene 19

(*As above;* HEMAN)

HEMAN (*rushing onstage from the left*) This is too much! Inflation is getting worse and worse!

ALL Master Heman!

AMMON The tailor.

HEMAN Where is a man to get money? Nobody pays; I must call in my outstanding debts.

NAZAEL I'd better be going. (*Runs away.*)

HEMAN (*Noticing* DANIEL, *approaches him.*) Aha! The blind man there pretends he doesn't see me; the gentleman still owes me for a suit from last year!

DANIEL (*with great feeling*) Stone him! Stone him!

HEMAN What? This is my payment?

CITIZENS Away with him! Away! (*They seize him.*)

HEMAN Oy vey!

JOACIM The mute has passed judgment on you. Away!

(*Several* CITIZENS *drag* HEMAN *away to the right.*)

JOACIM The ways of Heaven are truly amazing! The second sacrifice is to be a tailor!

AMMON I am that blind dummy's shoemaker. I'd better be careful not to say anything.

Scene 20

(As above; HOSEA)

HOSEA *(returning from the right)* Where is Daniel? *(to DANIEL)* You know what Nathan said just before his death? "Daniel will be sorry for this," he said, "I owe him three thousand guilders, and I have buried all my money and no one knows where. Nobody will get a penny after my death!"

(In desperate fury DANIEL endeavors to speak, but can only whimper inarticulately.)

ASSAD Now words have failed him again.

SEVERAL OF THE CITIZENS Serves him right!

ASSAD I'll kick him out of my house. Such a divinely inspired man I can do without. *(DANIEL falls to the ground and pummels his head with his fists.)*

HOSEA And I'll take him in. I'll lock him up in a room without any furniture except a big spike in the wall. Then I'll give him a length of rope to play with—maybe in the solitude he can come up with a practical idea. *(Exits with DANIEL.)*

ASSAD *(to the CITIZENS)* And we'll go to the high council and tell them to open the gates to Holofernes.

CITIZENS Yes, that's what we'll do. To the high council! *(All exit hurriedly to the left.)*

JOACIM Vey! Vey! *(Exits.)*

Change of scene: *the interior of Holofernes' tent. Stage left, the exit leading to the camp, covered by a curtain; stage right, the entrance to Holofernes' sleeping quarters, likewise covered by a curtain. Downstage left an ornate gilt sofa, before it a round gilt table and an ottoman.*

Scene 21

(HOLOFERNES, IDUN, CHALKOL, ZEPHO, and ACHIOR enter from the camp.)

HOLOFERNES The next time I ride out to reconnoitre, the cook will have to come along. (*to* ACHIOR) Wine! (ACHIOR *signals, a* SLAVE *enters, places a golden flagon an goblets on the table and exits.*)

IDUN Is my general hungry?

HOLOFERNES Captain, for that question I demote you to buck private.

IDUN I merely thought—

HOLOFERNES That is precisely your offense; I alone think, and whoever presumes to have thoughts is guilty of breaking and entering into my head. (*to* ACHIOR) Tell the cook to have a look at Bethulia; tomorrow I'm going to put it to the torch, and I'm not sure it will make him enough flame to cook my potato pancakes.

(*Takes several swallows.*)

ACHIOR Very well. I thought it was somethingÞlike that.

HOLOFERNES Bright fellow! Here, take this gold piece! (*Gives him money; exit* ACHIOR *in the direction of the camp.*)

Scene 22

(*As above except* ACHIOR)

IDUN (*softly to* CHALKOL *and* ZEPHO, *referring to* ACHIOR) He is allowed to think!

CHALKOL (*softly to* IDUN) Yes, a chamberlain can do a lot of things we can't.

HOLOFERNES Chalkol! How did you like that Hebrew girl that came through our camp?

CHALKOL Oh, tremendously! The sight of her pierced my heart like—

HOLOFERNES Like this? (*Runs* CHALKOL *through with his sword.*)

CHALKOL Agh! (*Sinks to the floor and dies.*)

HOLOFERNES That will teach you to look at girls who catch the eye of your sovereign. Damnation! (*to* ZEPHO) Have somebody seize her and set free a dozen Jews or so.

ZEPHO Why, my lord? We can take her captive anyway—

HOLOFERNES Would you have me play dirty tricks? Die! (*Stabs him.*)

ZEPHO Agh! (*Sinks to the floor and dies.*)

HOLOFERNES Well, Idun, what do you say? Isn't that Hebrew girl enchanting, cuddly, and gorgeous?

IDUN (*aside*) Now's my big chance to get in good with him. (*aloud*) Gorgeous? H'm—I haven't really noticed—

HOLOFERNES Have you so little regard for the taste of your master? Die, wretch! (*Stabs him.*)

IDUN Agh! (*Sinks to the floor and dies.*)

HOLOFERNES I'll teach you manners—no, on second thought, I won't bother to teach them anything any more.

Scene 23

(*As above;* ACHIOR)

ACHIOR (*reporting*) The charming and richly-adorned Hebrew girl wishes to pay her respects.

HOLOFERNES Aha, what else is new? But have the tent tidied up first. There are bodies lying around everywhere. No messiness, now! (*At* ACHIOR's *signal, several* SLAVES *enter and carry off* ZEPHO, CHALKOL, *and* IDUN.) (*to* ACHIOR) Three positions are vacant. Let the army be notified of the promotions. Have wine and food brought here, but nothing sweet. The wench herself shall be dessert.

(ACHIOR *opens the left curtain and* JOAB, *dressed as* JUDITH, *enters in sumptuous raiment, accompanied by the maid* MIRZA.)

Scene 24

(*As above;* JUDITH, MIRZA)

JUDITH (JOAB) (*to* HOLOFERNES)
    I asked them they should let me see his grace,
    The one and only Holofernes. This the place?

HOLOFERNES I wouldn't like it if there were another one. I got rid of all my mirrors because they had the effrontery to reflect my face, which in its way is quite unique. What's your name?

113

JUDITH (JOAB)

> Your most obedient servant, sir,
> Judith is my moniker.
> A young Old Testament girl am I,
> At times a dumb bunny, I cannot deny;
> A well-born widow, but so naïve,
> And innocent like you wouldn't believe!

HOLOFERNES They have innocent widows in Bethulia? Assyrian industry isn't that advanced.

JUDITH (JOAB)

> Thanks to fate I'm the only one there who, alas, is;
> And whose fault should it be that I am but Manasses'?

HOLOFERNES Manasses? Ah, he must be the sainted husband.

JUDITH (JOAB)

> A saint he was not, and neither am I.
> If it please you, just listen and I'll tell you why.
> My story will fill you with dread and dismay,
> In the end nothing came of it though, strange to say.

HOLOFERNES What a very interesting way to heighten the interest of the interested listener. Tell your story!

JUDITH (JOAB)

> My father, two others, and a fourth man beside,
> Got together and brought me, a newlywed bride,
> > To Manasses my spouse.
> > To get out of the house
> I was eager, for a voice in my ear
> Said no good was to come to me here.
> The others all left us alone there that night,
> The chamber was lit by the tallowy light
> Of three candles—he hugged me and put out the first;
> My heart pounded so that I feared it would burst;
> Then he gave me a kiss and—what could I do?—
> At that moment he snuffed out the second one too.
> My maidenly protests and pleas went unheard;
> He gave a big puff and like out went the third.

HOLOFERNES I am in agreement with the gentleman in question; I'd have done the same thing in his place. Yes, up to here I am entirely on Manasses' side.

JUDITH (JOAB)

> Now cavorting around and gay as a lark,
> He said, "Judith, I can see you still, there in the dark."

> Nu, of course he could see me, the moon was so bright,
> It came in at the window and made the room light.
> Unresisting, I let myself sink in a chair;
> Whereupon he sprang back and stood fixedly there,
>> Without moving—I trembled—
>> So much he resembled
>> A man that an evil dybbuk
>> Has bound by his feet to a rock.
> What's he up to? What is this, I wonder.
> Still he stood there, as though struck by thunder.
> "Would you scare me? Stop kidding," I cried.
> "Bad Manasses, come here to your bride."

HOLOFERNES Come on, he must have understood German— Hebrew, I mean.

JUDITH (JOAB)
> With the look of a sheep he stood fixed to the spot
> And repeated ten times in one breath, "I cannot!"

HOLOFERNES Oh, hapless Manasses!

JUDITH (JOAB)
> Wringing my hands and beginning to weep,
> I suddenly fell—

HOLOFERNES   In his arms!—

JUDITH (JOAB)
>   No, asleep.
> Not a word did he speak the next day;
> I also had little to say.
> Six months we led a quiet life,
> Though never as husband and wife.

HOLOFERNES But the subject must have come up? Was he hexed? Had somebody cast a spell on him? Or—

JUDITH (JOAB)
> On his deathbed he was when I first found the heart
> To enquire what it was that had kept us apart
> On our wedding night. "Nu," he replied, "I shall tell—"
> When bingo! His eyelids quite suddenly fell.
>> Death took his voice away, he sighed,
>> The riddle's answer with him died.
> And darkness eternal surrounds to this day
> The case of Manasses, I'm sorry to say.

HOLOFERNES That no longer matters. I could strike him dead, but I can't bring him back to life. But 'pon my honor, you're not a bad-looking morsel. I'm beginning to have some respect for Bethulia. It's a pity I have to put to the torch all the cities I respect. (*In the meantime* SLAVES *start serving a meal.*) By the way, to what do I owe this unexpected pleasure?

JUDITH (JOAB) (*coquettishly*)
> I've been told of the terrible things that you do—
> Never sparing men's lives—you naughty man, you.
> And I've also been told—though I simply refuse
> To believe it of a man like yourself—you eat Jews.

HOLOFERNES I'm not as bad as all that. I am merely in the habit of laying things waste. Sit down and dine with me. (*Reclines in the Greek manner on the sofa.*)

JUDITH (JOAB)
> I'm hungry. All right,
> I'll have a bite.

HOLOFERNES (*pointing to* MIRZA) In the meantime she can go into the kitchen.

JUDITH (JOAB)
> She may be of some use to me, don't make her go;
> It's my habit to lean on her often, like so.

(*Leans upon* MIRZA *in a picturesque fashion.*)

HOLOFERNES Very well—*prenez place!* (*She sits down.*)

JUDITH (JOAB) (*examining the table*)
> The great Holofernes eats so simple a meal?
> Only chicken with salad and a little piece veal?

HOLOFERNES I am more of a drinker. Now let's hear your request.

JUDITH (JOAB) (*sitting on the ottoman*)
> So listen: my people are digging their grave,
> They won't give up sinning and refuse to behave;
>   This Heaven will not permit,
>   That's the long and short of it.

HOLOFERNES (*growing tipsier by the minute*) What does that mean, "sinning?"

JUDITH (JOAB)
> Don't ask me such questions; even if I knew,
> I would never discuss such a matter with you.

HOLOFERNES Drink up and go on.

JUDITH (JOAB)
>Oh please, I'm no drinker and ought to decline;
>I'm too passionate anyway, without drinking wine.
>>(*Drinks and makes a wry face.*)
>H'm, I thought that *your* wine would be sweet and first-rate,
>Not a half-guilder *vin ordinaire* '48.[2]

HOLOFERNES Judith, how's about a little kiss?

JUDITH (JOAB)
>>Already? How forward you are!
>>Holofernes, you're going too far.
>I must say that I already regret coming here,
>I shall not give our people more reason to sneer.

HOLOFERNES Who's to sneer at you? By this time tomorrow there won't be any Jews left.

JUDITH (JOAB)
>What was that? Look how close I am standing to you, sir;
>I implore you to spare, oh please spare the Hebrew, sir.
>Just consider how forward it is of all Jewry
>To believe it can stir such a proud man to fury.

HOLOFERNES A good thought! If only it had been mine—oh well, it's yours, and I—I have no need of your thoughts. Therefore—therefore—your people will be burned, burned to a crisp.

JUDITH (JOAB) (*leaping up from the chair*)
>Then my people are not to be saved from the flame?
>I've got nothing to show for the loss of my name?

HOLOFERNES (*to himself*) How pushy she is! (*He rises unsteadily and calls.*) Chamberlain!

(ACHIOR *enters.*)

ACHIOR Your wish?

HOLOFERNES Where are you when I call "Chamberlain?" (*softly*) Listen, I don't trust her.

ACHIOR (*softly*) I trust no female.

HOLOFERNES (*softly*) You remember that dream I once had—you know—

ACHIOR (*softly*) I also remember what precautions were taken then.

HOLOFERNES (*softly*) Quite right! Well, those precautions must be taken again, at once—the same precautions, understand?

ACHIOR (*softly*) Perfectly. (*Exits into the sleeping tent.*)

HOLOFERNES (*to* JUDITH, *approaching her*) A kiss! By my wrath, give me a kiss!

JUDITH (JOAB)
>Wrath and kiss, how to make these two rhyme?
>(*seething with fury*)
>You had better take care I don't kill you sometime.
>Yes, it's Judith who speaks in this fashion,
>Overcome by a furious passion.

HOLOFERNES (*laughing*) Hoho! Hohoho! Am I supposed to be frightened? I'd be a sorry Holofernes then. Pity—I'm getting dizzy—

(ACHIOR *enters from the sleeping tent on the right, leaving the curtain open; within one can see the ornate interior and Holofernes' bed.* ACHIOR *exits left.*)

JUDITH (JOAB)
>You say "dizzy?" "Lit up" is what our people say;
>They lie down for a nap when they're feeling that way.

HOLOFERNES That's what I'll do. (*Removes his sword and places it on the table to the left. Haughtily to* JUDITH/JOAB.) Here lies my sword. You may stand guard over it— (*staggering toward the sleeping tent*)— to pass the time. (*lying down*) When I call "to arms!" you let me have—a kiss. To arms!—Kiss!— (*Lets the curtain fall.*)

MIRZA (*softly to* JUDITH/JOAB) I'm trembling all over. What risks you are taking, young master! Your young life—

JUDITH (JOAB) (*in his natural voice*) A woman doesn't risk anything here. But quiet!—Didn't you hear?—I think he is snoring, our gruesome general.

MIRZA (*listening*) It seems so to me, too; yes—

JUDITH (JOAB) Drunkenness is a bird that quickly takes wing. But what am I waiting for? Hurry up—give the Bethulians the signal to attack. Set off the concealed rocket; when it rises in the air, the head of Holofernes will fall to the ground.

MIRZA This one time I'll do it, but never again in my life will I go into a military camp. How all those warriors stared, and me without a veil—!

JUDITH (JOAB) Oh, get on with it.

MIRZA I'm going, I'm going! (*Exits.*)

JUDITH (JOAB) So I'm to stand guard here? (*Unsheathes the sword which lies on the table.*)
>I have risen in grade,
>Now *I'm* in command of the general's blade.
>Fate has found it meet
>That your head, Holofernes, should lie at your feet!

(*Rushes into the sleeping tent, closing the curtain behind him.* HOLOFERNES *peeps out with a sly grin from behind the right hand side of the curtain. From this moment on to the end of the play, melodramatic music accompanies the action.*)

(JUDITH/JOAB *enters from the tent after a short while with a papier-maché head similar to, though larger than that of Holofernes in his left hand and the sword in his right. Shouts, brandishing the sword.*)

JUDITH (JOAB) Got him already!

HOLOFERNES (*to himself*) No, I've got *you!*

JUDITH (JOAB) (*Rushing to the entrance of the tent, throws back the curtains and calls out in a loud voice.*)
>See, Assyrians, what I hold by the hair of the head!
>Your field marshal is headless!

VOICES FROM WITHOUT   Oh horrors! Oh dread!

JUDITH (JOAB) (*looking in the distance*) What is this drawing near in wild, Lützowian pursuit?[3]

VOICES FROM WITHOUT Woe! The Hebrews!

HOLOFERNES (*Signals to* ACHIOR, *who enters from the other side. They seize* JUDITH/JOAB.) Now we've got you!

JUDITH (JOAB) (*Screams at the sight of* HOLOFERNES *and lets the curtain drop.*)
>Oh, what is this? What an abundance of heads!

ACHIOR What's that commotion I hear going on out there? (*Rushes to the curtain and looks outside into the camp.*)

HOLOFERNES (*grimly to* JUDITH/JOAB) Now *your* head shall fall! (*calling*) In here! Four regiments in a hollow square!

ACHIOR My lord, there isn't anyone left out there. Everybody is running around yelling, "Our general has lost his head!"

JUDITH (JOAB) (*triumphantly*) Aha! Even the wrong head has produced the right result!

HOLOFERNES (*to* ACHIOR) Why don't they look at me, the idiots?

ACHIOR They're too busy running to look.

JUDITH (JOAB) (*to* HOLOFERNES)
That brouhaha you're hearing?
That's Israel cheering!

(HOSEA, ASSAD, BEN, NAZAEL, *and* NABEL *storm in with several other* HEBREWS.)

ASSAD Take him prisoner. Courage! (*pointing to* HOLOFERNES' *head*) He's been beheaded already; that one doesn't count.

BEN, NAZAEL, NABAL (*falling upon* HOLOFERNES) We've got you! (*They take him prisoner, put him in chains which one of the* HEBREWS *has brought along.*)

HOLOFERNES (*trying vainly to defend himself*) Army! Come to my aid! Where are you, you damned army?

JOACIM (*rushing in with several* BETHULIANS, *one of whom leads* DANIEL) What is this I hear? Joab my son!

JUDITH (JOAB) Papa!

HOLOFERNES (*furiously*) What? Judith a son?

JUDITH (JOAB) A Hebrew boy has outwitted you.

HOLOFERNES Fraud! Deception! Trickery!

JOACIM Vey, vey, three times vey!

DANIEL (*vis-à-vis* JOACIM, *regaining his powers of speech*) Stone him! Stone him!

HOSEA (*to* DANIEL) But that's our high priest!

ASSAD (*to* JOACIM) We have defeated Holofernes!

DANIEL (*vis-à-vis* HOLOFERNES) Stone him, stone him!

ALL Long live Judith! Victory for Israel!

(*Martial music. The curtain of the tent is torn down to reveal an open view into the camp.* JUDITH/JOAB *is lifted upon a shield and carried about triumphantly. Before him* HOLOFERNES *is led in chains. While the procession circles about within the tent, one can see the camp burning in the background. Triumphal shouts of the* HEBREWS.)

---

1. The Hannoverian Guard wore red uniforms.

2. 1848, though an indifferent year for wine, was a very good one for revolutions all over Europe.

3. A proverbial expression denoting great dash, derived from the celebrated mounted troops of Adolf, Freiherr von Lützow, a Prussian officer of the Napoleonic wars.

The House of Humors

Farce with Song in Two Acts

DRAMATIS PERSONÆ

MR. BOYLE a gentleman of means

ROBERT his son

WALBURGA his daughter

MR. YAWN a gentleman of means

EDMUND his son

AGNES his daughter

HUTZIBUTZ clothes cleaner

SLIPPY barber and hairdresser

MR. DOLE a gentleman of means

GUIDO his son

IRENE his daughter

MR. BLYTHE a gentleman of means

FELIX his son

MARIE his daughter

ISABELLA their maid

MR. STORM

MR. NAPP

} entrepreneurs from Straßburg

MR. PAINE

MR. JOY

MRS. KORBHEIM

MR. DARK

MRS. NIGHTSHADE
} relatives of Mr. Dole

JACOB servant of Mr. Storm

NANETTE housemaid

SUSANNE cook
} of the Boyle household

BABETTE housemaid

GERTRUDE cook

CYPRIAN valet
} of the Yawn household

LISETTE housemaid

BRIDGET housekeeper

MARGARET cook
} of the Dole household

THERESE cook

SEPHERL kitchenmaid
} of the Blythe household

NEEDLE tailor

LAST shoemaker

DR. HODGE physician

DR. PODGE physician

FLASHMAN

POYNTER

STARR
} friends of Mr. Blythe

FOUR NOTARIES, BALL GUESTS, MALE AND FEMALE STAFF

The action takes place simultaneously in two rooms on the first floor and two rooms on the second floor of the selfsame house. The placement of the four apartments, as seen by the audience, is as follows:

1	2
Choleric	Phlegmatic
(*red*)	(*yellow*)
3	4
Melancholy	Sanguine
(*gray*)	(*sky blue*)

Throughout the action Left and Right are referenced to the players.

ACT I

Choleric

Parlor of MR. BOYLE *on the second floor, right. Middle and side doors. Upstage right there is a small stove with a door which can be opened. The color scheme of the room is bright red.*

Phlegmatic

Parlor of MR. YAWN *on the second floor, left. Middle and side doors. Downstage an embroidery frame. The color scheme of the room is pale yellow.*

Melancholy

Parlor of MR. DOLE *on the first floor, right. Middle and side doors. Downstage right an easel with a half-finished picture on it; to the left a small table and chair. The color scheme of the room is gray with dark trim (as gloomy as possible).*

Sanguine

Parlor of MR. BLYTHE *on the first floor, left. Middle and side doors. Downstage left, a table covered by a cloth. The color scheme of the room is either sky blue or rose.*

Scene 1

Choleric: NANETTE, SUSANNE, *later* NEEDLE *the tailor and* LAST *the shoemaker.*

Phlegmatic: BABETTE, GERTRUDE, *later* CYPRIAN

Melancholy: LISETTE, MARGARET, *later* Drs. HODGE *and* PODGE

Sanguine: SEPHERL, THERESE, *later* FLASHMAN, POYNTER, STARR.

Choleric

NANETTE, SUSANNE (*a kitchen list in her hand*)
        It's nine o'clock, and how it goes
        With the grocery shopping, no one knows.
        The son of the house is arriving today,
        That sounds like a full course dinner, I'd say.

Phlegmatic

BABETTE, GERTRUDE (*a kitchen list in her hand*)
It's nine o'clock, etc.

Melancholy

LISETTE, MARGARET (*a kitchen list in her hand*)
It's nine o'clock, etc.

Sanguine

SEPHERL, THERESE (*a kitchen list in her hand*)
It's nine o'clock, etc.

Phlegmatic

CYPRIAN (*entering by the side door*)
The master's having a smoke just now,
Sees no one mornings, anyhow.
As for food, he simply doesn't care,
So long as it's good and there's plenty to spare.

Melancholy

DR. HODGE, DR. PODGE (*entering by the side door*)
It's agreed, then, a consultation.
In the end he'll die of this complication:
We insist upon a consultation.

Sanguine

FLASHMAN, POYNTER, & STARR (*before the side door and speaking to someone within*)
We're off, friend Blythe, adieu,
Look forward to seeing you!
(*stepping forward*)
Champagne at break of dawn is quite
The way to start the day off right.

Choleric

NEEDLE, LAST (*The former carrying a new tail-coat, the latter a new pair of boots, come running in by the side door.*)
There's no talking today with the gentleman again,
He rushes at one like a dog on a chain,
He's always in such an uproar,
We're not coming here any more!

NANETTE *and* SUSANNE
> You'd better leave us now. Adieu,
> Auf Wiedersehn, be seeing you!

NEEDLE, LAST
> We'd better leave you now. Adieu,
> Auf Wiedersehn, be seeing you!
> (*All exit through the middle door.*)

Phlegmatic

BABETTE *and* GERTRUDE
> We'd better leave you now. Adieu,
> Auf Wiedersehn, be seeing you!

CYPRIAN
> I'll take a nap, that's what I'll do,
> Auf Wiedersehn, be seeing you!
> (*All exit through the middle door.*)

Melancholy

LISETTE *and* MARGARET
> The gentlemen will say adieu.
> Goodbye, sirs, we'll be seeing you!

DR. HODGE *and* DR. PODGE
> We'd better leave you now. Adieu,
> Auf Wiedersehn, be seeing you!
> (*All exit through the middle door.*)

Sanguine

SEPHERL *and* THERESE
> The gentlemen will say adieu.
> Goodbye, sirs, we'll be seeing you!

FLASHMAN, POYNTER, STARR
> It's time for us to say adieu,
> Auf Wiedersehn, be seeing you!
> (*All exit through the middle door.*)

Scene 2

Choleric	Phlegmatic	Melancholy	Sanguine
BOYLE	YAWN	DOLE	BLYTHE

Melancholy

DOLE (*In dressing gown, arms folded, enters by the side door.*) Today, then, I am to see him again, my son, the firstborn of my prematurely departed bride! (*Sighing deeply, takes up a position before the portrait on the easel.*)

Sanguine

BLYTHE (*Enters, almost dancing, by the side door, also in a dressing gown.*) My boy's coming back, that's really something! He's probably turned into a real daredevil in these last three years, if he takes after his dad! (*Takes up a position before the mirror and adjusts his cravat with obvious satisfaction.*)

Phlegmatic

YAWN (*Enters by the side door in a dressing gown, a long pipe in his hand.*) So he's coming today, Edmund is. But if he doesn't, that's all right with me too. When children don't long for their homes it's a sign that things are going well with them. (*Sits down in an armchair and puffs on his pipe.*)

Choleric

BOYLE (*Bursts in through the side door in dressing gown.*) What's taking that young devil so long? He could have been here by eight o'clock. May lightning strike a son whose filial heart doesn't drive him back with all due haste into the loving arms of his father! (*Takes up a newspaper from the table and leafs through it hastily while pacing up and down.*)

Sanguine

BLYTHE He'll have me for a rival, and a formidable one, when he goes acourting. But he'll have plenty of time for that. My daughter, however, must tie the knot, a girl can never marry too early. But to a young buck like my son, domestic ills always come too soon. (*Tightens a loose string of the violin that lies on the table.*)

Phlegmatic

YAWN If only my daughter's fiancé were already here, I'd feel better. I don't like the idea of the girl remaining single. (*Puffs placidly on his pipe.*)

Choleric

BOYLE The arrival notices make my gorge rise! Everybody has come except my damned old chum from Straßburg. Such a lackadaisical fiancé ought to have firecrackers set off in his ears so that they may reach his cold heart and set fire to his sodden senses.

Melancholy

DOLE Soon my daughter will enter into holy wedlock. May the roses she receives bloom longer than did *these (pointing to the cheeks of the portrait)* of hers, who, herself a rose in bloom, now molders away in the night of the grave. (*Sits down at the easel and adds a few brush strokes to the portrait of his dead wife.*)

Scene 3

Choleric	Phlegmatic	Melancholy	Sanguine
BOYLE, WALBURGA	YAWN	DOLE	BLYTHE, MARIE

Sanguine

MARIE (*entering by the side door in an elegant negligée*) Well, how do you like me in this outfit, Papa?

BLYTHE Pretty, pretty as a picture. You're the spitting image of me!

Choleric

BOYLE (*yelling through the side door*) Walburga! Hi, Walburga!

Sanguine

MARIE Pretty girls are always at their prettiest in a negligée. Too bad it's not fashionable for one to go to a ball in a negligée; then we'd see who's pretty and who's not!

Choleric

BOYLE (*very angry*) Walburga, can't you hear—?

WALBURGA (*Enters by the side door.*) Here I am, Dad. I don't see why you have to shout so.

BOYLE Just one more time, —if you don't come the instant I call you, then—

WALBURGA (*vehemently*) I was three rooms away. That's where my room is, you know. While I am a quick person, it still takes some time to come through three rooms—

BOYLE Quiet! (*Paces heatedly up and down.*)

Sanguine

BLYTHE You might have saved that outfit to welcome your fiancé in.

MARIE What fiancé? Let's not go into that, Papa!

BLYTHE It won't be much longer now—in a few days, there'll be a wedding, and what a wedding—! (*Plays a Strauß waltz on the violin.*)

Choleric

BOYLE You shall marry!

WALBURGA Oh yes, I should hope so, I'm not one to sit around and become an old maid.

BOYLE And you'll marry whom I choose!

WALBURGA What if I don't like him?

BOYLE *I* like him, even though I haven't seen him for years. It's my old friend, Storm.

WALBURGA That is one storm that's not going to fan a flame in my heart. I shan't have him!

BOYLE You shall!

Sanguine

BLYTHE What's the matter with you? This is the first time I've ever seen you stand still when a german[1] was being played!

MARIE It's because I am to dance it with a bridegroom, and if he's not the one I want—

BLYTHE He is the one *I* want, my old friend Joy, whom I haven't laid eyes on since my student days.

MARIE You had better watch out, Papa, for I just might happen to dance away with someone else.

BLYTHE You wouldn't dare!

MARIE Wouldn't that be something— (*Sings the same german and dances about.*)

Choleric

BLYTHE I'll not be contradicted!

WALBURGA My lips may be sealed, but my heart will still contradict you!

BOYLE I'll stop that heart's mouth!

Sanguine

BLYTHE How the girl can dance—it's a joy to watch her! Now my own feet are itching! (*Waltzes once around the room with her, accompanying her as she sings the german, then exits by the side door.*)

Choleric

WALBURGA This is unjust coercion!

BOYLE (*grimly*) To your room, or else—

WALBURGA I'm going, but—

BLYTHE March, I say! (WALBURGA *leaves through the side door, visibly suppressing her anger.* BOYLE *follows her grimly.*)

Scene 4

Choleric	Phlegmatic	Melancholy	Sanguine
Empty Stage	YAWN, AGNES	DOLE, IRENE	Empty stage

Phlegmatic

YAWN (*After rising slowly, calls through the side door.*) Agnes!

AGNES (*following a pause, from within*) In a minute!

(YAWN *waits at the door.*)

Melancholy

DOLE (*painting*) Even after nineteen years, her features are still so vivid in my memory that I am able to paint her portrait. (*to the picture*) Your wishes, too, are unforgettable; to me they are holy commandments.

IRENE (*Enters weeping through the side door.*) Oh, my father!

DOLE You are weeping, Irene?

IRENE Does that surprise you? Do you not see me weeping every day?

DOLE Is there any particular ground for your sorrow today?

IRENE Isn't that sorrow deepest which is groundless?

Phlegmatic

YAWN (*calls again*) Agnes!

AGNES In a minute!

(YAWN *waits at the door.*)

Melancholy

DOLE Today let a sunbeam of joy pierce the misty veil of tears—a myrtle wreath beckons to you.

IRENE To bedeck my coffin?

DOLE No, to weave a bridal chaplet in your hair.

IRENE But who—?

DOLE A man to whom my word has been pledged since you were born; a friend of my youth, my long-awaited Paine.

IRENE Oh, unhappy me! (*Buries her face in her hands.*)

Phlegmatic

YAWN (*Calls again.*) If you don't come soon—I'll wait a little longer.

AGNES (*entering by the side door*) Here I am, Father.

YAWN What was I going to tell you? Oh yes, you're going to be married in a few days.

AGNES But why?

YAWN Because it is the custom. (*Sits down again.*)

Melancholy

DOLE (*rising*) You are surprised, Irene; this unexpected news has moved you deeply. Just think, over eighteen years ago this was the wish of your sainted mother; it must be as sacred to you as it is to me.

Phlegmatic

YAWN I used to have a chum named Napp. He has my word in writing.

Melancholy

IRENE I cannot, Father!

DOLE (*pointing to the picture*) You must, it was her wish!

IRENE Oh, heavens!

DOLE From up there she will bless this union. Come, my daughter! (*Leads her slowly out through the side door.*)

Phlegmatic

AGNES Father, I won't like him at all.

YAWN You must like him!

AGNES Oh stop it, Father! (*Sits down at the embroidery frame.*)

Scene 5

Choleric	Phlegmatic	Melancholy	Sanguine
Empty Stage	YAWN, IRENE	SLIPPY	HUTZIBUTZ

Melancholy

SLIPPY (*Enters by middle door during the ritournelle of the following song:*)

135

The sun's hardly up from the night's bed of down,
When I'm off on the rounds of my patrons in town.
I barber and style in the mode of the day,
For the head, although empty, must look recherché

Sanguine

HUTZIBUTZ (*Enters by the middle door during the ritournelle of the following song, carrying a clothes beater
and brushes, in addition to several pairs of freshly
polished boots.*)

The sun's hardly up from the night's bed of down,
When I rush to my customers all over town.
Cleaning clothing and boots is the world's hardest way
For a fellow to go about earning his pay.

together

Melancholy

SLIPPY

A hairdresser's through in the space of a minute,
Young men wear their hair short, there's no need to thin it.
It's amazing how easily barbering's done,
Of every ten hairs I need shave only one;
I grab each by the nose—you want to know why?
Because many are held altogether too high;
When I'm late and the client is making a blather,
I quiet him down with a mouthful of lather.

Sanguine

HUTZIBUTZ

Through thick and through thin they pursue maidens fair.
Then their boots, afterwards, become my sort's care.
When I'm out dusting britches, this question I pose:
Why isn't his lordship still here in his clothes?

Melancholy

SLIPPY

The head is the shop, the hair the display,
Indeed, as with storefronts is often the way,
The showcase is pretty and dazzles the eyes,
But that's all, in the store there is no merchandise.

What a state to compare with my own! I insist,
I live better by far than a capitalist.

Sanguine   together

HUTZIBUTZ

No estate's worse than mine! 'Pon my soul, I insist,
I'd rather by far be a capitalist!

Melancholy

SLIPPY A man has to know his way around in the world, that's the main
thing! Better to nick others than oneself; better to help someone else
get a wife than to take one oneself.

Sanguine

HUTZIBUTZ If I had to live on boot-blacking alone, it would be pure
misery. However, it's my good fortune to be a very clever fellow
who knows other ways of earning money.

Melancholy

SLIPPY There are two sides to everything, even to being a barber. If you
look at it superficially, it is a demeaning business. Lathering up,
snipping, curling—what does that amount to? If you reflect,
however, that we are the privileged messengers of secret love
affairs, that it is we who carry out the clandestine business of the
little blindfolded archer here on earth—if you look at it from that
angle, then there is a heap of poetry in our profession.

Sanguine

HUTZIBUTZ Four different gentlemen in this house are in love with four
different young ladies. The gentlemen go away, send their love
letters back to me, and rarely do I carry one in my bag over a week
before an occasion arises when the young lady in question is alone
in the house, whereupon I give her the letter, and well, that's a
masterstroke of intrigue.

Melancholy

SLIPPY That the love affairs in this house are not handled by me is an
oversight of fate, not to be explained and not to be forgiven. That a
person who carries seven pairs of boots in each hand should have
the impertinence to carry love letters in his waistcoat pocket; that a
person whose wits are as dim as the inside of a can of boot polish
should conduct intrigues! That he should wave love's magic wand,
instead of sticking to his clothes-beater. And handle the written

secrets of the heart with hands accustomed to wielding the shoe-brush! That is worse than a sharp stick in the eye!

Sanguine

HUTZIBUTZ Slippy the barber is plotting against me here in this house.

Melancholy

SLIPPY But those four lovers, along with their blessed *chargé d'affaires,* will pay for this. Whoever will not have me for a friend will have me for a foe.

My gorge rises at the mere sight of him, for whom it will be my highest pleasure to do a bad turn.

Sanguine

HUTZIBUTZ My gorge rises at the mere sight of him, for whom it will be my highest pleasure to do a bad turn.

together

Scene 6

Choleric	Phlegmatic	Melancholy	Sanguine
Empty Stage	YAWN, AGNES	SLIPPY, BRIDGET	HUTZIBUTZ, ISABELLA

Sanguine

ISABELLA (*entering through the side door*) Goodness gracious, here already? I'd much rather have waited till tomorrow! Truly your longing for me knows no bounds.

HUTZIBUTZ But Belle, think of the muddy weather! I've already cleaned nineteen pairs of boots!

ISABELLA Don't be so common!

HUTZIBUTZ That was some job, and I've got a splitting headache!

ISABELLA Oh come now, surely it can't have been that much of a strain on your brain!

Phlegmatic

AGNES (*at the embroidery frame*) Aren't you going out today, Father?

YAWN (*in a chaise longue, puffing on his pipe*) No, I have too much to
do.

Melancholy

BRIDGET (*entering through the side door*) Oh, are you here? I am so glad,
my dear Master Slippy.

SLIPPY Stop it, you know I can't stand all this silly flattery.

Sanguine

ISABELLA When a parlormaid condescends to love a clothes cleaner, then
the lucky dog should dash about like a greyhound in order to show
that—

HUTZIBUTZ Child, I do, but after nineteen pairs of boots—

ISABELLA Quiet, base slave!

Melancholy

BRIDGET There is great suffering in our house today.

SLIPPY That's the case every day in this tear-boutique of yours.

BRIDGET But especially today! The young lady is to be married to a man
she doesn't love.

SLIPPY What's that to me?

Sanguine

HUTZIBUTZ Base slave, you say? I don't see that you have the right to
give me that title. After all, you're in slavery all day long, I only till
ten in the morning. Many a gentleman has called me a blockhead in
the morning, only to bend a brotherly elbow with me in the evening
after running into me in a fog.

Phlegmatic

YAWN What are you embroidering, Agnes?

AGNES Haven't you looked at it yet, Father?

YAWN No, I haven't had time yet.

Melancholy

BRIDGET Master Slippy is in a pet today.

SLIPPY I'm no pet of yours, as you'll see; if you won't be quiet I'm leaving.

Sanguine

HUTZIBUTZ (*to himself*) Now I've made her angry. (*aloud*) Belle?

(ISABELLA *remains motionless, her face averted.*)

HUTZIBUTZ Won't you even look at me?

Melancholy

BRIDGET Would Master Slippy at least do me a favor?

SLIPPY That's a good question.

BRIDGET Take these three ducats and drink a little glass of wine to my health.

SLIPPY (*taking the money*) Well, we'll see—maybe—

Sanguine

HUTZIBUTZ You'll be getting a present from me today.

ISABELLA From you, you skinflint?

HUTZIBUTZ Be glad I am thrifty. I'll need the money when I marry you.

Melancholy

BRIDGET Isn't it true that you think of me just a little now and then? (*Caresses him.*)

SLIPPY Leave me alone.

BRIDGET Master Slippy is very finicky today.

SLIPPY Yes, I'm a discriminating fellow.

Sanguine

HUTZIBUTZ You might like to know I'm expecting some fine tips today.

ISABELLA From whom?

HUTZIBUTZ From the four young ladies, when I bring them the news that the four loves of their lives are returning today from the university.

ISABELLA They know that already!

HUTZIBUTZ All the same, when I bring them the news I will be in for an honorarium. Now fetch me your master's clothes; meanwhile I'll look in up at Mr. Boyle's.

ISABELLA All right. In expectation of the present I remain your undemanding Isabella. Adieu! (*Lets* HUTZIBUTZ *kiss her hand, then exits through the side door.*)

Melancholy

BRIDGET (*listening at the side door*) Miss Irene is coming.

SLIPPY What do I care?

BRIDGET Say something encouraging to her.

SLIPPY I don't see why I should. (BRIDGET *exits by the side door.*)

Sanguine

HUTZIBUTZ (*looking tenderly after* ISABELLA) Many are hitched to your wagon, yet you still look on me as the lead horse of the team, for I'm the one who'll lead you to the altar. (*Exits by middle door.*)

Scene 7

Choleric	Phlegmatic	Melancholy	Sanguine
HUTZIBUTZ	YAWN, AGNES	SLIPPY, IRENE	ISABELLA

Melancholy

IRENE (*Enters sobbing through the side door.*) Father says to tell you that you are to come back later.

SLIPPY As you wish, but what's the use? If I come back later, I'll still find Miss Irene in tears, and whenever I see anyone crying, my own eyes begin to burn, I get a catch in my throat, and before I know it I am crying along with her.

IRENE Compassion pours balm on a wounded heart.

SLIPPY To sprinkle balm on wounds is not only a general human obligation, but a specific barberly obligation.

IRENE Have you never been in love?

SLIPPY Oh, yes, I have often been infatuated, though I have loved deeply only sixteen times.

IRENE Is that possible? In me there is but one love, and this one is breaking my heart.

SLIPPY All hearts are not alike; some are more durable than others, some more elastic.

Phlegmatic

YAWN Agnes, doesn't it seem draughty to you in here with the door open?

AGNES I think so too. When Cyprian comes, I'll tell him to shut it.

Melancholy

IRENE Do you know that I am to give my hand to a man chosen by my father?

SLIPPY Then do it, take him. You couldn't find a better way to punish that unfaithful Master Felix!

IRENE Unfaithful, you say?

SLIPPY Oops, that just slipped out. Give me your word you won't tell on me. He's having an affair with someone in Prague, I got it from a friend of hers here; I shave her husband, he's one of my regular customers. You know, one hears all sorts of things. However, whether or not he's planning on breaking with you, I can't say. Maybe he adheres to the dictum: *unum debet fieri et alterum non omitti*—in English, "There's no need to be off with the old love, just because one is on with the new."

IRENE Ah, spring forth in torrents, you tears of blighted love, flow on, never to run dry! (*Buries her face in her hands and sinks into a chair.*)

SLIPPY (*to himself*) She must shed a power of tears in a year's time!

Choleric

HUTZIBUTZ (*Enters through the middle door and says in passing.*) Anyway, I know Belle is my friend. The thought of her is always like a ray of sunshine when I'm blacking boots and dark clouds envelop me. (*Exits through side door.*)

Sanguine

ISABELLA (*Enters through side door with several articles of clothing.*) Here are the clothes to be cleaned. I am really curious to see how Hutzibutz will fare. (*Hangs the clothing over the back of a chair, then exits through the side door.*)

Melancholy

SLIPPY (*to himself*) I made up all those things. I only said them to prepare a bad reception for Master Felix. So must it be. When I don't help someone, I harm him. I never remain neutral, whatever the cost; I must be the driving force, one way or the other. (*to* IRENE) Don't be angry with me!

IRENE You gave me truth instead of deception, and however sweet the deception and bitter the truth may be, I am nevertheless very much obliged to you. I shall always shed tears of friendly gratitude in your behalf.

SLIPPY Oh please, that's going too far! You'll need your tears for other occasions.

Choleric

HUTZIBUTZ (*Returning through the side door with articles of clothing draped over his arm, speaks back through the doorway.*) Right away, your lordship, right away. (*to himself*) I wish that man would put his personality in the cellar for a couple of hours to let it cool off. I have never in my life seen such a hothead. (*Exits by middle door.*)

Melancholy

IRENE And take this little something for your tender sympathy. (*Hands him a purseful of money.*)

SLIPPY It will be spent on toasts to your health.

IRENE Oh, no, nothing for my health. I have no desire to be healthy. I long for the grave, therein lies the end to my suffering. Now leave me alone with my pain!

SLIPPY As you wish. (*to himself*) If she goes on crying like this for three days running, we'll have a flood in the house. (*Exits by middle door.*)

Phlegmatic

YAWN But see here, Agnes, I am sitting about too much again. The doctor said I should take exercise. I'll go in and sit by the window, where I can watch the people pass by. (*Exits slowly through the side door.*)

AGNES My, how father is rocketing about from room to room today!

Scene 8

Choleric	Phlegmatic	Melancholy	Sanguine
NANETTE	AGNES, SLIPPY	IRENE, HUTZIBUTZ	MARIE

Phlegmatic

SLIPPY (*entering through middle door*) I'm glad I find you alone, Miss. I have things of the utmost importance to convey to you.

AGNES Wait a minute. (*Continues to embroider.*)

SLIPPY Your happiness, your peace of mind—everything is at stake.

AGNES Just wait until I finish with this thread.

Melancholy

IRENE Can he have betrayed me? Can Felix have broken his vows? But why should I be surprised? It had to happen so—it is my fate to know no joy in this world.

Phlegmatic

SLIPPY One might even say your very life is at stake.

AGNES Now you stop that! You're going to make me curious before long.

SLIPPY It is no doubt improper for me to intrude into others' secrets uninvited, but the danger is too great, too pressing.

AGNES That's really too much, I'm in danger and don't even know it.

SLIPPY Your relationship with young Master Boyle is no longer a secret, I learned of it the beginning of last month, and someone in Prague knows of it too.

AGNES Pshaw, pshaw, people will gossip about everything.

SLIPPY He'll be here today, and consider this: his mistress, to whom he made certain promises in Prague, is following him with the intention of murdering you. A good friend of mine wrote me about all this.

AGNES Now you stop that!

SLIPPY There's nothing left for you to do but to give this unfaithful fellow his walking papers, so as to avoid the terrible consequences.

AGNES Wait, give me a little time to think!

Melancholy

HUTZIBUTZ (*entering by middle door*) Miss Irene, I see a tear!

IRENE Oh, leave me alone!

HUTZIBUTZ Put on a happy face, I bring good tidings.

IRENE For me there can be none!

HUTZIBUTZ He's coming today!

IRENE Be quiet! (*to herself*) I must lock myself in my room, where I may give free rein to my tears. (*Exits by the side door.*)

HUTZIBUTZ (*alone*) But Miss! (*to himself*) Well, there goes my tip. H'm, h'm, what's eating her? It's really disconcerting when despair deteriorates into tip-denial. (*Leaves through the middle door shaking his head.*)

Phlegmatic

SLIPPY (*to himself*) There is no more fertile ground in the world than the human heart; once the seeds of mistrust are sown on it, they take root and shoot up. Everything moves slowly with her; nevertheless, the upshot will be the same.

Choleric

(*A bell rings at the side door.*)

NANETTE (*hurrying in through the middle door*) I think the master rang.

Right away, your lordship! (*Rushes out through the side door.*)

Phlegmatic

SLIPPY What have you decided, Miss?

AGNES I have decided that I am not going to make any decision right now; I must give this matter some thought. Take this for your kind consideration. (*Gives him money.*)

Sanguine

(MARIE *enters from the side door and looks out through the middle door.*)

Phlegmatic

SLIPPY Oh please, it is really too much!

AGNES If I'm ever in this sort of danger again, you let me know.

SLIPPY You may rely on your faithful Slippy. (*Exits by middle door.*)

Scene 9

Choleric	Phlegmatic	Melancholy	Sanguine
BOYLE, *later* NANETTE, WALBURGA	AGNES, *later* HUTZIBUTZ	Empty stage	MARIE, *later* SLIPPY

Sanguine

MARIE (*coming forward again*) Where is that Hutzibutz? I want to give him a reward for his loyal service as love's postillion. Also he must tell me when the express coach is to arrive. Ah, here he comes— (*Starts toward the middle door, then catches sight of* SLIPPY *entering.*) Is that you? I don't know if Papa wants his hair done now or not.

SLIPPY The young lady was expecting someone else.

MARIE That was a good guess.

Phlegmatic

AGNES (*embroidering*) Pshaw, pshaw, so he has been unfaithful to me! H'm, h'm.

Sanguine

SLIPPY I have no doubt you'd be more pleased to see the other fellow, since he always brings you good news.

MARIE What?—You couldn't know—

SLIPPY About your affair with Master Guido Dole? No, I never notice such things. Come now, a secret love affair to a hairdresser is like a truffle to a dog. We pick up the scent, we sniff it out, be it ever so deeply buried.

Phlegmatic

HUTZIBUTZ (*Enters through the middle door.*) Miss!

AGNES Leave me alone.

HUTZIBUTZ I have good tidings!

AGNES Go away and take your tidings with you.

HUTZIBUTZ But Master Robert—

AGNES Hush, I say!

Sanguine

SLIPPY By the by, I want to tell you—though only in passing, I know nothing definite—but concerning persons who always bring good news and good news only, the question always arises: is it true news?—but all this is only in passing, I really don't know anything.

MARIE What do you know?

SLIPPY That is to say, it depends on how you look at it—it's probably nothing.

MARIE Friend, you must tell me now. I'll not let you off.

SLIPPY Today I brought Miss Zi— oh, I almost said her name; no, I won't name names—you can't expect me to do that.

MARIE Without names then, but get on with it!

SLIPPY I brought her her curls and there on her dressing table lay a letter postmarked Prague and signed "Guido."

MARIE Guido!

SLIPPY It's a Christian name, anyone who wishes can be called Guido.

MARIE But the handwriting?

SLIPPY Well, it was, so to speak—peculiar.

MARIE Heavens, his very hand!

SLIPPY The final "o" was somewhat rounded.

MARIE No doubt about it. You just wait, you faithless monster! (*Stalks up and down.*)

Phlegmatic

HUTZIBUTZ Miss Agnes!

AGNES Out! Don't make me lose my temper. I've been very patient, but—

HUTZIBUTZ (*to himself*) Burned again! (*departing*) I couldn't get a tip if I stood on my head. The devil has gotten into these girls. (*Exits through the middle door.*)

Sanguine

SLIPPY Well, what are you going to do, Miss?

MARIE Oh, something will turn up. In any event, I am not going to die of grief. It always pleases the male of the species when the female tears out her hair for him. Oh, there will be none of that!

Choleric

BOYLE (*Enters with* NANETTE *through the side door.*) Where is he, that damned Hutzibutz?

NANETTE He said he was coming right away.

BOYLE May lightning—

NANETTE I'll just give this topcoat a quick brushing, then your lordship can go out.

BOYLE No, not now! He should be here, he has to be here—I am constantly badgered, from early in the morning till late at night! (*Paces restlessly up and down.*)

(NANETTE *exits through the middle door*.)

Sanguine

MARIE Friend, you have enlightened me. Please accept this small token of my gratitude. (*Gives him money*.)

SLIPPY (*taking the money*) I pray you will bear me no malice in the eventual disturbance of your soul's circumstantial tranquility.

MARIE Oh, I assure you it is only a temporary annoyance. It will pass, I assure you.

Choleric

WALBURGA (*coming in through the side door*) What has happened, Dad?

BOYLE Don't speak to me! Can't you see I am livid, you—creature, you!

(*Exits angrily through the side door*.)

Sanguine

SLIPPY I kiss your hand! (*to himself*) The lovers are going to have a fine time when they get here; then they'll learn what it means to turn up their nose at a barber and put their trust in a bootblack. (*Exits middle door*.)

Scene 10

Choleric	Phlegmatic	Melancholy	Sanguine
WALBURGA, then SLIPPY	AGNES	Empty stage	MARIE, *then* HUTZIBUTZ

Choleric

WALBURGA (*alone*) He's blown his top again! I don't understand how anyone can be as hotheaded as Dad.

Sanguine

MARIE (*alone*) It's true. Even though a man be six feet high, there is scarcely two inches of honesty in him, all the rest is sham and deceit. But why trouble my head with mathematical computations, this is no time for brooding. I must act now like a man, that is to say, I too must play false.

Choleric

SLIPPY (*Enters through middle door.*) I bid you a very good morning.

WALBURGA Have you brought me my curls?

SLIPPY No.

WALBURGA Why not, you horrid creature?

SLIPPY Because I have learned that the love of your life is returning today, and such a one should be received either in straight hair or in one's own curls, definitely not in artificial ones, for at such a reunion nothing should be false, neither curls nor hearts.

Phlegmatic

AGNES (*embroidering*) Well now, I do believe he is unfaithful.

Choleric

WALBURGA You're clever at talking yourself out of a hole.

SLIPPY Better that I talk myself cleverly out of a hole than for someone else to talk you cleverly into one.

WALBURGA What is that supposed to mean?

SLIPPY Ah, men, men! They're simply not to be trusted, men aren't. The way they—men, that is—lie to girls, you wouldn't believe. I know, I used to be a man myself—that is, a man who had love affairs. And most of all they lie to girls when they return from a trip. Then it's "Oh darling, every moment I was caught up in the memory of you, my every breath since our separation was a sigh for you, your words at our parting have echoed ceaselessly in the very depths of my soul, neither time nor space could ever erase your beloved image from my heart!" —That stuff just flows out, and all the while he has promised to marry two others, started up affairs, sent back letters from every stop, and the next day will pick up half a dozen at the general delivery window. Oh, they are terrible creatures, men!

WALBURGA (*seized with mistrust*) He'd better not—

BOYLE (*calling from within*) Walburga!

WALBURGA In a minute! (*to herself*) This is infuriating! (*to* SLIPPY) Wait a moment, I'll be right back. Take this for your time and trouble, I'll be right back. (*Gives him money and rushes out through the side door.*)

SLIPPY (*to himself*) Got her!

Sanguine

MARIE (*looking into the mirror*) They don't look like this, girls who are despondent over unfaithful men.

HUTZIBUTZ (*Enters through middle door.*) Miss Marie, my humblest wishes for your happiness!

MARIE I don't need the kind of happiness you wish me; my only wish is that you go away, and you will be happier if you do so at once.

HUTZIBUTZ (*to himself*) How high-spirited she is in her joy. (*aloud*) In half an hour the mail coach will arrive carrying four postmarked young men, one of whom is registered and addressed to your heart.

MARIE Get out of my sight! You can see I am in no mood to listen to your stupid prattle.

HUTZIBUTZ May the dear couple be united in years to come, just as they are today, their happy hearts filled with the love of life—

MARIE Shut your mouth!

HUTZIBUTZ (*to himself*) All my efforts are in vain!

MARIE Out! You can see I'm not in a good mood.

HUTZIBUTZ (*to himself*) That's just great! All year long she is in a good mood, and now when it's time for her to pay up, she's in a bad mood.

MARIE Out, I say!

HUTZIBUTZ (*to himself, on leaving*) Fate, I'm going to sue you for damages!

(*Exits by middle door.*)

Choleric

WALBURGA (*returning through the side door*) Now speak up, you know something about Edmund!

SLIPPY Well, oh law, I don't know anything definite—

WALBURGA The least hint will suffice. Take this purse, —much more will follow—but speak as my friend, as the friend of truth, as the enemy of falsehood and treason!

SLIPPY As you know, there is a milkmaid in the house next door. Well, the servants are always gossiping with her about their work, tittling and tattling, picking their masters to pieces, as has been the way of servants and milkmaids for thousands of years.

WALBURGA Go on, go on!

SLIPPY Well, one of the servants says, after complaining about low wages, long hours, no opportunities for cheating, she says: "Today Miss Boyle's fiancé is coming back to her." "Oho?" says the milkmaid, "oho?" —and laughs, so to speak, a milkmaidenly laugh into her pail.

WALBURGA The milkmaid laughed? That's enough! Too much, in fact, for a loving heart!

SLIPPY Naturally, no milkmaid laughs without cause.

WALBURGA No doubt this woman had heard from one of the servants that Edmund was having an affair with her mistress—notes exchanged—promises—protestations—endearments—vows—ha! I can see it all!

Sanguine

MARIE Not to worry, that is the first rule when one is upset about something. (*Trips singing out through the side door.*)

Choleric

SLIPPY It's probably so; men, they are capable of anything.

WALBURGA Leave me alone now, I am working out a hideous vengeance. Revenge, I shall have revenge!

SLIPPY The house of love is now on fire in every corner. (*Exits by middle door.*)

Phlegmatic

AGNES (*as above*) I must say, this business comes as a surprise to me.

Choleric

WALBURGA (*as above*) Wretch! Betrayer! Perjurer!

152

Scene 11

Choleric	Phlegmatic	Melancholy	Sanguine
WALBURGA, HUTZIBUTZ	AGNES (*still embroidering placidly*)	Empty stage	ISABELLA

Sanguine

ISABELLA (*entering*) What has happened to Miss Marie? She sings and tears the ribbons from her dress, laughs and at the same time stamps her feet. It's too much for me!

Choleric

HUTZIBUTZ (*entering by middle door*) Miss Walburga!

WALBURGA Ha! The second assistant fiend! He no doubt knew all about it and lent a hand in betraying me! (*Takes some books from the table and throws them furiously at* HUTZIBUTZ.) Away, villain, before I grind you to dust in my wrath!

(HUTZIBUTZ *exits quickly through middle door.*)

WALBURGA A thousand volcanoes are erupting in my breast! Woe be unto him who gets in the way of the lava flow! (*Exits through side door.*)

Scene 12

Choleric	Phlegmatic	Melancholy	Sanguine
WALBURGA	AGNES	IRENE	ISABELLA, MARIE

Phlegmatic

AGNES I am embroidering this tobacco pouch for him—he doesn't deserve it. I ought to tear it into a thousand pieces, but since I am already so far along, I'll think I'll just go ahead and finish it.

Sanguine

MARIE (*entering, to* ISABELLA) Say, what is the name of the gentleman who passes by my window every day half a dozen times on horseback and eight more times in his carriage?

ISABELLA Mr. Weather.

MARIE Give Mr. Weather this note the next time you see him (*handing her a note*) and tell him there has been a change of weather in my heart that promises him sunshine. Have you got that?

ISABELLA But Miss Marie—

MARIE You tell him what I told you!

Melancholy

IRENE (*Enters through the side door, takes a box from a cupboard, and removes the medallion which hangs about her neck.*) In this medallion I kept a lock of his hair. It is black as his soul, black as my fortune. Rest here locked away, dark curls, while mine fade in the sorrow of injured love!

Choleric

WALBURGA (*Enters through the side door carrying a large packet of letters.*) I'll throw his letters in the stove! Turn to ashes, you lie-besmirched pages! You deserve death by fire! (*Flings the letters into the stove with vehemence.*)

(*Outside, the sound of the post horn.*)

Scene 13

Choleric	Phlegmatic	Melancholy	Sanguine
WALBURGA (*busy at the stove*)	AGNES (*placidly embroidering*)	IRENE, *later* DOLE, GUIDO	ISABELLA, MARIE, *then* BLYTHE, FELIX

Sanguine

ISABELLA There's the post coach!

MARIE My brother is coming!

ISABELLA And your lover with him!

MARIE Don't speak of him to me! It's over, all over, forever!

ISABELLA I must go see— (*Hurries out quickly through middle door.*)

Melancholy

DOLE (*entering by side door*) It seemed to me I heard the post horn.

IRENE The sound pierced my heart like a death knell.

Sanguine

BLYTHE (*Leaps in through the side door, making the motions of blowing a post horn.*) Did you hear it? My son is here!

Melancholy

GUIDO (*Enters sadly through middle door.*) Oh, my father!

DOLE Guido, my Guido! Oh, why must your features remind me so painfully of her who is no more?

GUIDO (*looking at the portrait*) Oh, my mother! Oh, why can't she be here to take part in the joy of our reunion? (*Weeping, he hurls himself into his father's arms.*)

Sanguine

ISABELLA (*Enters by middle door followed by* FELIX, *who pinches her.*) What are you doing? (*Exits by side door.*)

FELIX Pop, you have always had pretty housemaids, but this one's a pip!

BLYTHE You just wait, I'll teach you to flirt instead of throwing yourself into your father's arms! Come here, Felix, let me give you a hug! (*Embraces him.*)

FELIX Pop, you are a real pop!

Scene 14

Choleric	Phlegmatic	Melancholy	Sanguine
WALBURGA,	AGNES,	IRENE,	ISABELLA,
then ROBERT,	*then* YAWN,	DOLE,	MARIE,
BOYLE	EDMUND	GUIDO	BLYTHE, FELIX

Phlegmatic

YAWN (*entering by the side door*) I say, I think Edmund is here.

EDMUND (*entering by middle door, very languid in tone and manner*)

155

I kiss your hand, Father. How are you, Agnes?

AGNES Thank you, so-so.

Melancholy

GUIDO (*to* IRENE) My sister, the sight of you fills me with profound melancholy.

IRENE Oh, you cannot know my suffering!

Phlegmatic

YAWN (*very calmly*) Well, I'm quite pleased to see you looking so well after three years.

AGNES (*to* YAWN) He is well, but you will make yourself ill if you give in to such transports of joy.

Melancholy

DOLE (*with deep suffering*) Guido! (*Rushes out, choking back the tears, through the side door.*)

Sanguine

FELIX How have you been, Marie?

MARIE How could a young, rich, pretty girl be anything other than well?

FELIX I'm glad to hear it!

Choleric

ROBERT (*Storms in through middle door.*) The devil take those post horses! The wishes of the passengers are shackled to their rotting bones! Everything ought to be driven by combustion, there should be nothing but steam coaches; with ours only the horses were puffing.

WALBURGA (*still at the stove*) Robert, my brother!

ROBERT Greetings! What are you doing there?

Sanguine

BLYTHE I'd better pop upstairs and see if I still have a bottle of champagne left. (*Exits by the side door.*)

Phlegmatic

AGNES Father, scenes like this excite you far too much. Why don't you go inside?

YAWN You are right. (*Exits through the side door.*)

Choleric

BOYLE (*In a towering rage, enters through the side door, to* ROBERT.) So! The young master is finally here? Pretty slow, —but then why not? Why hurry? What does it matter if he see his father a few hours earlier or later? You could have stayed away altogether! If you think nothing of me, I certainly think even less of you.

ROBERT You wrong me, Dad. At every stop I swore impatiently, as only the best of sons can swear. At the postillions, the horses—

BOYLE Quiet! It's not true!

ROBERT I never lie, Dad! I don't know why I should be lying now!

BOYLE You dare to contradict me? Out of my sight! I want nothing more to do with you.

ROBERT But Dad—

BOYLE Not another word. I'll teach you to respect your father! (*Exits in a fury by the side door.*)

Scene 15

Choleric	Phlegmatic	Melancholy	Sanguine
ROBERT,	EDMUND,	GUIDO,	FELIX,
WALBURGA	AGNES	IRENE	MARIE

Choleric

ROBERT This is too much—this reception—

WALBURGA Oh, it takes a meek nature like mine to put up with Dad.

Phlegmatic

EDMUND Agnes!

AGNES Edmund!

EDMUND If Father should ask for me, I'll be right back. (*Goes slowly, though not ludicrously so, out the middle door.*)

AGNES Very well.

Sanguine

FELIX Say what you will, even if I vex her, I cannot help it, I'm champing at the bit, my heart is about to burst, I must go to her! (*Exits quickly by middle door.*)

MARIE You're going to be in for it again!

Melancholy

GUIDO (*to himself*) How shall I find her? (*to* IRENE) Sister, a difficult moment lies before me. Farewell! (*Exits by middle door.*)

IRENE Farewell!

Choleric

ROBERT I must be off.

WALBURGA Where to?

ROBERT How can you ask such a stupid question?

WALBURGA Don't be so rude!

ROBERT I'm going to my Agnes. Woe be to her if she no longer loves me! (*Exits by middle door.*)

Scene 16

Choleric	Phlegmatic	Melancholy	Sanguine
WALBURGA	AGNES	IRENE	MARIE

Melancholy

IRENE Now it is here, the moment I have long awaited with scalding tears. How darkly it lowers over me!

Sanguine

MARIE The coward is bound to come here, he thinks I know nothing. This will be a scream, then adieu, game's over!

Phlegmatic

AGNES If only Robert will not call on me; I might become enraged, and that I must avoid on account of my health.

Choleric

WALBURGA He is not coming, that is the clearest proof of his guilt! But tremble in your boots, coward! Your infamy will turn the lamb into a tiger, the dove into a hawk!

Scene 17

Choleric	Phlegmatic	Melancholy	Sanguine
WALBURGA,	AGNES,	IRENE,	MARIE,
EDMUND	ROBERT	FELIX	GUIDO

Melancholy

FELIX (*entering through middle door*) Irene, my dear love, my adorable, heavenly, divine Irene!

IRENE Felix, you have broken my heart. Farewell forever.

FELIX What? What's this? You speak of farewell forever, just when I've come about seeing you forever in the indissoluble bond of love?

(*They continue to speak in pantomine.*)

Phlegmatic

ROBERT (*storming in through the middle door*) Agnes, my Agnes!

AGNES You startled me. Can't you ever knock?

ROBERT Does my coming here upset you? And you address me so formally, abandon all warmth and affection to assume a cold formality towards one who burns with love for you, in whose bosom the most ardent flame blazes with an all-consuming passion!

AGNES Stop it, don't play Simon Pure with me!

ROBERT Agnes—! (*Can speak no longer because of the feelings raging within him.*)

Sanguine

GUIDO (*Enters by middle door and speaks in a lugubrious tone.*) Marie, my Marie!

MARIE Ah, it's you! Why so mournful? Is it perhaps because your sly dodges have been found out? Oh, nothing is so finely spun that it will not some day come to light.

GUIDO I do not understand you. Your speech is so strange, so distant. Can it be that all-devouring time with its insatiable appetite has also consumed my happiness?

MARIE I didn't understand that.

GUIDO We understand one another no more. I feared as much from our unhappy separation.

Choleric

EDMUND (*Enters through middle door.*) Dear Walburga!

WALBURGA Ha, beast! Scum of the earth, you dare show yourself to me! Can you dare lift your treacherous gaze to her whom you have cheated, deceived, betrayed, deluded, and slain?

EDMUND I don't know what you mean; however, I think you wrong me.

WALBURGA Wrong? Wrong you, the picture of deceit, the mirror of falsehood, the very personification of dishonor?

EDMUND I am astounded!

BOYLE (*calling from within*) Walburga! Why don't you come when I call you ten times?

WALBURGA (*angrily*) Ten times! He hasn't even called once. Dad is driving me mad today with his incessant calling! (*very angrily to* EDMUND) Wait, wretch!

EDMUND (*placidly*) I shall wait.

(WALBURGA *exits through the side door.*)

Melancholy

FELIX So that's the way it is, Irene? Look at me frankly and truly, eye to eye. —Am I capable of deceit? I have never thought of anything else, nor shall I ever think of anything else than making you happy and because of you, being happy myself.

IRENE Is it true? Oh, then let me shed tears of joy on your breast!

FELIX Joy laughs, love of my life. You must give up this incessant weeping!

Phlegmatic

ROBERT May seven thousand monsters tear him limb from limb who would say such a thing about me! I can swear you ten thousand oaths—

AGNES That would all be well and good, if one could believe them.

ROBERT Then you don't believe me?

AGNES Once I'm in doubt, it's not easy for me to get out again.

Sanguine

GUIDO It pains me deeply to see that you utterly, utterly misjudge me—

MARIE Oh, a book is known by its cover—cowards in plain brown wrappers often conceal all sorts of off-color contents in their hearts.

GUIDO I see you do not wish to believe in my fidelity, otherwise your mind could not erect such a towering structure of mistrust on such flimsy foundations. I shall go—would to heaven these steps were my last. (*Makes as if to leave.*)

MARIE Guido!

GUIDO What else do you want of me?

MARIE (*to herself*) I may after all be doing him an injustice. (*aloud*) You needn't be so desperate! One has the right to show a little jealousy now and then.

Choleric

WALBURGA (*returning through the side door*) Well, have you memorized your excuses? I have been courteous enough to give you time to get your lies ready.

EDMUND What do you mean?

WALBURGA Ha! This cold detachment would try the patience of a saint! Must I endure the ridicule of a person who has made me the laughing-stock of milkmaids?

EDMUND (*placidly as ever*) What milkmaid has laughed at you, and why did she laugh at you, this milkmaid?

Melancholy

FELIX So our love is in peril and you are to wed another?

IRENE Oh, woe is me!

FELIX No, it is well for you and me! Thank heaven for this danger! I shall meet it boldly head-on! Danger calls for timely action, and timely action leads to its goal. I wish to attain my goal; therefore, my wish will be fulfilled precisely because of the danger.

Phlegmatic

ROBERT Who is this designated fiancé and where is he? If you show him the least favor I shall murder you both.

AGNES All right, go ahead. Murder people by pairs! I told you I don't care for him, I care only for you, if only I could believe your assurances.

Sanguine

GUIDO You are to belong to another? I am lost! All, all is lost!

MARIE How so? All may yet be won if you think of a clever plan to make me yours.

GUIDO That I shall do, but I fear it will fail.

MARIE What? I care for you again, am prepared to believe you have been wrongfully accused, and you dare to fear anything?

Choleric

WALBURGA (*to herself*) Now it weighs upon my heart like a millstone; he could be innocent. He is, most certainly; his calm demeanor is the clearest proof of it. Who knows what the milkmaid might have been laughing about? It is she who deserves my wrath, that creature, but he—my love, my passionate, undying love. (*aloud*) Edmund, my Edmund!

EDMUND Reflect upon everything rationally and hold me in your arms.

WALBURGA Reflection be damned! Henceforth only blind faith in you and in your fidelity shall dwell in my soul! (*Embraces him passionately.*)

Melancholy

IRENE Go now, Felix, write me; you know my father is not well disposed toward you. It would be terrible if he were to come in.

FELIX Nothing is terrible, Irene, all is well and what is not well will soon be so.

Sanguine

MARIE I think I hear Papa.

GUIDO (*sadly*) Then I must depart.

Phlegmatic

ROBERT Agnes, if you are resolved to make any sacrifice for love, speak, oh speak quickly!

AGNES Go on, you never give one time to think. And don't shout like that; father might hear you and that would spoil everything.

Choleric

WALBURGA You must deliver me from this detestable rival—by force, if necessary!

EDMUND I shall give the matter mature consideration.

WALBURGA Now go before Dad sees you; he is in a terrible mood today! Farewell!

EDMUND (*in a manner consistent with his personality*) Goodbye!

(EDMUND *exits by middle door,* WALBURGA *by side door.*)

Phlegmatic

AGNES Farewell!

ROBERT Goodbye!

Sanguine

MARIE Farewell!

GUIDO Goodbye!

Melancholy

IRENE Farewell!

FELIX Goodbye!

together, all in a manner consistent with their personalities

(ROBERT, GUIDO *and* FELIX *exit by middle doors;* AGNES, MARIE *and* IRENE *by side doors.*)

Scene 18

Choleric	Phlegmatic	Melancholy	Sanguine
Empty stage	YAWN	DOLE	SLIPPY, FELIX, GUIDO, ROBERT, EDMUND, HUTZIBUTZ

Phlegmatic

YAWN (*Enters through the side door alone, smoking.*) Edmund! Edmund! He must have left already. That's the worst thing about the boy, he gets his restless blood from his father, must be on the go constantly, just like me. (*Sits down.*)

Melancholy

DOLE (*Enters by the side door, alone.*) Guido!—He is not here!—He has fled—the son flees from his father in the first hour of their reunion? I now know there can be but one joy for me—the painful memories of her whom I shall never forget. (*Sits before the portrait for a while, then begins to paint.*)

Sanguine

SLIPPY (*Enters by middle door.*) The lovers are over there in the coffeehouse with their heads together like sheep when it thunders:

the storm of jealousy must have broken over each of them. But so what? Such a thunderstorm is invariably followed by a downpour of feminine tears, a gale of masculine protestations, the clouds of doubt are scattered and the sunshine of love reappears in full splendor, more brilliant even than had there been no storm. That's no good. What should I have gotten out of it? Nothing but a few tips which, were the lovers to discover the truth, would be followed by a considerable *numerus retardatus* of blows. None of that! Revenge is my trade! Revenge on Hutzibutz! They must come to ruin who build upon the support of a clothes cleaner. I'll drag their joy through the dust until he'll never be able to brush it out again! (*Sounds are heard from the doorway.*) Here they come. Now we'll see how things stand. (*Hides under the table.*)

(FELIX, GUIDO, ROBERT *and* EDMUND *enter by middle door.*)

FELIX It's the only way. A quick decision is called for—a single stroke brilliantly executed, bring home the bride, that's the ticket.

GUIDO Yes, but if—

ROBERT To hell with your "but ifs!" You and Edmund, you are incapable of a bold thought!

EDMUND Why do you always have it in for me? I do everything you wish.

FELIX First we must get word to our young ladies—though it's not advisable to speak to them, since each of us, interestingly enough, is detested by the father of his beloved. Therefore we shall have to resort to written communication. (*Distributes sheets of notepaper around the table.*)

GUIDO With my proverbial bad luck, this thing is bound to take a turn for the worst.

ROBERT (*to* GUIDO) Tell me, what bad luck have you actually suffered?

GUIDO None—but I have premonitions, terrible premonitions that must surely come to pass.

ROBERT I too have a premonition, and mine has already come to pass.

GUIDO What's that?

ROBERT That you are a fool.

FELIX Quickly now! Take up your pens, everything you need is at hand.

165

EDMUND I shall go along with everything and calmly await the outcome.

(*All four sit down at the table and speak as follows while writing.*)

ROBERT I'll see to the coach.

FELIX Fine.

GUIDO And where is this perilous journey to take us?

FELIX To Zittendorf.[2]

SLIPPY (*to himself, peeking out from beneath the tablecloth and taking a sheet of paper from his pocket*) I'd better take notes of the most important details. (*Writes on the floor.*) So it's to Zittendorf.

FELIX Zittendorf lies two hours beyond the frontier. My old tutor is the magistrate there.

SLIPPY (*to himself*) Aha, an elopement is in the offing!

FELIX We'll be back by evening, and each of us shall spin the father of his beloved a tale of a secret wedding. First there will be a storm, but it will soon pass, and afterwards we'll have his consent willy-nilly; then we'll own up to our deception, fall to our knees before him again, receive forgiveness, blessings, arise again for embraces all around between daughter, father, bride, bridegroom and father-in-law; corks will be popped, toasts drunk, "Viva!" shouted; there will be laughter, kissing, joking, and by the close of day we'll be the four happiest couples in the city.

SLIPPY (*to himself*) I may be no cook in love, but I'll put some salt in their soups.[3]

GUIDO I foresee bad luck hanging over our heads.

SLIPPY (*to himself*) Missed! The bad luck lies at your feet.

ROBERT Shut your mouth, you bird of ill omen! (*Stamps his foot indignantly, then speaks to* EDMUND, *who sits beside him.*) Forgive me for stamping on your foot.

SLIPPY (*to himself*) It was my hand!

EDMUND I felt nothing.

SLIPPY (*to himself*) I can believe that, but I—!

(*All four continue to write.*)

Phlegmatic

YAWN I wonder if my son has learned anything in these last three years? If he hasn't, no matter—too much knowledge gives one headaches, and although I have never had a headache in my life, I understand it is a very unpleasant sensation.

Sanguine

HUTZIBUTZ (*Entering by middle door, observes the four lovers.*) How they sit together and write! It's really nice when boys are so hardworking, they must be a joy to their parents.

FELIX Ah, Hutzibutz, it's good you are here. You will have four letters to deliver.

GUIDO Couldn't each of us just hand over the appropriate letter to his sister?

FELIX None of that! We must be off, we still have arrangements to make abroad and besides, what are we paying him for? (*to* HUTZIBUTZ) And you, take careful note of the addresses, so as not to confuse the letters—remember, it happened once before.

HUTZIBUTZ (*half to himself*) That wouldn't be any catastrophe. More than likely they all say the same thing. The writing of love letters could be entirely done away with, and a printer could make a killing. All one needs are four forms: one for a declaration of love, one for jealousy, one for reconciliations and promises, and one for the final break. If one could only buy them made up like checks, then one would only need to fill in the names and dates, and the world of lovers would be taken care of forever. (*The four lovers fold their letters.*)

FELIX I see we don't have any seals; well, no matter. The affair's no secret to him, anyway. (*indicating* HUTZIBUTZ)

ROBERT Now all is ready. (*to* HUTZIBUTZ) Hurry up! (*Each of the four lovers gives him his letter.*)

HUTZIBUTZ By the way, do you know about the new enemy we have just made?

ALL FOUR Enemy?

HUTZIBUTZ My cleverness is a thorn in the side of Slippy the barber. For that reason he is trying to foil my efforts on your behalf.

FELIX It must have been he who was responsible for that bad scene with our sweethearts.

GUIDO & EDMUND No doubt about it!

ROBERT (*leaping up*) Bring him here so that I may trounce him, crush him, shred him!

SLIPPY (*under the table, to himself*) My situation is beginning to look questionable.

ROBERT (*furiously*) Hutzibutz, bring him here right away. He will have from me the most prodigious walloping that has ever been dealt out on this earth!

Melancholy

DOLE (*lost in contemplation of the portrait*) Oh, sweet memory, you rage too violently in me, my heart will be swept away by melancholy.

Sanguine

ROBERT Get him here, your reward will be six ducats.

SLIPPY (*under the table, to himself*) A price has been put on my head.

FELIX This is no time for thoughts of revenge, the execution of our plan must come first. Come with me now—wait—where is—? (*Searches his pockets.*) I have lost my wallet with Irene's picture in it.

HUTZIBUTZ It must have fallen under the table while you were writing. (*Goes to the table as if to search for it.*)

EDMUND You asked me to hold it for you at the last stop; here it is.

FELIX Oh, of course!

ROBERT To work, then!

EDMUND What did I do with my gloves? (*Searches his pockets.*)

HUTZIBUTZ They are probably under the table.

EDMUND Look for them! (HUTZIBUTZ *goes to the table as if to search for them.*) Oh, here, I have them.

HUTZIBUTZ Oh? I look under the table for everything that is lost; you wouldn't believe what may be lying under a table. For instance, I myself have lain under this very table. (*to* GUIDO) It was on your account, when I was suspected of carrying notes. The old man came home, and I was left with no other refuge but this table. You should have seen it! There stood Mr. Blythe, there Miss Marie, there the parlormaid, and I was lying right there. I'll show you. (*Starts to crawl under the table.*)

FELIX Come on, we don't have time to listen to your stories! (*to his friends*) Come! (*All four exit by the middle door.*)

HUTZIBUTZ (*alone*) They still won't believe that I am one of the most cunning fellows of my time. I have an idea that will astonish them and put this Slippy to shame. To deliver the letters would be a simple matter, but no! I will deliver the letters to the girls right under the noses of the father and my enemy the barber, and when I'm finished I'll say to Slippy: "See, *I* did that, you mutt!" That will be an everlasting triumph! Then everyone will have to respect my brains. Really, it's a pity fortune didn't give me a higher station in life, for I'm not young, I'm not handsome, I'm not rich, I am merely a mastermind. In me nature made many oversights, but she created a model brain. What an odd mismatch. (*Exits by middle door.*)

Scene 19

Choleric	Phlegmatic	Melancholy	Sanguine
Empty stage	YAWN	DOLE	SLIPPY

Sanguine

SLIPPY (*crawling out*) I could now publish the most beautiful account of a journey through the wilds of mortal terror. What one can feel *under* a table no one *at* a table can imagine—I know, I have felt it! No wonder every fiber of my being, which two minutes ago trembled in terror, now glows with lust for revenge. I have always been the guardian angel of love—at least when there was something in it for me—but now I must play an evil spirit, an avenging ghost, a Eumenidian Fury! To such lengths can circumstances drive a barber! (*Exits by middle door.*)

Phlegmatic

YAWN (*smoking*) Will my son do anything now? I feel sorry for him. Every job is a tribulation. Should he marry? Being single, being rich, being nothing—these together make up the most comfortable condition. What's the use in marrying if he gets an ill-tempered shrew for a wife?

Melancholy

DOLE (*gazing fixedly at the portrait*) That was she! The very image of an angel—just as she stands here before me in this portrait.

Phlegmatic

YAWN What a creature, what a bore!

Scene 20

Choleric	Phlegmatic	Melancholy	Sanguine
Empty stage	YAWN	DOLE, SLIPPY, IRENE, HUTZIBUTZ	Empty stage

Melancholy

SLIPPY (*entering by middle door*) Your humble servant, Mr. Dole! Would it please you to be shaved now?

DOLE Please me? Friend, nothing on this earth is pleasant for me. For all I care, you may shave me. (*Sits down.*)

SLIPPY (*wrapping an apron about his neck and lathering him*) There are things in life one cannot avoid, among them being barbered. Still it is most bearable when done by a barber, when one gets shorn by a relative—

DOLE You are speaking figuratively. My daughter—she who is my one joy—happy the man who has such a daughter!

SLIPPY Well, she hasn't shorn you yet, but— (*as if breaking off, but adding pointedly*) you've been softsoaped already.

DOLE (*taking his meaning*) What! — You cur! — What do you mean by that?

SLIPPY (*stropping the razor*) You're all soaped up and I am about to start shaving you.

DOLE No, no, don't deceive me. You meant it another way.

SLIPPY (*shaving him*) Well, even if I did mean it another way, take comfort, it happens to plenty of people.

DOLE In such comfort lies an ocean of mischief! Speak plainly, if you have any feeling for what goes on within a father's breast.

170

SLIPPY (*shaving him*) I have feeling for all kinds of things—head to the other side a little, please—I'll tell you, your lordship, I have come upon something, and so as not to prolong your agony I'll tell you straight away what it is: your daughter is planning to elope with that no-good Master Felix from next door.

DOLE (*Buries his face in his hands.*) My daughter! —Is it possible?

SLIPPY But your lordship, now you have the soap on your hands instead of on your face; I'll have to start all over again. (*Relathers him.*)

DOLE Irene, my good, gentle Irene!

Phlegmatic

YAWN (*puffing on his pipe*) Yes, yes, the worst, the most fatal annoyances are the domestic ones.

Melancholy

SLIPPY Let me finish shaving you!

IRENE (*Enters by side door.*) You called me, my Father?

DOLE Called?

SLIPPY Control yourself!

DOLE (*quietly*) The sight of her rends my heart.

SLIPPY If you jerk your head around like that again, I'll rend your nose.

IRENE (*to* DOLE) Did you want something?

DOLE No, I want nothing more.

HUTZIBUTZ (*Carrying a bundle of clothing over his arm, enters by middle door.*) Here, I've brought back the clean clothes.

DOLE Just put them on the chair.

(HUTZIBUTZ, *in doing so, shows* IRENE *a letter behind her father's back and puts it into the pocket of a coat which he then hangs on the chair-back.*)

SLIPPY (*Glancing at* HUTZIBUTZ *out of the corner of his eye while continuing to shave* DOLE, *speaks softly to him.*) Your lordship, he showed her a letter just now and slipped in into your topcoat pocket.

DOLE For shame! For shame!

SLIPPY Control yourself!

HUTZIBUTZ Will your lordship be requiring anything more?

DOLE (*in a broken voice*) No, nothing more.

HUTZIBUTZ (*to himself*) Triumph Number One accomplished! (*Exits by middle door.*)

SLIPPY (*softly to* DOLE) Now, your lordship, pay close attention to your daughter—you see, she is already sneaking over to it.

DOLE (*loudly*) Irene!

IRENE (*in the process of approaching the chair to get the letter, startled*) Father—?

DOLE You know I love solitude, go to your room!

IRENE Right away. (*to herself*) Heavens, if he should find the letter—! (*Exits through the side door.*)

SLIPPY (*collecting his shaving gear*) So, I have got your face fixed up now; if it comes unglued because of the letter, it's not my fault. (*Exits by middle door.*)

Scene 21

Choleric	Phlegmatic	Melancholy	Sanguine
Empty stage	YAWN, *later* SLIPPY, AGNES, HUTZIBUTZ	DOLE	Empty stage

Melancholy

DOLE (*alone*) Ah, must I suffer this calamity too? Every calamity falls upon me save the final one which will put an end to life.

Phlegmatic

SLIPPY (*entering by middle door*) Your lordship!

YAWN What is it you wish, Mr. Slippy?

SLIPPY To do your hair, your lordship.

YAWN Let us put it off until tomorrow.

SLIPPY Tomorrow? Who know whether there'll be anything left to comb tomorrow, your lordship?

YAWN I do not understand you, Mr. Slippy.

SLIPPY If your lordship should happen to tear out your hair today, what shall I have to comb tomorrow?

Melancholy

DOLE (*Takes the letter from the coat pocket, unfolds it and reads.*) "Beloved Irene, this morning I shall come for you." —Horrors!

Phlegmatic

YAWN Under no circumstances shall I tear out my hair.

SLIPPY Not even if your daughter should elope today with young Mr. Boyle?

YAWN Elope? With young Mr. Boyle? H'm, h'm, h'm, h'm.

SLIPPY What do you say to that, your lordship?

YAWN I say nothing to that.

SLIPPY Well, then, happy journey!

YAWN There will be no journey.

SLIPPY But how will you prevent it, your lordship? It will be hard.

YAWN If a thing is hard, I let someone else take care of it; I don't do hard work.

Melancholy

DOLE (*reading*) "You must take a little trip with him who would travel to the ends of the earth with you."

Phlegmatic

AGNES (*coming in through the side door*) Father, will Edmund be home for dinner?

YAWN Yes, or perhaps not.

SLIPPY The cook should make her plans according to *that?*

Melancholy

DOLE (*reading*) "Love will guide our steps; Fortune, Happiness and Rejoicing beckon from the finish line." (*Paces up and down, his hand to his forehead.*)

Phlegmatic

HUTZIBUTZ (*Enters through middle door.*) Here, I've brought the boots.

YAWN I'm not going out today, I am too tired.

HUTZIBUTZ They are polished to perfection.

SLIPPY (*softly to* YAWN) I'll pretend to comb out your lordship's hair and we'll see what happens. (*Takes a comb and begins to arrange* YAWN'S *hair.* YAWN *sits center stage,* AGNES *stands to the right,* HUTZIBUTZ *to the left.*)

HUTZIBUTZ (*to himself*) She is not looking my way. I'll say something about marriage, that always electrifies girls. (*aloud*) These boots are so beautiful one could dance at a wedding in them. (*to himself*) Aha! She is already looking this way! (*Surreptitiously shows her the letter.*)

SLIPPY (*softly to* YAWN) You see, your lordship, he is showing her a letter.

YAWN H'm, h'm!

(HUTZIBUTZ, *after communicating in pantomime with* AGNES, *places the letter in Yawn's tobacco pouch, which lies open on the table.*)

SLIPPY (*softly to* YAWN) He put it in the tobacco pouch just now.

YAWN H'm, h'm!

HUTZIBUTZ I kiss your hand, your lordship. (*to himself*) Triumph Number Two! (*Exits by middle door.*)

AGNES (*in order to get to the letter*) Shall I make a pipe for you, Father?

YAWN No, I haven't finished this one yet.

AGNES I believe you are out of tobacco. (*Starts toward the pouch.*)

YAWN Are you going or not? To your room, march!

AGNES You certainly are irritable today, Father!

YAWN No one is to meddle in my tobacco-affairs.

AGNES (*to herself*) If that letter should fall into his hands—what is to be done? I must wait it out patiently. (*Exits through the side door.*)

SLIPPY The tobacco pouch now contains everything; tamp your uncertain head full of conviction and light the affair in the flames of your righteous indignation. I kiss your hand, your lordship! (*Exits by middle door.*)

Scene 22

Choleric	Phlegmatic	Melancholy	Sanguine
Empty stage	YAWN	DOLE, *then* BRIDGET	BLYTHE, MARIE, *then* SLIPPY, *then* HUTZIBUTZ

Melancholy

DOLE I'll put the letter back now.

Phlegmatic

YAWN I'll get the letter now.

Melancholy

DOLE I know all now.

Phlegmatic

YAWN I don't really know anything yet, at least nothing definite.

Melancholy

DOLE My daughter is guilty. (*Puts the letter back into the coat pocket and hangs the coat over the chairback.*)

Phlegmatic

YAWN The girl could be innocent. (*Takes the letter from the tobacco pouch and opens it slowly.*)

175

Sanguine

BLYTHE (*Enters through the side door with* MARIE, *who is busy arranging flowers on a bonnet.*) That makes fourteen people all together; that is far too few for me, you must tell me who else should be invited.

MARIE Felix is sure to have some acquaintances.

BLYTHE If he were only here, that boy!

Phlegmatic

YAWN (*reading*) "Soul of my soul, life of my life!" What a nincompoop!

Sanguine

SLIPPY (*Enters by middle door.*) Mr. Blythe!

BLYTHE Well, you have certainly taken your own sweet time!

SLIPPY Please be seated, I'll have your hair done right away.

BLYTHE (*sitting down*) You're going to neglect my head so long that one of these days I'll come down on yours.

Melancholy

DOLE (*calling through the side door*) Bridget!

Sanguine

SLIPPY (*Putting down the alcohol burner and taking up the curling iron, speaks softly to* BLYTHE.) Send your daughter away!

BLYTHE (*softly*) What for?

(HUTZIBUTZ *enters by middle door with several articles of clothing on his arm.*)

SLIPPY (*seeing* HUTZIBUTZ, *softly*) That did it, now it is too late! He is already here.

BLYTHE (*softly*) Who?

SLIPPY (*softly*) The helper's helper!

Melancholy

BRIDGET (*entering through the side door*) Your lordship called?

DOLE My hat!

(BRIDGET *exits by side door.*)

Sanguine

HUTZIBUTZ Well, everything is clean again; but the way your lordship soils his clothes, that is really something!

BLYTHE Put everything over there! (*Points to a chair downstage left.*)

Phlegmatic

YAWN (*reading*) "All is ready for our flight!"

Sanguine

HUTZIBUTZ (*to himself*) That is stupid, she's standing clear over there. (*Lays the clothing on the chair.*)

Phlegmatic

YAWN (*reading*) "I'll come for you this morning." —H'm, h'm!

Sanguine

(SLIPPY *and* BLYTHE *are center stage,* MARIE *to the right,* HUTZIBUTZ *to the left.*)

SLIPPY (*while combing* BLYTHE'S *hair, softly*) You'll see something in a minute. Just keep an eye on Hutzibutz and do nothing!

MARIE (*to herself*) Can it be that Hutzibutz has no news for me?

Phlegmatic

YAWN (*reading*) "Until the end of eternity, with burning passion and ardent desire, your Robert." (*Shakes his head.*) H'm, h'm!

Sanguine

(HUTZIBUTZ *surreptitiously shows* MARIE *the letter.*)

SLIPPY (*softly to* BLYTHE) Did you see that?

BLYTHE (*softly*) Oh, what devilment! A letter!

SLIPPY (*as before*) Quiet now!

Melancholy

DOLE I shall find out for sure and then—

Sanguine

(HUTZIBUTZ *hangs a coat from a nail in the wall downstage left and sticks the letter through its collar like a pigtail.*)

MARIE (*begins to laugh furtively*) How that Hutzibutz carries on!

SLIPPY (*combing* BLYTHE'S *hair, softly*) Did you see where he put the letter?

BLYTHE (*suppressing a laugh*) Just like a pigtail!

Phlegmatic

YAWN (*shaking his head*) H'm, h'm—h'm, h'm.
Sanguine

HUTZIBUTZ (*aloud to* BLYTHE) Your humble servant! (*to himself, exiting*) The way I paper the whole world, it's really something! (*Exits by middle door.*)

Melancholy

BRIDGET (*bringing the hat*) Here is your hat. I don't know why, but your lordship seems somehow so thoughtful.

DOLE Thoughtful? I have thought everything through.

Sanguine

MARIE (*looking for an excuse to get to the letter*) How carelessly he put the clothes down—

BLYTHE Leave them there and go inside. I have something to talk over with Mr. Slippy.

MARIE But—

BLYTHE Inside, I said!

MARIE (*to herself*) It's impossible now to get at it.

Melancholy

BRIDGET Where is your lordship going? Which way?

DOLE It's all the same, all roads lead to the dead. (*Exits by middle door.*)

(BRIDGET *looks after him sadly, then exits through the side door.*)

Sanguine

MARIE If Papa discovers the correspondence, what a pretty kettle of fish that will be! (*Exits, giggling and looking toward the letter, through the side door.*)

BLYTHE (*to* SLIPPY) Just what is going on here?

SLIPPY *On,* nothing; but something might be going *off.*

BLYTHE I'm beginning to see the light!

SLIPPY Wait till you've read the letter. Your hair is done, —your humble servant. (*Exits by middle door.*)

Scene 23

Choleric	Phlegmatic	Melancholy	Sanguine
BOYLE, *then* SLIPPY, WALBURGA, HUTZIBUTZ	YAWN	Empty stage	BLYTHE

Phlegmatic

YAWN (*alone*) H'm, h'm! In the end I shall be compelled to make a decision.

Sanguine

BLYTHE (*alone*) Just wait, I'll get to the bottom of your scheme! (*Takes the letter.*)

Choleric

BOYLE (*entering through side door*) Robert! Robert! —Why does the boy take so long when I call him? He is going to make me lose my temper yet. (*Someone is heard at the middle door.*) And how he crawls along! (*Seizes* SLIPPY *as he enters and drags him forward.*)

You just wait, my lad, I'll get you moving!

SLIPPY But Mr. Boyle—

BOYLE Oh, is it you? I thought it was my son.

SLIPPY I thank you for the fatherly welcome. Your lordship may yank his son about as he likes, but—

BOYLE It can do you no harm either. Why can't you be more punctual? Shave me! (*Sits down.*)

SLIPPY Right away! (*Sets out his shaving gear.*)

Sanguine

BLYTHE (*reading swiftly*) "My darling, you must flee with me, even if only for a short while, our uncertain destiny demands such measures."

Choleric

BOYLE Well, shave me, damn it!

SLIPPY (*lathering him*) Right away!

BOYLE (*aping him*) Right away, right away—you should be finished by now.

SLIPPY But I must lather you first!

BOYLE Shut up!

Sanguine

BLYTHE (*reading*) "Should this fail, should we not be united in life, then we shall be in death."

Choleric

SLIPPY That's the way it goes. Ingratitude is the world's reward. I get here a little late because I have been working in your behalf, watching over the honor of your house, and you mistreat me.

BOYLE You have done all this? Forgive me, noble friend, come to my heart! (*Throws himself on* SLIPPY'S *breast.*)

SLIPPY What are you doing? You're getting me all soapy.

BOYLE Speak up, friend, what have you done for the honor of my house? (*Sits down.*)

Phlegmatic

YAWN (*shaking his head*) Really, I must say—h'm, h'm!—

Choleric

SLIPPY (*beginning to shave* BOYLE) I have spied out something, a plot to elope with your daughter.

BOYLE (*Jumps up and seizes him by the shirtfront.*) Villain, you lie!

SLIPPY Let go of me!

BOYLE Give me proof, villain, or beneath my fists you shall breathe your last!

SLIPPY Then hear me out!

BOYLE (*enraged*) Proof!

SLIPPY Let me get a word in!

BOYLE Speak up, then!

SLIPPY Sit down, one can talk and shave at the same time, otherwise how could barbers talk so much? (BOYLE *sits down and* SLIPPY *continues to shave him.*) You see, it was like this— (WALBURGA *enters from the side door.*) your daughter—

WALBURGA Tell me, Dad—

BOYLE (*vehemently*) No, you tell me—

SLIPPY (*softly to* BOYLE) Quiet, you mustn't give anything away yet!

HUTZIBUTZ (*Enters by middle door.*) Here are the clothes. (*Carries clothing and a man's hat on his arm.*) This hat was all out of shape, as if it had been bashed in.

SLIPPY (*softly to* BOYLE) Here is the secret lettercarrier.

Sanguine

BLYTHE That mopey bird of ill omen is not going to have my girl. I know what I'll do! (*Pushes the letter back through the collar of the coat hanging on the wall.*) This will be a splendid joke! (*Takes his hat and hurries, laughing, out the middle door.*)

Choleric

BOYLE (*vehemently*) Hell and damnation! (WALBURGA *and* HUTZIBUTZ *draw back in fear.*)

SLIPPY (*to cover up Boyle's explosion*) I almost severed a couple of the gentleman's arteries. (*softly to* BOYLE) Quiet, your lordship, quiet!

(HUTZIBUTZ, *after exchanging signs of understanding with* WALBURGA, *tosses the letter into the hat.*)

SLIPPY (*observing the above, softly to* BOYLE) The letter is now in the hat.

BOYLE (*softly*) I'm suffocating with rage.

HUTZIBUTZ (*to himself*) Here the task was most difficult; but it is done. (*departing*) Really, my achievements fill even me with wonder! (*Exits middle door.*)

WALBURGA The hat is all out of shape, he said. (*Starts toward the hat.*)

BOYLE (*hotly*) What is that to you?

WALBURGA I was only—

BOYLE The only thing you have to do is get out of my sight!

WALBURGA (*departing*) If Dad comes upon the letter, he'll tear the house to pieces. (*Exits through the side door.*)

Phlegmatic

YAWN I'll put the letter back where it was. (*Does so.*)

Choleric

BOYLE (*leaping to his feet*) Now let me at that treasonous document! (*Snatches the letter from the hat, and unfolding it angrily, reads.*) "I have given everything careful consideration, dear Walburga; the pretense of flight is the only means which will bring us to our goal. The hour of decision seems near. Await me in the morning with a calm demeanor. Your Edmund." (*after he has finished reading*) Murder! Death! Poison! Plague! Hell and damnation! (*Throws the letter to the floor and stamps on it.*) Tremble, you vipers—tremble before my wrath! (*Rushes with half-shaven face out the middle door.*)

SLIPPY But your lordship is only half-shaved! (*Quickly picks up the letter, folds it, and puts it back into the hat.*) I must go after him! (*Hurries out through the middle door.*)

Phlegmatic

YAWN I shall take the part of a dispassionate observer. (*Takes his hat and exits by middle door.*)

Scene 24

Choleric	Phlegmatic	Melancholy	Sanguine
WALBURGA	AGNES	IRENE	MARIE

Sanguine

MARIE (*entering through side door*) Papa is gone, and the letter is still here! (*Takes the letter up quickly and reads it silently.*)

Choleric

WALBURGA (*Enters through side door and looks around carefully.*) Dad is no longer here, now the question is: does he have the letter or does he not? (*Hurries to the hat.*) He doesn't have it! (*Exultantly holds up the letter and reads it in silence.*)

Melancholy

IRENE (*Enters by side door and looks around carefully.*) Father has found the letter, an evil premonition tells me so. (*Goes hesitantly to the chair on which the clothes hang and searches in the pocket of the coat.*)

Phlegmatic

AGNES (*Enters by side door.*) Father has disappeared, we'll see if the letter has also. (*Looks toward the tobacco pouch.*)

Melancholy

IRENE He has not found it. (*Unfolds the letter and reads it silently.*)

Phlegmatic

AGNES Ah, he hasn't got it. (*Opens the letter and reads it in silence.*)

Sanguine

MARIE I'm to be carried away! (*Laughs.*) How transporting!

Choleric

WALBURGA I shall follow him! No power on earth shall separate us!

Melancholy

IRENE His wish shall be mine, though it will all end tragically; I know my destiny.

Phlegmatic

AGNES So I'm to go away with him? Well, we can give it a try.

Sanguine

MARIE My Guido!

Choleric

WALBURGA My Edmund!

Melancholy

IRENE My Felix!

Phlegmatic

AGNES My Robert!

Scene 25

Choleric	Phlegmatic	Melancholy	Sanguine
WALBURGA	AGNES	IRENE, *later* BRIDGET	MARIE, *then* ISABELLA, HUTZIBUTZ

Choleric

WALBURGA (*alone*) Above all, I must make myself ready for the journey. (*Exits by the side door.*)

Melancholy

IRENE (*calling through the side door*) Bridget!

Sanguine

MARIE If only Belle were here!

Phlegmatic

AGNES What shall I wear? (*Exits pensively through the side door.*)

Melancholy

(BRIDGET *enters by side door.*)

IRENE My hat and shawl! (BRIDGET *exits by side door.*)

Sanguine

HUTZIBUTZ (*Enters with* ISABELLA *through the middle door.*) Soon they'll be here, the four cavaliers.

MARIE And I am not ready yet. Quickly, Belle, my sky-blue hat!

ISABELLA Right away!

MARIE No, rather the rose. Rose is more appropriate for eloping.

ISABELLA In such cases one doesn't waste time choosing. I'll bring whatever comes to hand first. (*Exits through side door.*)

Melancholy

BRIDGET (*Enters by the side door, bringing a shawl and a hat.*) Are you going out, Miss Irene?

Sanguine

HUTZIBUTZ Well, how are you, Miss Marie?

MARIE Oh, I am so happy I could dance on air. Such an adventurous undertaking is absolutely divine!

HUTZIBUTZ Yes, packing off has its charms, no doubt about it.

Melancholy

IRENE Don't ask me whither! An inner voice tells me I shall soon see you again in tears of anguish. (*Falls upon* BRIDGET'S *breast.*)

Choleric

WALBURGA (*Enters by the side door with hat and shawl.*) What's taking him so long? I am consumed with impatience!

Phlegmatic

AGNES (*Enters with hat and shawl by the side door.*) Never in my whole life have I dressed so quickly as today.

Sanguine

(ISABELLA *returns with hat and shawl.*)

Scene 26

Choleric	Phlegmatic	Melancholy	Sanguine
WALBURGA, *then* EDMUND (*via middle door*)	AGNES, *then* ROBERT (*via middle door*)	IRENE, *then* FELIX (*via middle door*)	MARIE, ISABELLA HUTZIBUTZ, *then* GUIDO (*via middle door*)

Choleric

EDMUND My Walburga!

Phlegmatic

ROBERT My Agnes!

Melancholy

FELIX My Irene!

Sanguine

GUIDO My Marie!

together

Choleric

WALBURGA Are you finally here? Oh, how I have longed for you!

Phlegmatic

AGNES Are you here already?

Sanguine

MARIE You've come just in time; Papa is gone, now let's have our outing in the world.

Melancholy

IRENE You have come to fetch me—oh, if only I could overcome my premonitions. (*Sinks weeping on* FELIX'S *breast.*)

FELIX Don't cry, we'll return soon to joy and merrymaking.

Phlegmatic

AGNES Let me think if I am forgetting anything.

ROBERT You'll forget the main thing if you don't hurry!

Sanguine

MARIE (*taking the hat and shawl from* ISABELLA, *to* GUIDO) What's the matter with you?

GUIDO I palpitate for our success!

MARIE Not bad, a man palpitating!

Choleric

WALBURGA Let us hurry!

EDMUND Put something about your shoulders, you might catch cold.

WALBURGA No, no, we have no time to lose.

Sanguine

HUTZIBUTZ (*to* ISABELLA) I am sorry our relationship can't lead to such interesting arrangements.

ISABELLA How so?

Choleric

EDMUND Come, my love!

(*Makes to leave with* WALBURGA *through middle door.*)

Phlegmatic

ROBERT Come, my love!

(*Makes to leave with* AGNES *through middle door.*)

Melancholy

FELIX Come, my love!

(*Makes to leave with* IRENE *through middle door.*)

Sanguine

GUIDO Come, my love!

(*Makes to leave with* MARIE *through middle door.*)

together

Scene 27

Choleric	Phlegmatic	Melancholy	Sanguine
EDMUND, WALBURGA, BOYLE, *then* SLIPPY	ROBERT, AGNES, YAWN	FELIX, IRENE, DOLE	GUIDO, ISABELLA, MARIE, HUTZIBUTZ, BLYTHE

Choleric

BOYLE (*Enters by middle door.*) Back, cur!

WALBURGA Ah!

EDMUND Oh fatal coincidence!

Phlegmatic

YAWN (*Enters by middle door.*) What's the meaning of this?

AGNES Oh.

ROBERT Damnation!

together

Melancholy

DOLE (*Enters by middle door.*) Now my cup of misfortune is full!

IRENE Alas!

FELIX Damn!

Sanguine

BLYTHE (*Enters by middle door.*) Halt! Got you!

MARIE Uh-oh, it's Papa!

GUIDO Oh, horrors!

ISABELLA Your lordship!

HUTZIBUTZ Oops!

} together

Melancholy

IRENE (*falling at* DOLE'S *feet*) My Father!

Phlegmatic

YAWN Next time I'm not going to overlook this.

Melancholy

DOLE I am no longer myself; consider yourselves cursed. (*Sinks exhausted into a chair.*)

Choleric

BOYLE (*to* WALURGA) Quake before my fury, wanton! And (*to* EDMUND) you, you shameless seducer, —you—you— (*Can no longer speak for anger.*)

Sanguine

BLYTHE (*to* GUIDO) Get a move on! (GUIDO *totters upstage. To* MARIE.) Just wait, I'll teach you to elope. (*to himself*) I've caught them beautifully! (*laughing*)

Choleric

BOYLE (*to* EDMUND) Woe be unto you!

SLIPPY (*entering by middle door*) The show is on!

Scene 28

Choleric	Phlegmatic	Melancholy	Sanguine
EDMUND,	ROBERT, AGNES,	FELIX, IRENE,	MARIE, GUIDO,
WALBURGA,	YAWN,	DOLE,	ISABELLA,
BOYLE,	GERTRUDE,	MARGARET	HUTZIBUTZ, BLYTHE,
NANETTE,	BABETTE,	LISETTE,	FLASHMAN,
SUSANNE, LAST,	CYPRIAN	DRS. HODGE & PODGE,	POYNTER, STARR,
NEEDLE		BRIDGET	SEPHERL, THERESE

(*The persons entering form the chorus.*)

Choleric, Phlegmatic, Melancholy, Sanguine

CHORUS

What have we here? Alack, alas!
What's come to pass, what's come to pass?

(*The curtain falls as the group crosses the stage.*)

---

1. *german:* an early form of the waltz.

2. Zittendorf is a small community on the Czech side of the border.

3. "Die verliebte Köchin versalzt die Suppe" (The cook in love oversalts the soup), a proverb referring to the absentmindedness of one in love.

ACT II

Scene 1

Choleric	Phlegmatic	Melancholy	Sanguine
BOYLE, YAWN, DOLE, BLYTHE (*all seated*)	EDMUND, ROBERT, GUIDO, FELIX (*pacing up and down in conversation*)	IRENE, MARIE, WALBURGA, AGNES	SLIPPY, HUTZIBUTZ, ISABELLA

Choleric

BOYLE We are in luck to have Slippy on our side. (*All four continue to talk in dumb-show.*)

Phlegmatic

FELIX Let us rejoice that we have won Slippy over!

Melancholy

(IRENE *sits, weeping, downstage; by her,* AGNES; MARIE *and* WALBURGA *stand at their sides.*)

MARIE Now that Slippy is our ally, I have the highest hopes.

Sanguine

SLIPPY (*In conversation with* HUTZIBUTZ, *flirts meanwhile with* ISABELLA.) Our hostilities are over, we are united in a common cause.

HUTZIBUTZ (*still somewhat miffed*) I could have done it all by myself; my brains—

SLIPPY Are not adequate in such a complicated affair.

Phlegmatic

ROBERT (*grudgingly*) We have Slippy to thank for this; after all, he is the one who upset our apple-cart!

FELIX Only so as to right it again as a victory chariot and celebrate his cleverness.

Choleric

BOYLE (*to* YAWN) You don't take exception to the fact that I won't have your son as my son-in-law, do you?

YAWN No more than you do that I won't have yours—

BLYTHE All four of us are in the same boat; for that reason, none of us can take exception.

BOYLE (*to* YAWN) I have nothing against your daughter.

YAWN And I have nothing against yours.

BLYTHE (*points to* DOLE) It's the same with us. All four of us have made other arrangements for our daughters, and as far as I am concerned the son can marry whom he pleases—

BOYLE, DOLE, YAWN I say the same!

BLYTHE But daughters must obey!

BOYLE If not, deuce take—!

DOLE I am an unhappy father!

BLYTHE How so?

Melancholy

IRENE I am an unhappy creature!

MARIE Oh, be reasonable!

Choleric

BLYTHE The goal will still be reached. The girls shall marry our old friends just as planned.

Sanguine

SLIPPY We must stand by one another as faithful allies. (*Takes* HUTZIBUTZ *by one hand and* ISABELLA *by the other.*)

HUTZIBUTZ That is, the two of us will stand by one another. But this hand (*pointing to* ISABELLA) will not be taken by the hand by anyone but me when she gives it to me at the altar.

Melancholy

IRENE It is all over!

WALBURGA You are about to make me lose my temper!

Choleric

YAWN If only our four old friends don't find out that our four girls already have four sweethearts!

BOYLE I'll see to that! I'll strike like thunder and lightning!

BLYTHE Sure, why not?

Phlegmatic

ROBERT (*rising*) I could tear him limb from limb, that scoundrel Slippy.

EDMUND Calmly, calmly. Let us consider this dispassionately.

GUIDO It is hopeless, you'll see.

Sanguine

SLIPPY (*to* HUTZIBUTZ) Let me explain what you are to do.

HUTZIBUTZ (*to* SLIPPY, *observing that the latter keeps eyeing* ISABELLA) Why do you always look over there when you are explaining something to me? She knows everything.

ISABELLA Don't be silly, Hutzibutz.

SLIPPY Now pay attention— (*Continues to explain.*)

Choleric

BLYTHE Before the old tales come out, the new engagements will have taken place.

Melancholy

AGNES (*very complacently*) I've been so caught up in emotions to-day—love, dread, terror, despair.... I fear I am going to be ill.

Choleric

BLYTHE Our friends left Straßburg on the same day, each by the express coach.

BOYLE They should have been here by today.

Sanguine

SLIPPY The fiancés from Straßburg have already arrived and are staying at The Sign of the Long Nose.[1]

ISABELLA A prophetic sign for the gentlemen.

Choleric

BLYTHE It is not yet evening; surely they are coming. It would be a shame if they didn't. (*to* BOYLE *and* YAWN) We have already invited guests for the announcement party. Well, goodbye—I have a few errands to run.

Sanguine

SLIPPY That's why I have tried to get the fathers out of the house.

Choleric

YAWN The carriage is waiting for me. Slippy told me a drive is good after a traumatic experience.

BOYLE He recommended a tavern to me, to wash down my anger.

DOLE Slippy suggested I divert myself by going for a stroll in the cemetery. That's what I think I shall do.

Sanguine

HUTZIBUTZ You are a fine fellow, the way you make fools of people!

Choleric

BLYTHE Goodbye, then, until we have our daughters out of the house and in a coach bound for Straßburg with our old friends. (*All four exit through the middle door.*)

Sanguine

ISABELLA Remember, Hutzibutz, do your job well! (*Exits through side door.*)

Scene 2

Choleric	Phlegmatic	Melancholy	Sanguine
Empty stage	EDMUND, ROBERT, GUIDO, FELIX	IRENE, MARIE, WALBURGA, AGNES, *then* ISABELLA	SLIPPY, HUTZIBUTZ, *then* BLYTHE ISABELLA

Sanguine

SLIPPY Now first of all you are to go—

HUTZIBUTZ No, first of all, I'm going to stay! (*jealously, to himself*) I am not going to leave him alone in a Certain Presence!

Melancholy

WALBURGA The nearness of danger thrills me, victory or death is the cry that echoes through my soul!

Phlegmatic

FELIX If his scheme succeeds, even a hundred ducats isn't too much.

ROBERT Not even a thousand!

EDMUND Oof!

Sanguine

SLIPPY Are you perchance waiting for the thrashing Mr. Blythe owes you?

HUTZIBUTZ No, I'll let him have it on time.

SLIPPY But if you were to insist on a down payment—

BLYTHE (*Enters through middle door.*) Ah, Slippy, I'm glad to find you here! (*noticing* HUTZIBUTZ) Out!

HUTZIBUTZ I only wanted to see if there were any boots to be cleaned.

BLYTHE No, but there is a pair of britches to be dusted, namely yours— Oh, if only I had a cane!

Phlegmatic

FELIX Twenty-five apiece is not too much.

Sanguine

HUTZIBUTZ Oh, I beg of you, don't trouble yourself; I'll take care of the brushing. (*Hurries out through middle door.*)

SLIPPY Your lordship mustn't scare him off, I can get all kinds of information through him.

BLYTHE (*very hurriedly and secretively*) Fine, fine. But Slippy, I have something to tell you in confidence.

SLIPPY What?

(ISABELLA *starts to enter through the side door, but steps back to eavesdrop.*)

BLYTHE I am in love!

SLIPPY Intentions honorable?

BLYTHE Marriage, marriage! I have no desire to remain a widower, and the widow Korbheim is weary of widowhood.

SLIPPY Understood. May I perhaps be of assistance? She is one of my clientele.

BLYTHE Really? Oh, you are a prince of a fellow!

SLIPPY Precisely. And since I am a prince, I am to be dealt with only in crowns.

BLYTHE If I give you these three crowns, will you then turn my misunderstanding with Mrs. Korbheim—

SLIPPY Into the most beautiful of understandings.

Phlegmatic

GUIDO Don't speak with such assurance of success!

Sanguine

(ISABELLA *enters through the side door.*)

SLIPPY Isabella! (*Waves, nods to her affectionately.*)

(ISABELLA *exits, acknowledging Slippy's nods with a smile, through the middle door.*)

BLYTHE I hope she didn't hear anything! This matter is one of the strictest secrecy, I haven't even told my children yet, only after Marie is married—

SLIPPY All right, all right!

Melancholy

ISABELLA (*entering through middle door*) Pardon me, Miss Marie—

MARIE Belle! (*to the others*) She has played an important part in turning our enemy Slippy into a friend.

ISABELLA In spite of my feelings and my principles.

Sanguine

BLYTHE But tell me, what is going on between you and Belle?

SLIPPY Did your lordship notice something?

Melancholy

ISABELLA I am pretending to be in love with Slippy.

Sanguine

BLYTHE But she belongs to Hutzibutz.

SLIPPY She is quite mad about me.

Phlegmatic

FELIX (*discussing the same subject with the others*) Isabella is leading Slippy around by the nose.

Melancholy

ISABELLA And the idiot believes it!

Phlegmatic

ROBERT A clever girl, that Belle!

Melancholy

ISABELLA And when we no longer have need of his services, I'll tell him fare-thee-well, the game's over!

Sanguine

SLIPPY Hutzibutz, of course, is under the illusion that he is cock of the walk, while it is I—

Phlegmatic

ROBERT What a stupid dolt that barber is, he doesn't suspect a thing!

(ROBERT, EDMUND, *and* FELIX *laugh.*)

Sanguine

BLYTHE What a fine joke!

Melancholy

MARIE A person like Slippy deserves after all to be made a laughing-stock.

(MARIE, AGNES, *and* WALBURGA *laugh.*)

Sanguine

SLIPPY One can only laugh at such an ass. (*Laughs very loudly with* BLYTHE.)

BLYTHE But tell me now, what am I to do with regard to my love?

SLIPPY Attentiveness, the purchase of gifts, visits to her when I say so, or —but wait! Hasn't she often been a guest in your home?

BLYTHE Certainly, but—strained relations—

SLIPPY I shall undertake to have her at your daughter's engagement party here today.

BLYTHE Man, angel, if only you could—!

SLIPPY Go shopping and leave everything to me.

BLYTHE Wonderful, wonderful Slippy, Slippy of my heart, I place myself in your hands. (*Exits by side door.*)

SLIPPY (*alone*) What a triumph, to discover *his* weakness! To put the screws to the others will be mere child's play. (*Exits by middle door.*)

Scene 3

Choleric	Phlegmatic	Melancholy	Sanguine
Empty stage	EDMUND, ROBERT, GUIDO, FELIX, *then* SLIPPY	IRENE, MARIE, WALBURGA, AGNES, ISABELLA, *then* SLIPPY	Empty stage *then* BLYTHE

Melancholy

ISABELLA And to you, Miss Marie, I have a huge, tremendously important secret to impart.

ALL FOUR (*curious*) A secret?

ISABELLA (*to* MARIE) Yes, concerning your Papa! (*Speaks softly into* MARIE'S *ear.*)

WALBURGA This is something new, this whispering into one another's ears.

AGNES It seems as though we aren't worthy of a solemn trust.

IRENE From a friend, this hurts one cruelly.

Phlegmatic

SLIPPY (*moving to center stage*) With your permission, gentlemen—!

FELIX What is it you want?

ROBERT (*endeavoring to suppress his anger at the sight of* SLIPPY, *to himself*) My fingers are itching to get hold of him!

SLIPPY Only to ask if you are in agreement on all points of our operation, as I have outlined it to you.

ALL FOUR Entirely! In complete agreement!

SLIPPY Excellent, gentlemen, excellent; for now, your servant. (*Hurries out through middle door.*)

Sanguine

BLYTHE (*Enters by side door, still arranging his suit.*) If I don't look like a bridegroom, I don't know why not—now to pass by her window a couple of times, that should make a favorable impression. (*Exits by middle door.*)

Melancholy

MARIE (*to the others*) You'll soon know all, friends, but not just yet.

WALBURGA (*very piqued*) Oh, we have no desire to know your secrets.

AGNES You can keep them entirely to yourself.

IRENE But even as your lips, so shall our hearts be sealed to you forever.

MARIE I don't know what to make of you.

WALBURGA We shan't impose our friendship upon anyone.

AGNES Thank God we have no need to, but this is really too much!

WALBURGA Yes, it is—I cannot find words to express it.

MARIE I don't know whether I should laugh or cry.

AGNES What a friend you are!

AGNES *and* WALBURGA Haha!

IRENE (*at the same time*) Alas!

SLIPPY (*entering through the middle door*) Ladies, I observe here less than perfect accord— (*aside*) Whenever women get together—

WALBURGA We would be in accord except that Marie—

MARIE I'd be, but Walburga and Agnes and Irene—

SLIPPY Set aside your differences until after the wedding and keep your eyes fixed on the main goal. The enemy is near, love is in peril, I have been appointed commander, and as such I order this debate postponed.

MARIE I shall have forgotten the whole silly affair in five minutes.

WALBURGA I shall make an effort to bridle my righteous indignation.

AGNES It is really not worth getting upset about.

IRENE I shall say no more; however, a thing such as this leaves the iron in one's soul.

Phlegmatic

FELIX Our gathering place, the headquarters from which all our operations will proceed, will be the coffeehouse across the street.

EDMUND, ROBERT, GUIDO Fine!

Melancholy

SLIPPY Now listen to what you are to do according to the newly-forged plan.

ALL FOUR Speak!

SLIPPY (*to himself*) They all four said that in unison; the only thing all women agree upon is that they must speak. (*aloud*) The main task is this: the designated fiancés must renege of their own free will, and each of your lovers must win the heart of the respective father, who at present still detests him. Two easy chores fall to you: the first will be easy for you because you are *women:* you must pretend to be in love with the fiancé who comes to you. The second will also be easy for you because you are *lovable* women: you must make the fiancé who comes to you fall in love with you.

WALBURGA But that is entirely at odds with our objective!

SLIPPY Peace, peace! An interesting reversal is to be arranged.

Phlegmatic

ROBERT Adieu, then!

Melancholy

MARIE How so? Explain it to us—

SLIPPY There's simply no time!

Phlegmatic

EDMUND, GUIDO, FELIX Adieu! (*All exit save* EDMUND.)

Melancholy

SLIPPY The commander has spoken, and that's that!

WALBURGA All right. Come, Agnes, let us go! (*Exits with* AGNES *through the middle door.*)

MARIE Adieu, Irene!

IRENE (*to* MARIE) I forgive your betrayal of our friendship, but I cannot forget it. (*Exits through the side door;* MARIE *and* ISABELLA *exit through the middle door.*)

Scene 4

Choleric	Phlegmatic	Melancholy	Sanguine
WALBURGA, NANETTE	EDMUND, *then* AGNES	SLIPPY, *then* PAINE, *then* JOY	HUTZIBUTZ, *then* MARIE *and* ISABELLA, *then* JOY, PAINE, SLIPPY

Sanguine

HUTZIBUTZ (*entering through middle door, alone*) The tyrant of the house is gone, perhaps there may be a chance meeting. I must have a serious talk with Belle—she has a pure soul, Belle does, but the dust of vanity lies upon it, and that will lead the dear girl into danger.

Melancholy

SLIPPY I can't imagine where those fiancés can be!

Sanguine

MARIE (*to* ISABELLA *as they enter through the middle door*) You mustn't let that bother you.

HUTZIBUTZ Belle—

ISABELLA Leave me alone. Can't you see I am talking to Miss Marie? (*Exits with* MARIE *through the side door.*)

Melancholy

PAINE (*In traveling clothes, enters sadly through the middle door.*) Does Mr. Dole live here?

SLIPPY (*to himself*) Aha! (*aloud*) No, Mr. Blythe lives here.

Sanguine

JOY (*In traveling clothes, enters cheerfully through the middle door.*) Does Mr. Blythe live here?

HUTZIBUTZ (*aside*) Aha, my work begins! (*aloud*) No, Mr. Dole lives here.

JOY Bravo! Missed the minute I walked into the house.

Melancholy

SLIPPY Have I the honor of addressing Mr. Paine?

PAINE Yes.

Sanguine

HUTZIBUTZ You must be Mr. Joy?

JOY Yes.

Melancholy

SLIPPY Mr. Dole lives right next door.

PAINE I see—thank you, my friend. (*Exits through middle door.*)

Sanguine

HUTZIBUTZ Mr. Blythe lives right next door.

JOY Oh! Hahaha! Wouldn't it have been a joke had I come to the wrong place! (*Exits laughing through the middle door.*)

Phlegmatic

AGNES (*Enters through the middle door.*) Ah, Edmund, I tell you, I still can't get over this business.

EDMUND Let me think this over calmly!

Sanguine

HUTZIBUTZ (*alone*) Didn't I handle him nicely! No doubt about it, I am one of the great intriguers of the century.

Melancholy

SLIPPY (*alone*) That's one taken care of. I only fear that Hutzibutz may do something stupid, for his wits will never rise above the level of his monumental stupidity.

JOY (*entering through the middle door, to himself*) If only I can surprise him!

Sanguine

PAINE (*entering through the middle door*) Is Mr. Dole at home?

HUTZIBUTZ (*to himself*) Dole? Aha, here's a boob already! (*aloud*) He is out.

Melancholy

JOY (*to* SLIPPY) Is he in that room there?

SLIPPY Who?

JOY My friend Blythe.

SLIPPY (*to himself*) Blythe? (*aloud*) He is not home at the moment, but his daughter— (*Points to the side door.*)

JOY So much the better. I'll surprise her; after all, it is because of the daughter that I am here! (*Laughing slyly, runs on tiptoe through the side door.*)

Sanguine

HUTZIBUTZ Would it please you to stroll over to the young lady?

PAINE (*with deep significance*) The young lady ... but will she be *my* lady? (*Sighs and exits through the side door.*)

Melancholy

SLIPPY Can this really be the work of Hutzibutz? I must go find out. (*Hurries out through the middle door.*)

Sanguine

HUTZIBUTZ Now I wonder—did I do that right or not?

Phlegmatic

AGNES And everything upsets me so!

EDMUND Farewell, sister! (*Exits through middle door.*)

AGNES Adieu! (*Exits through side door.*)

Sanguine

SLIPPY (*Enters through middle door.*) Did you send him over to me?

HUTZIBUTZ Yes, and did you send me the other one?

SLIPPY Yes!

HUTZIBUTZ It's working like a charm!

SLIPPY See what a clever plan can do?

HUTZIBUTZ Well, yes, but you'll have to admit that it was not all on account of your cleverness; luck too has earned itself a tip.

SLIPPY Yes, that's quite right. If it weren't for luck, how many ventures in the world would succeed? Luck is the mother's milk on which every plan must be suckled if it is to grow up strong and successful. You don't understand that. Now first of all go up and see if Cyprian at Mr. Yawn's can be trusted. Meanwhile I'll come to an understanding with Boyle's Nanette.

HUTZIBUTZ With Nanette?

SLIPPY (*Lays his finger across his lips.*) Pst! Come now! (*Exits through middle door.*)

HUTZIBUTZ And he dares to look at my Belle? Just you wait, Slippy! (*Shakes his fist threateningly at* SLIPPY *behind his back and follows him.*)

Choleric

(WALBURGA *and* NANETTE *enter through middle door.*)

WALBURGA (*crossing the stage*) Then Dad didn't ask about me before he left?

NANETTE No, he was with the other gentlemen—

WALBURGA All right, all right! (*Exits through side door.*)

(NANETTE, *preparing to exit through middle door, is met by* SLIPPY.)

Scene 5

Choleric	Phlegmatic	Melancholy	Sanguine
NANETTE, SLIPPY, *then* STORM, NAPP, WALBURGA	CYPRIAN, HUTZIBUTZ, *then* NAPP, STORM	Empty stage	Empty stage

Phlegmatic

CYPRIAN (*entering through middle door*) Too much is too much! The fuss and bother in this house—! (*Exits through side door.*)

HUTZIBUTZ (*entering through middle door*) I could have sworn I heard Cyprian.

Choleric

SLIPPY (*Enters through middle door.*) Pretty Nanette, a word with you in confidence.

NANETTE Confidence? I have none in you!

Phlegmatic

CYPRIAN (*dragging a chaise longue with difficulty through the side door*) Oh Lord! (*Pushes it to downstage right.*) This'll be the death of me!

HUTZIBUTZ What's with the chase lounge?

CYPRIAN His lordship wants it here when he gets back from his drive so he can collapse in it and recover.

Choleric

SLIPPY I hope not to have an enemy in you?

NANETTE No, not quite that, but not a friend either.

Phlegmatic

HUTZIBUTZ Say, Cyprian—

CYPRIAN I can't say anything more today, I am too overworked in this house. (*Exits through middle door.*)

HUTZIBUTZ My, what a lazy fellow!

Choleric

SLIPPY (*holding* NANETTE, *who tries to escape him*) You won't get away that easy!

NANETTE Someone's coming!

STORM (*entering in traveling clothes through middle door*) So there we are! Dallying around with each other instead of receiving visitors in the foyer!

(NANETTE *runs out through middle door.*)

Phlegmatic

NAPP (*entering in traveling clothes through middle door*) Is this the residence of—? (*yawns*)

Choleric

SLIPPY Your lordship wishes—?

STORM I want to speak with my friend Boyle!

SLIPPY With him?

Phlegmatic

HUTZIBUTZ If you have the time, would you mind telling me who you're looking for?

NAPP My friend Yawn.

HUTZIBUTZ (*aside*) Oho!

Choleric

SLIPPY He lives next door, turn left as you go out.

STORM The deuce! They gave me the wrong address! The whole world's gone mad! (*Storms out through middle door.*)

Phlegmatic

HUTZIBUTZ He lives next door to your right, you've come to the wrong place.

NAPP (*catching sight of the chaise longue.*) Pity, pity ... that lovely long chair....

HUTZIBUTZ Mr. Boyle lives here!

NAPP H'm, h'm, h'm, h'm. (*Exits slowly through middle door.*)

Choleric

SLIPPY (*alone*) I must alert Miss Walburga right away.

Phlegmatic

HUTZIBUTZ (*grinning smugly*) Really, I'm getting better at this every time; if I had to send a couple more to another quarter, I'd outdo myself.

Choleric

NAPP (*entering through middle door*) Announce me!

SLIPPY (*aside*) This must be Mr. Napp, I can see it written all over his face. (*aloud*) You wish to see Mr. Yawn?

NAPP Yawn father and daughter.

Phlegmatic

STORM (*entering through middle door*) Is the master of the house in?

HUTZIBUTZ No.

STORM The daughter?

HUTZIBUTZ Yes! (*Hurries, alarmed by Storm's harsh manner, through middle door.*)

Choleric

WALBURGA (*entering through side door*) What is the meaning of—? (SLIPPY *signals to her and exits quickly through middle door.*)

Scene 6

Choleric	Phlegmatic	Melancholy	Sanguine
WALBURGA, NAPP	STORM, *then* AGNES *then* HUTZIBUTZ	Empty stage	Empty stage

Choleric

WALBURGA (*continuing her speech but suddenly changing tone*) —this pleasant surprise?

NAPP Your servant, Miss.

Phlegmatic

STORM (*alone*) Who was that person? What's he up to? Why is he skulking around so suspiciously in the vicinity of my fiancée?

Choleric

NAPP (*to himself, after viewing* WALBURGA *with obvious pleasure*) What a charming person!

WALBURGA Have I perhaps the pleasure of making the acquaintance of Mr. —?

NAPP (*flattered*) Yes, you have the pleasure, or rather I have the pleasure of hoping that we two shall find pleasure in one another.

Phlegmatic

AGNES (*entering, somewhat unwillingly, through side door*) What's going on, who is that shouting so?

STORM Forgive me—

AGNES I do not understand, this impertinence—

(SLIPPY *opens middle door and signals to* AGNES; *she takes his meaning, and he leaves quickly.*)

AGNES (*Continues her previous speech in an altered tone of voice.*) —this inattentiveness of the servants, to fail to announce such a visitor promptly.

Choleric

WALBURGA It is difficult, when one is handed over to a stranger by a despotic command, yet it becomes easier and easier when one feels one's own heartfelt wishes corresponding to the parental will.

NAPP (*to himself*) What a dear person!

Phlegmatic

STORM Then you know who stands before you, Miss?

AGNES If my intuition doesn't deceive me, I behold before me the man who, according to my father's wishes—

STORM Is to be yours. You've got it!

Choleric

NAPP (*to himself*) How accommodating she is. Just as I was about to declare my love to her, she declares hers to me!

Phlegmatic

STORM I must tell you, you are an angel, you please me unspeakably!

AGNES I take that to be a compliment, and hope through obedience and meek submission to earn the approval of my husband.

STORM That's nice; I love soft, complaisant women, since I myself am so damned soft and yielding.

Choleric

WALBURGA One should really be a little better acquainted before entering into such a bond—

NAPP You'll soon come to know me. I have only one passion, sleep, and I shan't concern myself with yours; with the result that perfect harmony shall reign.

WALBURGA Won't you have a chair?

NAPP Oh, yes, a nice roomy one, if I may. (*to himself*) What an exemplary person!

Phlegmatic

STORM I have no faults save jealousy, and that is a proof of love.

AGNES I shall never give you an occasion for it.

STORM Oh, your charms are sure to attract throngs of admirers, but then I'll break their arms and legs for them!

Choleric

WALBURGA (*drawing up a chair*) I regret that we have no chaise longue.

NAPP (*sitting down*) From you even a milkstool is a bed of ease. Now I shall sketch you a little picture of the domestic bliss that lies in store for us.

Phlegmatic

HUTZIBUTZ (*entering through middle door*) Miss, I'd like to—

STORM (*snapping at* HUTZIBUTZ) What would you like to do with the young lady?

HUTZIBUTZ (*very taken aback*) Nothing, nothing at all! (*Exits hurriedly through middle door.*)

STORM (*to* AGNES) You know, this is very suspicious!

AGNES What do you mean by that? He is a servant!

STORM The devil he is! Pardon me, but I don't know whether to believe that or not! I shall soon— (*Makes to leave.*)

AGNES Where are you going?

STORM I must keep that fellow in my sights, follow his footsteps! Death and arson! (*Exits angrily through middle door.*)

Choleric

WALBURGA (*to* NAPP, *who has already dropped off to sleep*) Mr. — (*aside*) I don't even know his name— (*aloud*) Would you perhaps care to—he is asleep—my, what a singular specimen of a fiancé! At any rate, my arrows of love appear to have pierced his thick heart; thus my task is accomplished! (*Exits through side door.*)

Phlegmatic

AGNES Oh, that's too much, he's jealous of Hutzibutz! (*Exits laughing through side door.*)

Scene 7

Choleric	Phlegmatic	Melancholy	Sanguine
NAPP	YAWN, CYPRIAN	BRIDGET, IRENE, *then* HUTZIBUTZ	SLIPPY, ISABELLA, *then* HUTZIBUTZ

Melancholy

BRIDGET (*entering through middle door*) The fateful hour has struck for my poor mistress!

Sanguine

SLIPPY (*entering through middle door*) I must see how things are progressing. (*Peeps through the keyhole of the side door.*) Charming; he is wailing a declaration of love to her even now.

Melancholy

IRENE (*entering through side door*) Ah, Bridget, just imagine—!

HUTZIBUTZ (*entering through middle door*) Slippy wants to know if he is already in love with you; I am to bring word to him in the coffeehouse.

Sanguine

SLIPPY Here comes Belle!

ISABELLA (*entering through side door*) You are here?

SLIPPY Yes, and I am happy to find you alone at last.

Melancholy

IRENE Tell him that the stranger is already madly in love with me.

Sanguine

ISABELLA Ah, every time I see you it is like a millstone falling on my heart.

SLIPPY That's only natural; heavy hearts are the result of love and tenderness.

Melancholy

HUTZIBUTZ (*only now noticing* BRIDGET) Oh my, we are speaking so intimately, and a third party is present.

Sanguine

ISABELLA Whenever I see you, I want to run away.

SLIPPY That's nice, shyness is the little violet in love's bouquet.

Melancholy

IRENE She'll not oppose the plans of her beloved Slippy.

HUTZIBUTZ What? She is in love, this third party?

BRIDGET Ah!

HUTZIBUTZ With Slippy? And would this third party marry him?

BRIDGET Ah!

HUTZIBUTZ What a relief!

Sanguine

ISABELLA When I think of how I am treating poor Hutzibutz, I feel like a criminal.

SLIPPY That's good.

Melancholy

HUTZIBUTZ Now that I am relieved about Slippy and relieved about Belle, I take my leave doubly relieved. (*Exits through middle door.*)

Choleric

NAPP (*in his sleep*) Most charming bride!

Phlegmatic

YAWN (*entering through middle door, followed by* CYPRIAN) My, how it takes it out of one to ride three-quarters of an hour without rest! (*Sinks into the easy chair.*) Oh, chaise divine!

CYPRIAN Your lordship, the fiancé has arrived.

YAWN I have no time to take notice of the fact just now.

CYPRIAN That's all right; he has left already.

Melancholy

BRIDGET (*to* IRENE) All will turn out well for you, but I am wretchedly, hopelessly in love!

Phlegmatic

YAWN Let a man rest! (CYPRIAN *exits through middle door,* YAWN *falls asleep.*)

Sanguine

ISABELLA I am in love with you, but I cannot rejoice in it because I know how much Hutzibutz will be hurt.

SLIPPY But that's just what gives it spice!

ISABELLA Go on; how could I be so malicious?

SLIPPY It must be so; the spice in every joy is the pinch of malice which goes into it. If I have money I rejoice, but the piquant part is that others have none; if I have a carriage I rejoice, but the interesting part is that others must go on foot. If I have a mistress or a wife I rejoice, but the essential thing is that others envy me her. Therefore a mistress who does not give up another because of me and leave him half-dead with lovesickness, such a one could never make me happy.

ISABELLA Oh, what a naughty man you are!

Melancholy

(BRIDGET *exits through middle door.*)

Sanguine

SLIPPY Be that as it may, let us seal our love with a kiss.

HUTZIBUTZ (*entering through middle door, baffled*) I was looking for you in the coffeehouse and couldn't find you there.

SLIPPY Naturally not; as you see, I am here.

HUTZIBUTZ But you said—

SLIPPY That I was going to the coffeehouse, and so I am, right now. (*Exits through middle door.*)

Scene 8

Choleric	Phlegmatic	Melancholy	Sanguine
NAPP, WALBURGA	YAWN	IRENE	ISABELLA, HUTZIBUTZ, *then* MARIE

Phlegmatic

(YAWN *sleeps on peacefully.*)

Sanguine

HUTZIBUTZ Isabella!

ISABELLA Well, why the long face?

HUTZIBUTZ Your treatment of me has crossed over into the area of mis-treatment.

Choleric

WALBURGA (*Enters through the side door.*) The room ought to be empty. If only I could get him out of here! (*trying to wake him*) Mr. Napp—!

Sanguine

ISABELLA Hutzibutz, you are a fool!

HUTZIBUTZ What is not can come to be.

ISABELLA We agreed that I was to pretend to be attracted to Slippy.

HUTZIBUTZ Yes, but I thought it was only to be a joke!

ISABELLA You can't believe I am serious!

Choleric

WALBURGA This won't be easy. (*Calls louder.*) Mr. Napp!

Melancholy

IRENE No girl on this earth has ever been so miserable as I! (*Sits down in the chair with her head bowed and remains in this posture.*)

Sanguine

HUTZIBUTZ I found him alone with you!

ISABELLA Yes, of course; was I to throw him out?

Choleric

WALBURGA I must—there's no other way. (*Shakes the chair.*) Mr. Napp!

NAPP (*waking up and yawning*) Wha—what's going on? Ah, my betrothed!

Sanguine

HUTZIBUTZ He embraced you, I suppose that was just a joke too?

ISABELLA Stop it, you're about to make me lose my temper.

Choleric

WALBURGA You're tossing and turning so here; wouldn't you rather move over to the sofa?

NAPP Sofa? Oh, divine word! I hasten to obey, lovely lady! (*Stumbles drunk with sleep through the side door.*)

Sanguine

MARIE (*Enters laughing through the side door.*) Oh, this Mr. Paine is absolutely carried away by love-pains! But what long faces do I see here?

HUTZIBUTZ Miss Marie, this person is carrying on, — I can think of no milder term than "carrying on"—and I—I thought it was only to be a joke! (*Exits holding back his tears.*)

Choleric

WALBURGA Thank Heavens, the coast is clear! (*Exits by middle door.*)

Scene 9

Choleric	Phlegmatic	Melancholy	Sanguine
Empty stage	YAWN (*sleeps on peacefully*)	IRENE, JOY, *then* BRIDGET, LISETTE, MARGARET	MARIE, ISABELLA, PAINE

Sanguine

PAINE (*sadly from the side door*) Why does my fiancée flee me?

Melancholy

JOY (*very merrily from side door*) Where's my true love hiding? And why so downcast?

Sanguine

MARIE Even when I am away, how can you be sure my thoughts haven't remained with you?

Melancholy

JOY (*aside*) What a darling pet! We'll cheer her up yet, with patience. She must become as merry as I!

Sanguine

PAINE Even as the northern lights glimmer above the pole at midnight, so your love rises on the horizon of my life, to cast a faint ray of light into my heart's gloom.

ISABELLA (*to herself*) Such are the newfangled gallantries that we hear nowadays.

Melancholy

JOY I have an idea, my dearest. Where are the servants? (*calling through the middle door*) Hoy! Come aboard, all hands! (*to* IRENE) We'll arrange a little ball for this evening.

IRENE A ball? What are you thinking of? Father loves quiet and solitude.

JOY Oh, I'm going to introduce an altogether different tone in this house!

Sanguine

MARIE (*to* PAINE) You must forgive me if I can't stay and listen to your charming conversation, but the preparations for this evening's ball—

PAINE Ball? Ball? Unbearable word! Where is this ball to be?

MARIE Here! Father arranged it for this evening to celebrate our engagement.

PAINE It must be cancelled!

Melancholy

(BRIDGET, LISETTE *and* MARGARET *enter through middle door.*)

BRIDGET Your lordship wishes?

JOY Scout out whatever you can quickly; hire musicians, buy food, anything that's expensive and good. And wine, plenty of wine! And lots of wax candles! Here's some money! (*Gives* MARGARET *a purse.*) Now on your way, look lively! (LISETTE *and* MARGARET *exit through middle door.*)

Sanguine

PAINE A ball, that would be the death of me! (*to* ISABELLA) Send out the word at once, everywhere: no ball, definitely not; everything is cancelled!

Melancholy

BRIDGET But—

JOY The old girl is to come with me; I'll give her so much to do it will make her head swim!

Sanguine

ISABELLA Yes, but—

PAINE I shall take full responsibility upon myself.

MARIE It must be so, if my fiancé wishes it.

ISABELLA Very well. (*Exits through middle door.*)

Melancholy

JOY (*to* IRENE) I have brought with me from Straßburg a friend and his two daughters, fine, amiable people; I'll go fetch them. They have many acquaintances here; I too have a few acquaintances from former times. They must all come, these acquaintances, this will be a ball to remember, improvised on the spot! (*Hurries out through middle door, dragging the reluctant* BRIDGET *in his wake.*)

Sanguine

PAINE I have brought along my aunt and her brother-in-law, two soul-mates of mine, quiet, sombre creatures; except for them I wish to see no guests at our engagement.

MARIE Oh, I am so looking forward to making their acquaintance! I'll be back in a moment. (*Exits through middle door.*)

Scene 10

Choleric	Phlegmatic	Melancholy	Sanguine
Empty stage	YAWN, CYPRIAN, *then* STORM	IRENE (*alone*)	PAINE, *then* BLYTHE

Melancholy

IRENE (*alone*) Heavens, what will come of all this?

Sanguine

BLYTHE (*from outside*) Then he's already here?

PAINE My friend Dole is coming home.

BLYTHE (*entering through middle door*) Friend, old pal!

PAINE At last I may pour out my tears upon your breast! (*Falls sobbing on* BLYTHE'S *breast.*)

Phlegmatic

CYPRIAN (*entering through middle door*) He is coming back, even now he is storming up the stairs. (*to* YAWN, *as he approaches him*) Your lordship—

Sanguine

BLYTHE Come now, pull yourself together. Tears of joy came to my eyes too, but to carry on like this—

PAINE Oh, don't begrudge me this pleasure!

Phlegmatic

STORM (*Barges in through middle door.*) I couldn't catch the fellow, but patience, patience, he'll fall into my hands yet, and when he does I'll tear the scoundrel limb from limb!

CYPRIAN Softly, softly, his lordship is sleeping!

STORM How? What? Is this he? The father sleeps while his daughter's reputation is in peril? Up, you old dodderer, let the voice of honor sound the knell to your rest! Up, wake up! (*Shakes him.*)

Sanguine

BLYTHE But friend, aren't you about through?

PAINE No, never—never!

Phlegmatic

YAWN Wha—what is it?

STORM What is it? A girl pursued by a relentless seducer—your daughter, that is; an irate fiancé—that's me; and a drowsy father—namely you!

Sanguine

BLYTHE Is something wrong with you?

PAINE The memory of our youth—!

BLYTHE Is altogether jolly!

Phlegmatic

CYPRIAN (*to* YAWN) This is the gentleman from Straßburg!

YAWN My old chum! So glad to see you!

STORM I however am not at all glad to see what I have seen here. Your daughter is an angel, but that—that—

YAWN (*assuming* STORM *to be speaking of Robert*) My Lord, the young man is head over heels in love with her, and youth—youth—

STORM (*referring to Hutzibutz*) Oh, he's not all that young! But the devil take him if he ever runs after her again!

YAWN Friend, no one runs all the way to Straßburg!

STORM You take lightly this thing which infuriates, enrages, maddens me! But he'll not escape me, I'll find him, I must find him, I won't rest till I do. (*Exits angrily through middle door.*)

Sanguine

PAINE (*ruefully shaking his head*) Memory is a malicious reminder of beautiful times gone by; for this reason reunions are the source of such deep, ineffable sorrow!

Melancholy

IRENE (*taking a notebook from the drawer of the table*) Oh, my diary, chain of bitter torments, receive today the bitterest yet! (*Sits at the table and writes in diary.*)

Sanguine

PAINE I must leave you for a moment—it is too much for me— (*in an outpouring of emotion*) my heart is bursting—! (*Hurries out through side door.*)

Phlegmatic

YAWN What a terrible person! How he has changed over the years since I last saw him—it's almost as if he weren't the same person—

Sanguine

BLYTHE (*alone*) It's as if he were a changeling.

Scene 11

Choleric	Phlegmatic	Melancholy	Sanguine
BOYLE, SLIPPY (*disguised as a braggart soldier*), *later* EDMUND	YAWN, *then* AGNES	IRENE (*alone*)	BLYTHE, MARIE

Sanguine

(MARIE *enters through middle door.*)

BLYTHE Marie, have you seen your fiancé yet?

MARIE Oh, yes—!

BLYTHE Well, how do you like him?

MARIE Fine, just fine! Papa, I am greatly obliged to you for your choice! (*Exits through side door.*)

Choleric

BOYLE (*followed by the disguised* SLIPPY) Sir, I have had enough, get off my back!

SLIPPY No, I am going to get *on* your back; you have offended my honor, and I must have blood!

BOYLE Leave me in peace!

SLIPPY No, that cannot be, for you have left me none!

Sanguine

BLYTHE (*alone*) She likes him!

Choleric

BOYLE What I did to you was as much as nothing.

SLIPPY You stepped on my boot in the tavern and injured my honor.

BOYLE Is your honor then in your boot?

SLIPPY Yes, because I am in my boot, and my honor is in me: therefore it is in my boot, even as I am.

Phlegmatic

YAWN (*Calls through the side door.*) Daughter!

Choleric

BOYLE But I didn't see your foot under the table.

SLIPPY This blatant disregard for my person is an insult in itself. We must come to blows.

Melancholy

IRENE (*writing*) Such blows cut deep!

Choleric

BOYLE In a moment I shall have my servants throw you out!

SLIPPY I'll hold fast to you and you'll fly out with me.

BOYLE What in the devil's name do you want?

SLIPPY Nothing less than your blood!

Sanguine

BLYTHE (*alone*) What regrettable taste the girl has! (*Paces up and down shaking his head.*)

Choleric

SLIPPY Honor is the fine linen which clothes the soul of a cultivated man; this is why the honor must often be vigorously washed, though not with soap and water. No, it is only with the blood of the offender that one may wash one's honor clean.

BOYLE (*feeling himself ever more driven to the wall by Slippy's imposing, blustering manner, to himself*) What a damnable business! (*aloud*) I am too old to fight duels!

SLIPPY That's no fault of mine. Why didn't you insult me twenty years ago? But that wouldn't have been possible, I was only a little boy then. No, there is no getting out of it, here are pistols! (*Draws two pistols from his pocket.*)

BOYLE (*to himself*) Damn! How am I to get rid of this fellow?

SLIPPY I always carry a loaded pair on me, to have them handy at all times.

Phlegmatic

YAWN (*as before*) Daughter!

Sanguine

(BLYTHE *examines several trinkets which he has brought along in a box.*)

Choleric

SLIPPY Choose! (*Holds out the pistols.*)

BOYLE No, I say!

SLIPPY Sir, if you decline, I'll shoot you like a dog! (*Advances toward him.*)

BOYLE The fellow's mad! Hi, anyone! Come here! Help!

EDMUND (*entering through middle door*) What's going on here?

BOYLE This man wants to kill me!

SLIPPY He won't fight.

Phlegmatic

AGNES (*Enters through side door.*) You called, Father?

YAWN Have you seen him!

AGNES Yes.

Choleric

EDMUND (*after exchanging signs of understanding with* SLIPPY) Mr. Boyle, you are entirely right to decline to duel; you are in far too violent a mood, and pistols call for cold nerve and a steady hand. It will be my pleasure to give this swashbuckler a harsh lesson in your stead. (*to* SLIPPY) I take it it is a matter of indifference to you whether you duel with me or with this gentleman?

SLIPPY Total indifference; the insult calls for blood, whether the offender's or the substitute's, it is all the same to me.

EDMUND Then come, sir!

SLIPPY To the woods outside the wall! In five minutes you shall take the mortal blow above the fourth button of your waistcoat. Blood, that's the ticket! (*Exits with* EDMUND *through middle door.*)

BOYLE (*recovering from his astonishment at Edmund*) The man is going to fight for me, and if I remember aright, I gave him a beating only this morning! It's too much, too much!

Phlegmatic

YAWN Well, how do you like him?

AGNES Fine, just fine!

YAWN Well, I don't!

Choleric

BOYLE H'm, even cold-blooded people are good for something. I really must give up starting quarrels everywhere, it could easily lead to something serious.

Phlegmatic

YAWN I must see where he went, if only he doesn't embarrass me here in the house! Steady now, steady! (*Exits through middle door.*)

Choleric

BOYLE But there was someone in the tavern who laughed at me when I was challenged. I must speak to him, perhaps he is still there, the scoundrel! (*with growing vehemence*) I won't let him get away with it! (*Exits through middle door.*)

Scene 12

Choleric	Phlegmatic	Melancholy	Sanguine
Empty stage	AGNES, *then* ISABELLA, HUTZIBUTZ, SLIPPY, STORM, YAWN	IRENE, *then* DOLE, JOY	BLYTHE, *then* ISABELLA

Phlegmatic

AGNES (*laughing*) Father's on the run today!

ISABELLA (*entering through middle door*) I kiss your hand, Miss Agnes. Slippy says I am to ask you to unlock the door that leads from the back room to the stairs.

AGNES All the keys are in there on my table; if you will be so kind, Belle, as to find the right one and open up the door.

ISABELLA Right away, Miss Agnes, right away. (*Exits through side door.*)

HUTZIBUTZ (*Enters through middle door.*) Was that Belle? What's Belle doing here?

AGNES Slippy wants—

SLIPPY (*Enters through middle door.*) Pardon me, has the other door been unlocked yet?

AGNES Belle has gone for the key just now.

SLIPPY It is essential—one can never know—retrograde movements— (*Exits quickly through side door.*)

HUTZIBUTZ (*anxiously*) Now he's going into the room where Belle is!

AGNES So? What's the harm in that?

HUTZIBUTZ Oh, Miss Agnes, you can't imagine, my dear Miss Agnes—

AGNES Oh Hutzibutz, be reasonable—!

STORM (*Enters through middle door; on hearing Hutzibutz's last words, dashes forward.*) Aha! All is discovered!

Sanguine

BLYTHE (*still occupied with the examination of his purchases*) The surprise is here, but I don't know by whom to send it over.

Phlegmatic

STORM "My dear" is what you said to the young lady, and she admonished you in vain to be reasonable. You are a presumptuous fop, whoever you may be; but now you have me to deal with!

HUTZIBUTZ (*greatly taken aback*) I beg your lordship—

STORM Not another word, or—! (*to* AGNES) Leave us alone, Miss!

Melancholy

DOLE (*Enters through middle door.*) Is he here already?

IRENE (*rising*) Yes.

Phlegmatic

AGNES Surely you don't believe—

STORM I know you are innocent, but your persecutor here has earned himself a thrashing. Leave us!

AGNES (*leaving, to herself*) Now he'll be all over Hutzibutz! (*Exits giggling through middle door.*)

STORM Now, sir, you'll not escape me again!

HUTZIBUTZ Oh, what's going to happen to me? (*to himself*) I'm scared to death!

(STORM *locks the side door.*)

HUTZIBUTZ (*to himself*) Now he's locking Slippy and Belle in together. (*aloud, indicating the side door*) Whatever you do, don't lock that door!

STORM No escape shall be open to you! (*Locks the middle door.*)

Melancholy

DOLE (*to* IRENE) Have you nothing to say?

Phlegmatic

HUTZIBUTZ I am in a terrible fix!

Melancholy

IRENE I shall behave like an obedient daughter.

Phlegmatic

STORM Now, sir, what do you have to say for yourself?

HUTZIBUTZ I thought it was only to be a joke! (*glancing anxiously toward the side door*)

STORM The young lady is my fiancée, and you have the effrontery—

YAWN (*from without, knocking on the middle door*) Open up in there! What foolishness is this?

Sanguine

BLYTHE If only Slippy were here! (*Exits through middle door.*)

Phlegmatic

HUTZIBUTZ Mr. Yawn! Thank God! Help, your lordship, help!

STORM (*grimly*) That won't help you! (*Opens the middle door.*)

HUTZIBUTZ This is going to take ten years off my life.

YAWN (*entering through middle door*) What's going on here?

Sanguine

ISABELLA (*Enters through middle door.*) That's taken care of! (*Exits through side door.*)

Phlegmatic

STORM (*pointing to* HUTZIBUTZ) I have captured your daughter's persecutor!

Melancholy

DOLE How do you like him?

Phlegmatic

YAWN (*assuming Hutzibutz to have brought another letter from Robert*) So the bootblack still won't give up?

STORM Bootblack?

Melancholy

IRENE It was a good choice you made.

Phlegmatic

YAWN (*to* HUTZIBUTZ) Out, lettercarrier, helper's helper! March!

HUTZIBUTZ I am going, but please, your lordship, unlock that door! (*Points entreatingly to the side door and exits through middle door.*)

Melancholy

JOY (*entering through middle door, to* DOLE) Just wait, I'll teach you not to be at home when company comes! Come here, a handshake, a hug, a kiss on the cheek, and now our old friendship is as good as new!

Phlegmatic

STORM What? This man is—

YAWN My bootblack.

Melancholy

DOLE Is it really you? You have changed so!

JOY (*ever jovial*) Only on the outside; heart and spirit are young and fresh as ever! Don't I please you? Oh well, I please your daughter, and that's all that matters!

Phlegmatic

YAWN And you are carrying on so wildly in the house!

STORM But you said, "lettercarrier, helper's helper!" I must get to the bottom of this; I must have light! (*Dashes out through middle door.*)

Melancholy

DOLE (*shaking his head, to himself*) It's uncanny how the years have changed him!

Scene 13

Choleric	Phlegmatic	Melancholy	Sanguine
Empty stage	YAWN, *then* SLIPPY, HUTZIBUTZ, CYPRIAN, ROBERT	DOLE, IRENE, JOY	Empty stage

Phlegmatic

YAWN (*alone*) He's gone out of his head—and Agnes likes him: I can't understand how a daughter of my own flesh and blood could have such bizarre taste.

229

SLIPPY (*Enters by middle door, dressed as a regimental band member and disguised by a false beard and altered tone of voice.*) Is my buddy here?

YAWN (*surprised*) What is your buddy to me?

SLIPPY The same as I am; we're both to be quartered with you. (*Hands him a paper.*)

YAWN (*shocked*) Quartered?

Melancholy

JOY "Happy-go-lucky" is my motto.

DOLE My only happiness lies with the dead.

Phlegmatic

SLIPPY Be glad you didn't get crude, uncouth men; me and my buddy, we're each as cultured as the other. (*Flings himself onto the chaise longue.*)

YAWN (*utterly bewildered*) Quartered? Can it be—the paper says so, but soldiers are so seldom quartered here—

SLIPPY All the more reason to put up with a little inconvenience!

YAWN Thanks!

Melancholy

JOY Old friend— (*to himself, amazed*) My, how he has changed since his youth!

Phlegmatic

YAWN Who exactly are you, sir?

SLIPPY I am the band blackamoor. Our old moor, who was a wizard on the cymbals, passed away, my cymbalistic talent was discovered, and now I am the regimental moor.

Melancholy

JOY (*to himself*) I'd rather concentrate on the fiancée. (*Strikes up a conversation with* IRENE, *during which time* DOLE *is lost in melancholy contemplation of the portrait.*)

230

Phlegmatic

HUTZIBUTZ (*Disguised as a caricature of a grotesquely fat regimental musician, enters through middle door.*) Ah, already here, buddy? Where's the old walrus we're to be quartered with?

SLIPPY (*to* YAWN) Don't pay any attention to him; he doesn't know what he's saying. (*softly to* HUTZIBUTZ) Pretend you're drunk!

HUTZIBUTZ (*softly to* SLIPPY) I don't know how!

SLIPPY (*as above*) Pretend it is nine-thirty in the evening, you can't go wrong.

HUTZIBUTZ (*shouting*) Yoo-hoo! Wine here! Wine! (*to* YAWN) Get someone to run down to the cellar and bring up a bottle of your best, if you want us to treat you right!

SLIPPY (*to* YAWN) Quick, look lively, it ought to be here already!

YAWN (*anxiously, to himself*) What terrible men! (*Calls through the side door.*) Agnes, bring some wine!

SLIPPY (*to* HUTZIBUTZ) Are our weapons here?

HUTZIBUTZ I left 'em out in the hall.

YAWN Weapons?

SLIPPY Don't worry, there'll be no shooting, no sword play here—we are members of the band.

HUTZIBUTZ Our weapons are our musical instruments. But we need to practice—practice, practice, practice!

SLIPPY Yes, siree! (*Calls through side door.*) Bring them in here! (*to* YAWN) The new march we are learning is pretty hard. (*Throws two scores down on the table.*)

Melancholy

JOY (*to* IRENE, *who has shown him her diary*) I presume I too shall become an entry under today's date?

Phlegmatic

(CYPRIAN *enters panting, carrying a very large Turkish drum, drumsticks, and cymbals.*)

231

YAWN You don't mean to—

HUTZIBUTZ Ah, my wood and leather instrument!

SLIPPY (*to* YAWN) You can hold the scores for us, and (*pointing to* CYPRIAN) you too.

YAWN Gentlemen, this simply won't do, this behavior—I will complain to your chief of staff, and then you'll get the staff. (*Mimicks a flogging.*)

SLIPPY Heaven—!

HUTZIBUTZ The devil—!

SLIPPY Bloody murder—!

HUTZIBUTZ Thunder and lightning—!

SLIPPY Stay! So we're to be threatened, are we? Complain to anyone you want, but not before you have helped us with our music practice, or else you won't leave this room a whole man. By Heaven—!

HUTZIBUTZ The devil—!

SLIPPY Bloody murder—!

HUTZIBUTZ Thunder and lightning—!

SLIPPY Stay!

CYPRIAN Humor them, your lordship, or else we are dead men! (YAWN *takes a score,* CYPRIAN *another, one stands before* HUTZIBUTZ, *the other before* SLIPPY; HUTZIBUTZ *beats the Turkish drum and* SLIPPY *clashes the cymbals.*)

YAWN (*in desperation*) I can't stand this noise!

HUTZIBUTZ (*Yells at* YAWN *with musical gusto.*) Now you made me lose my place! This last bumbumbum is so hard, and you broke my concentration! Once more! (*Beats the drum several times, accompanied by* SLIPPY *on the cymbals.*)

SLIPPY Damn! I got the whole passage wrong!

HUTZIBUTZ I can't bring out the half-tones!

Melancholy

JOY (*to* DOLE) Why the sighs?

Phlegmatic

SLIPPY (*to* YAWN) This is all your fault, you have provoked us. Do you think we've come here just to listen to your insults?

HUTZIBUTZ A band member is just as good as anybody!

SLIPPY We settled that question ten years ago.

Melancholy

JOY (*to* DOLE, *who shows him the portrait*) Your spouse?

Phlegmatic

HUTZIBUTZ At the storming of the stone pontoon-bridge.

SLIPPY The bridge stood thus— (*Overturns the chaise longue and swings it around so that its back lies on the floor, downstage.*) —grape-shot filled the air, blocking out the sun. The men had lost heart, then the order came through for the band to move up to the head of the bridge and play a stirring march. The men filed by with renewed courage in quintuple-time through the rain of bullets, followed by the band in triumph. (HUTZIBUTZ *beats enthusiastically on the drum,* SLIPPY *on the cymbals, and the two march across the overturned chaise longue, so that it breaks with a crack.*)

YAWN (*wringing his hands*) My chaise longue! This is my final hour!

ROBERT (*entering through middle door*) Hell fire, what a sight!

YAWN Oh, you won't believe—

ROBERT The chair demolished—? An act of violence has been perpetrated here!

SLIPPY (*pretending to be terrified, to himself, but so that* YAWN *cannot help but overhear*) Oh Lord, a friend of our bandmaster! (*softly to* HUTZIBUTZ) Pretend you are frightened!

ROBERT (*with feigned gravity*) I know your superior and shall report you at once.

HUTZIBUTZ (*pretending to be terrified*) Have pity on us, we could get into trouble.

Melancholy

JOY (*consolingly to* DOLE) One must come to terms with such things.

Phlegmatic

YAWN (*breathing a sigh of relief, to* ROBERT) You are truly a friend in need!

SLIPPY (*softly to* HUTZIBUTZ) The old man fell for it like a charm!

ROBERT It was only my neighborly duty.

Melancholy

JOY (*to* DOLE) Grief has taken up permanent quarters with you.

Phlegmatic

ROBERT We must do something about this quartering. (*Exits through middle door.*)

HUTZIBUTZ Permit me—

SLIPPY If you please—

} together

(*Both hurry out anxiously after* ROBERT.)

Scene 14

Choleric	Phlegmatic	Melancholy	Sanguine
NAPP	YAWN, AGNES	JOY, DOLE, *then* SLIPPY, HUTZIBUTZ	Empty stage

Phlegmatic

AGNES (*Enters through the side door with a bottle and glasses.*) Here is the wine, Father.

YAWN You certainly come quickly when you are called.

Melancholy

JOY (*to* DOLE) Now, now, let's hear no more of your painting. To portray the central figure in a scene of mourning in a white ball gown! Give it up!

DOLE Ball gown—ball—what a horrible word! You are quite right, I should have painted her in black crepe!

Choleric

NAPP (*coming through the side door*) A blacksmith must live next door! I had much more peace and quiet in here. (*Sits down in the chair and falls asleep again.*)

Melancholy

DOLE The entire picture, my last remaining joy, is now as good as ruined for me!

Phlegmatic

YAWN (*Has told his daughter of the incident.*) And my friend and supposed-to-be son-in-law-to-be was no help, all he can do is run around having jealousy tantrums.

AGNES A sure sign that I mean more to him than anything else.

Melancholy

JOY (*to* DOLE) You really are an awful person!

DOLE (*very meekly*) Leave me to my sorrow! You were correct in your observation concerning my picture, I have botched it. But you cannot deprive me of the sad realization that through my own incompetence I have destroyed my last consolation! Come, Irene, come away! (*Exits with* IRENE *through side door.*)

JOY (*alone*) What a personality! I've never seen anything like it!

Phlegmatic

YAWN I don't know what to make of you!

Melancholy

JOY So that he won't remain upset with me, I must fulfill his silly desire and as a happy surprise—

(SLIPPY *enters in his usual dress through middle door.*)

JOY Ah, it's good to see you again, friend! Could you find me a painter in a hurry? All he has to do is paint this dress black.

SLIPPY A painter?

(HUTZIBUTZ *enters through middle door, dressed as usual.*)

SLIPPY (*pointing to* HUTZIBUTZ) Here you are! (*aside*) Maybe in this way I can arrange a flogging for Hutzibutz.

JOY (*to* HUTZIBUTZ) Ah, I have met this gentleman before. So you are a painter?

HUTZIBUTZ (*somewhat taken aback*) I—? Oh sure, I'm a painter (*collecting himself*) —but I only work in dark tones.

JOY Just what I need!

Phlegmatic

AGNES Isn't that something! I do believe Father isn't pleased that I am an obedient daughter. This man about whom you are grumbling, didn't you yourself choose him to be my bridegroom?

YAWN Don't talk so much, you are driving me mad! I have already been far too agitated and upset today! (*Exits through side door.*)

Melancholy

JOY (*to* HUTZIBUTZ) Here, sir, for your trouble. (*Gives him money.*) Please paint (*pointing to the picture*) the entire dress black.

HUTZIBUTZ As you wish; all over high-gloss black.

JOY But quickly, please, quickly! (*Exits through side door.*)

Phlegmatic

AGNES (*laughing*) Father is already more than half won over to Robert. (*Exits through side door.*)

Melancholy

HUTZIBUTZ (*not quite knowing what he is to do*) Now I don't know—

SLIPPY Go out and get two guilders worth of paint, then paint the dress black; that's all there is to it!

HUTZIBUTZ All right. That's no problem for a professional bootblack. (*Exits through middle door.*)

Scene 15

Choleric	Phlegmatic	Melancholy	Sanguine
NAPP (*sleeps on peacefully*)	Empty stage	SLIPPY	Empty stage

Melancholy

SLIPPY (*alone*) Just now I actually came within a hair of becoming melancholy myself, and that's the humor I can abide least of all. Even at that, it has happened to me a couple of times. But after all, who can remain long in any one humor? Circumstances dictate that man must reel about in all four.

1

Though in marriage one's conduct be four-square and stern,
One can easily have all four humors in turn.
First the bliss of the honeymoon comes into flower,
And sanguine delight holds the soul in its power.
But this doesn't last long, one awakes with a start,
And one's judgment sits down for a chat with one's heart,
Pointing out how reality differs from folly;
This brings on an attack of acute melancholy.
The young bride is pretty, admirers pursue,
For most of them have nothing better to do,
The boldest press on till they get through the door,
Cholerically then one chucks out three or four.
The wife longs for finery, the account's in the red,
So one says to her, "Angel, put it out of your head."
Then she faints and has seizures three times a day;
One becomes a phlegmatic then, turning away.

2

Whenever I go to a dance-hall, I know
In one night I'll experience all four in a row.
When I see all the girls in decolleté dress,
I'm instantly sanguine—*quel embarras de richesses!*
I fall madly for one, but to my chagrin,
Her partner, the lackey, won't let me cut in!
The fellow depresses me, I go in to dine,
And say melancholically, "Waiter! Some wine!"
Nine glasses I drink, no more and no less,
But the waiter says eleven, I have no redress,
And I have to watch out and do nothing unwise,
For hackles choleric are starting to rise.

I look to the dance-floor, it's the end of the ball,
And there's my ideal, humping round in the hall,
Hair undone, rumpled, sweaty—a pitiful sight!
I go home a confirmed phlegmatic that night.

3

Women have, one may say with complete confidence,
No less than a hundred or more temperaments.
The merrily sanguine, which teases and jests,
Lasts only as long as their looks make conquests.
As the years come and go and there's no fiancé,
Nor so much as a lorgnette directed their way,
They perceive that to be an old maid is their fate,
And melancholy takes over, sad to relate.
No woman has ever been able to abide
Another one's praises, it hurts deep inside;
Say another is fair, and one falls from their graces,
Cholerically blood rushes up in their faces.
The worst, though, is when they believe one has money,
Then discover he hasn't—it's not even funny,
No "Can't live without you," in accents heartwracking,
Oh no—they phlegmatically send one a-packing.

4

Even poets are subject to humors withal,
Save for one, about which they know nothing at all.
When one brings out a play, and it has a few flaws,
Optimistically sanguine, one awaits the applause,
And then, when particular noises are heard—
It may be the rattling of keys[2] or "the bird"—
Struck with dread to the heart at this pitiless volley,
One puts on a face of profound melancholy.
Next day, friends will tell you they're sorry to see
You have had such a flop. But the thinly-veiled glee
That their eyes in the meantime are clearly revealing
Makes the poet choleric, and he goes through the ceiling!
But when one has a hit, and it's all going well,
And the applause in the house is beginning to swell,
There's a warm, thankful feeling that routs all past strife.
Shall one be phlegmatic, then? Not on your life!

Scene 16

Choleric	Phlegmatic	Melancholy	Sanguine
NAPP (*sleeps on peacefully*)	Empty stage	HUTZIBUTZ, *then* WALBURGA, IRENE	MARIE, ISABELLA, *then* MRS. KORBHEIM, GUIDO, *later* BLYTHE

Sanguine

MARIE (*Hurries in through the side door with* ISABELLA.) Mrs. Korbheim is coming and Guido is with her.

ISABELLA This must be Slippy's doing.

MRS. KORBHEIM (*Enters with* GUIDO *through middle door.*) Dear Marie—!

MARIE (*hurrying to her and kissing her hand*) Oh, Mrs. Korbheim, you are really so kind—

MRS. KORBHEIM And why shouldn't I be? Why shouldn't I be concerned about my future daughter-in-law's affairs of the heart? I only wish you had confided in me earlier!

MARIE Only today did I learn by chance about your relationship with Papa—he has been so secretive!

MRS. KORBHEIM (*to* GUIDO) Now, Mr. Dole, pay court to me as if your life depended on it. Slippy's idea is a good one.

GUIDO I fear, I fear— (*Speaks in pantomime with* MRS. KORBHEIM, *then with* MARIE, *while* MRS. KORBHEIM *strikes up a conversation with* ISABELLA.)

Melancholy

HUTZIBUTZ (*Enters through middle door carrying a mug of boot polish and a brush.*) Slippy says I should pay two guilders for black paint—that would be like throwing money away when I have my own polish right here. Now then, to the work of art! The main thing is to give it a try. Who knows, I may have talents I don't even know about. (*Sits down and begins to paint the dress black.*) Ha! It's going on slick as grease!

Sanguine

BLYTHE (*Enters through middle door.*) Your humble servant, dear lady. (*Kisses her hand and converses with her with much gallantry until he notices* GIUDO, *then balks.*)

Melancholy

HUTZIBUTZ (*painting vigorously*) What fine highlights—there's nothing like lampblack and Frankfurt coal dust! (*Finished, he regards his work with satisfaction.*) Really, it's even better than I expected!

Sanguine

MRS. KORBHEIM (*to* BLYTHE) I know of the tension that has reigned between you and young Mr. Dole, but all that is past now; he relinquishes all claim to your daughter, yet will remain a friend of the house.

BLYTHE (*unpleasantly embarrassed*) Your obedient servant—!

Melancholy

HUTZIBUTZ I wonder how it would be if I put a black veil over her face? Yes, I'll give free rein to my fancy. (*Paints over the entire face, so that the portrait is no longer recognizable.*)

Sanguine

MRS. KORBHEIM (*pointing to* GUIDO) He has been so highly recommended by my aunt in Prague that I intend to introduce him everywhere I visit.

GUIDO You are too kind, dear lady!

BLYTHE (*to himself*) Yes, I think so too!

Melancholy

HUTZIBUTZ (*finished*) *Magnifique!* It only goes to show what talents may lie hidden in a man! I never dared to dream I was an artist. Now I'll stand it up against the wall to dry; it would be a terrible shame if someone brushed up against it. (*Stands the picture, together with the easel, against the wall, so that only the back can be seen.*) It's a pity I can't give it a good buffing with the brushes!

WALBURGA (*Hurries in through the middle door.*) Irene! Irene!

IRENE (*entering through side door*) Who is calling? Oh, it's you!

WALBURGA Have you seen Slippy?

IRENE No.

WALBURGA I am so afraid Dad will see right away that my fiancé is not the right one, for I've heard him mention quite a few times that his friend Storm is noticeably pockmarked. Dad is very nearsighted, but he is still apt to notice a thing like that. I'd like to consult with Slippy about what to do.

HUTZIBUTZ (*stepping forward*) Where is this fiancé?

WALBURGA Ah, are you here? Mr. Napp is taking a nap upstairs.

HUTZIBUTZ (*struck by an idea*) If only he's sleeping soundly!

WALBURGA Oh, not even a cannon could wake *him!*

HUTZIBUTZ And he is supposed to be pockmarked? Not to worry; I'll take care of it!

WALBURGA Fine, fine; be so good as to ask Slippy for advice. Adieu, Irene, I must go; I'm expecting Dad any minute. (*Exits quickly through middle door.*)

IRENE Farewell, Walburga! (*Exits through side door.*)

Sanguine

MRS. KORBHEIM Come, Marie! (*to* GUIDO) Mr. Dole, accompany us! (*Exits with* MARIE *and* GUIDO *through side door.*)

Melancholy

HUTZIBUTZ (*alone, pondering*) He is a sound sleeper. What do we need Slippy for? A genius like me needs only a little red paint and nothing else. One more work of art quickly done, and my reputation as an artist is made! (*Runs out through middle door.*)

Scene 17

Choleric	Phlegmatic	Melancholy	Sanguine
NAPP, WALBURGA, HUTZIBUTZ	Empty stage	DOLE, *then* SLIPPY, *then* HUTZIBUTZ	BLYTHE, ISABELLA, *then* SLIPPY, *then* HUTZIBUTZ

Choleric

WALBURGA (*Enters through middle door.*) Dad's not home yet, that's good! (*Exits quickly through side door.*)

Sanguine

BLYTHE (*restlessly pacing up and down*) Belle, what do you say to this?

ISABELLA I? I have nothing to say, but it does seem peculiar to me.

BLYTHE Doesn't it! There's something very peculiar indeed about Mrs. Korbheim and this Master Guido!

Choleric

HUTZIBUTZ (*Enters through middle door holding a mug of paint, a brush, and a stick. Observes* NAPP, *who continues to sleep soundly.*) He seems to be sound asleep—so he's supposed to be pock-marked?—Downstairs we brushed; up here we'll spatter! (*Holds the stick in one hand, the brush in the other, and spatters* NAPP'S *face in the manner of a house painter.*)

Melancholy

DOLE (*Enters through the side door.*) He is right—it is unforgivable! Black, yes, yes, it must be black! But where is—? (*Sees the picture standing against the wall.*) Who put it there against the wall!

Choleric

HUTZIBUTZ If he doesn't look right now, my shoebrushes are velvet. (*Exits through middle door.*)

Melancholy

DOLE (*Turns the picture around and sees what has been done to it.*) Ye heavenly powers, who has done this to me?

SLIPPY (*Enters through middle door.*) What's wrong, your lordship?

DOLE (*pointing to the picture in despair*) The most ghastly, the most horrible thing!

SLIPPY (*feigning surprise*) What the devil—? (*Approaches the picture.*) I smell boot polish! This smacks of Hutzibutz!

DOLE Has everything, then, conspired to bring about my downfall?

Sanguine

BLYTHE I don't like the smell of her familiarity towards that young man!

ISABELLA (*to herself*) Hooked through both gills!

Melancholy

HUTZIBUTZ (*Enters unsuspecting through middle door.*)

SLIPPY (*to* HUTZIBUTZ) Mr. Dole would like to have a word with you. (*Exits through side door.*)

Sanguine

BLYTHE (*to* ISABELLA) If I only knew whether Slippy has already been to see her, —Mrs. Korbheim, that is!

SLIPPY (*Enters through middle door.*) He has.

BLYTHE So? And noticed nothing!

SLIPPY (*craftily*) With regard to Guido? Well—at the moment he's her protégé, but how long or how far her patronage may go, only time will tell.

BLYTHE This accursed business! (*Paces restlessly up and down;* SLIPPY *and* ISABELLA *meanwhile continue to bait him with words and shrugs.*)

Melancholy

HUTZIBUTZ (*to* DOLE, *who, lost in grief, pays no heed to him*) What does your lordship wish?

DOLE You dare approach me, wretch? Who planted this black deed in your soul?

HUTZIBUTZ Your lordship don't like it?

DOLE I'd like to throttle you, but grief has sapped my strength. I'd like to curse you, but sobs catch in my throat—

HUTZIBUTZ Is art rewarded thus? I'm going now, but I want you to know I couldn't help it, I was only the instrument. That foreigner, your lordship's daughter's fiancé, gave me twenty-five guilders to do it.

DOLE What? He did?

HUTZIBUTZ My hands are clean, I can swear to that! (*Holds up his paint-blackened right hand and exits through middle door.*)

243

Sanguine

(BLYTHE *exits hurriedly through side door.*)

SLIPPY (*to* ISABELLA) Well, what do you say, are my plans working or aren't they?

ISABELLA Ah, go on, you're quite the intriguer!

SLIPPY One must do what one must do.

(HUTZIBUTZ *enters through middle door.*)

SLIPPY (*observing him, to himself*) So, the bad penny Hutzibutz turns up again! (*Exits through middle door.*)

HUTZIBUTZ (*stepping forward with an accusing look*) There he was with you again!

ISABELLA Yes, is that any wonder, when one is caught up in such plans?

HUTZIBUTZ You seem to have forgotten what I keep telling you, that I only went along with this as a joke!

ISABELLA Yes, but how am I to—?

HUTZIBUTZ I've seen this twice, and if I see it one more time—

ISABELLA What then?

HUTZIBUTZ (*with great seriousness*) Then I'll have seen it a third time. (*Exits through middle door.*)

ISABELLA I can't help laughing at that crazy Hutzibutz! (*Exits side door.*)

Scene 18

Choleric	Phlegmatic	Melancholy	Sanguine
BOYLE, NAPP, *then* WALBURGA	Empty stage	DOLE	BLYTHE

Melancholy

DOLE (*alone*) How shocking! And that the blow should come from the hand of a friend! (*Sinks into the chair, burying his face in his hands.*)

Sanguine

BLYTHE (*Enters through side door, greatly upset.*) My chosen one is utterly smitten with young Dole. The way she allows him to pay court to her—I can't bear to watch them in there—I must have another look— (*Hurries out through side door.*)

Choleric

BOYLE (*Enters through middle door.*) He has flown the coop, the rascal who laughed at me! But I'll find him yet—! (*Notices* NAPP, *who is sleeping in the chair.*) What's this—? My friend Storm, perhaps? No doubt about it! Storm, friend of my youth? Wake up! Damn, he's a sound sleeper! Storm! (*Shakes him.*) Hi there, wake up!

NAPP (*awakening with difficulty*) All right, all right, who is it!

BOYLE Your friend, embracing you with warmest fervor after all these long years!

NAPP All right, all right, but I was resting so well just now!

BOYLE What? Sleep is dearer to you than waking in the arms of your friend!

NAPP But I was having the sweetest dreams.

WALBURGA (*Enters through the side door.*) I hear the voice of my betrothed!

NAPP Oh my beloved!

Melancholy

DOLE Air! Air! A great weight lies on my chest! I must have fresh air! (*In great agitation runs out through middle door.*)

Choleric

NAPP (*to* WALBURGA) Permit me but one kiss upon this hand of hands!

BOYLE (*aside, but loudly*) He pays absolutely no attention to me!

NAPP (*to* BOYLE) We shall have plenty of time for talk. Now I must see that the second part of my dream continues the theme of the first. (*Kisses* WALBURGA'S *hand and falls asleep again.*)

Sanguine

BLYTHE (*Enters angrily through side door.*) It is getting worse and worse— Slippy—! If only Slippy were here, I must see if I can find him! (*Runs out through side door as if his hair were on fire.*)

Choleric

WALBURGA What a dear man!

BOYLE (*vehemently and angrily*) He is a sloth, an unthinking, unfeeling block of wood!

WALBURGA Yet he does feel something, love for me!

BOYLE You're not going to—

WALBURGA I trust you will permit me to love the man whom you yourself have chosen for me.

BOYLE To your room!

WALBURGA I'm going, but—

BOYLE Without another word!

(WALBURGA *exits with feigned reluctance.*)

BOYLE It's enough to drive one mad! (*looking at* NAPP) You—you—walrus! (*Exits through side door.*)

Scene 19

Choleric	Phlegmatic	Melancholy	Sanguine
NAPP, *then* NANETTE	CYPRIAN, *then* STORM	HUTZIBUTZ, JOY, *then* LISETTE, MARGARET, THE COMPANY, IRENE, DOLE	BLYTHE, PAINE, *then* DARK, MRS. NIGHTSHADE, SLIPPY

Melancholy

HUTZIBUTZ (*entering through middle door with* JOY) You have really got me in a pickle.

JOY (*hurriedly*) I have no time now to listen to you, dear painter. If only someone were at hand—the guests are already arriving! (*to*

HUTZIBUTZ) Help me get things ready for the ball and I'll make it worth your while. Take these wax candles (*gives him a package*) and put them in the candelabra and light them. Quickly now! Light! Let's have some light in here! (*Rushes out through middle door.*)

HUTZIBUTZ Fine with me. (*Does as* JOY *has ordered.*)

(LISETTE *enters through middle door with four lamps, places two on the table and takes the remaining two through the side door.*)

Choleric

NANETTE (*Enters through the middle door with four lamps, places two on the table and says to* NAPP, *who sleeps on peacefully.*) I wish you a very good evening! (*She carries the other two lamps through the side door, returns a bit later and exits through middle door.*)

Sanguine

PAINE (*Comes in with* BLYTHE *through the side door.*) I didn't want to say anything to you in there; you keep talking about the ball—I have cancelled it.

BLYTHE What? My ball, that I was so much looking forward to, you cancelled it?

PAINE I love solitude, quiet, gloom!

Melancholy

HUTZIBUTZ (*busy with the lighting of the candles*) The illumination is almost complete. (*to the returning* LISETTE) Will you help me, Miss? (LISETTE *take a light and helps him; before they are finished,* JOY *arrives with the company.*)

Phlegmatic

CYPRIAN (*Enters with four lamps, places two on the table and carries the other two through the side door.*) This job is too much! (*Exits through side door. He returns a bit later, after the music has begun, and exits through middle door.*)

Sanguine

BLYTHE (*very out of sorts*) But I invited such merry, amusing guests—

PAINE All has been cancelled. You should make the acquaintance of others who will offer a more suitable alternative to your boisterous pleasures.

Melancholy

(*The* COMPANY *enters with* JOY *during the ritournelle.*)

Chorus with solo

CHORUS (*to* JOY)
>Responding to your call, we've come to you.
>The question now is, are we welcome too?

(IRENE *enters through side door and with much shyness welcomes the guests introduced by* JOY.)

Sanguine

(*Dumb-show between* BLYTHE *and* PAINE.)

(ISABELLA *enters through middle door with lamps and takes them to the side room.*)

(SEPHERL *enters simultaneously from middle door and places two lamps on the table, then exits.*)

(*The music assumes a very sombre quality as* DARK *and* MRS. NIGHTSHADE *enter through middle door, both dressed in mourning. They are introduced to* BLYTHE *by* PAINE *and pay their respects to him in the following mournful duet.*)

>We are pleased to discover that fortune condones
>Our meeting with you in this valley of bones.

(BLYTHE *is utterly bewildered and does not know how to conceal his annoyance with this disquieting company. Towards the end of the music* SLIPPY *enters by middle door.*)

Melancholy

(*Music merry, as before*)

CHORUS
>So let us dedicate these hours to delight,
>And rejoice in our new friends with all our might!

(*The orchestral music ends.*)

JOY (*after the music has ended*) In with the musicians! Out with the furniture! (*Four* MUSICIANS *enter and* LISETTE *and* MARGARET *move aside some of the furniture.*)

Sanguine

SLIPPY (*softly to* BLYTHE) What the devil kind of company does your lordship keep?

BLYTHE (*softly to him*) What a crew of crepehangers my old friend has brought along, he who used to be the jolliest of companions! I don't know what to do!

SLIPPY (*as above*) For the moment nothing can be done.

Melancholy

JOY Play on, we'll start dancing right now! Now to make some quick arrangements—I'll turn the kitchen and cellar inside out! (*Hurries out through middle door, followed by* HUTZIBUTZ.)

IRENE (*to herself*) I tremble to think of Father's return!

Sanguine

PAINE This evening we shall devote to a reading. I have here an edifying volume.

DARK It's a pity I don't have my eyeglasses with me, or else I'd do the reading.

PAINE My eyes are already filled with tears, I cannot. (*to* BLYTHE) Here, friend, could you—?

BLYTHE Leave me out of it!

PAINE (*to* SLIPPY) Here stands a superfluous fellow. (*Hands him the book.*)

SLIPPY If you will be so kind— (*All sit down around the table.*)

Melancholy

(*A waltz is played and dancing begins. The dance music continues throughout the entire scene.*)

Sanguine

SLIPPY (*reading*) "Almanac of Sorrows for the Woebegone, An Anthology of Doleful Reflections...."

BLYTHE (*to himself*) I could get along nicely without such a book.

SLIPPY (*reading*) "Hope is the light which promises to guide the traveler through the forests of the night to the long-awaited shelter, yet it is only a will-o'-the-wisp that leads one into the quagmire of misery and then mockingly vanishes." That's beautiful.

DARK *and* MRS. NIGHTSHADE Marvelous! Marvelous!

BLYTHE (*aside*) I'm about to be sick!

Melancholy

HUTZIBUTZ (*Entering through middle door with a tray of refreshments, speaks in the manner of a theater vendor.*) Lemonade, ices, almond milk, Barbaras,[3] punch! (*Serves those not dancing.*)

Sanguine

SLIPPY (*reading*) "Whenever you kiss a pretty girl, remember that behind those rosy cheeks lies corruption!"

DARK *and* MRS. NIGHTSHADE True, how true!

SLIPPY And so lovely!

BLYTHE (*aside*) This is too much for me!

Melancholy

JOY (*Having entered through middle door sees* HUTZIBUTZ *standing by idly.*) But why isn't the painter dancing?

HUTZIBUTZ (*to himself*) There aren't any customers of mine among the guests; fine, I'll play the painter. (*to* JOY) By your leave, sir. (*Asks a* YOUNG LADY *to dance and waltzes very clumsily downstage.*) Why, I'm a dancer too, and didn't even know it! Really, sometimes I even outdo myself!

DOLE (*Enters through middle door.*) What's this? (*Stands thunderstruck; the music stops.*)

JOY (*to* DOLE) They are only acquaintances of mine, I invited them.

DOLE (*struggling manfully to contain his fury*) Servants! You servants! Excuse me— (*Exits through side door, followed by* IRENE.)

Sanguine

SLIPPY (*continuing to read*) "Before the discovery of wine, mankind lived to a much more advanced age; reflect, therefore, each time you drink a glass of wine, you are taking a sip from the goblet of mortality."

BLYTHE (*aside*) I can't stand any more of this, I'm getting up and leaving. (*Exits through side door.*)

Phlegmatic

STORM (*Enters with* CYPRIAN *through middle door.*) My servant still hasn't come from the inn?

CYPRIAN No!

Melancholy

JOY (*to the* COMPANY) Let's to it! He's not going to embarrass us! (*to the* MUSICIANS) A galop, a galop!

HUTZIBUTZ Gallop or trot, it's all the same to me! (*The music resumes, and a galop is danced.*)

Phlegmatic

STORM (*haranguing* CYPRIAN) Why isn't that rascal here yet?

CYPRIAN (*taken aback*) It's not my fault! (*Exits through middle door.*)

(STORM *paces impatiently up and down.*)

Sanguine

DARK Where did our host go? We must follow him.

(DARK, MRS. NIGHTSHADE, PAINE, *and* SLIPPY *exit through side door.*)

Melancholy

JOY (*during the galop*) That room in there is larger! (*pointing to the side door*) Let's go! Keep on dancing! (*All dance out through the side door.*) You musicians, come along! (*The* MUSICIANS *follow the company, continuing to play the galop.*)

Scene 20

Choleric	Phlegmatic	Melancholy	Sanguine
NAPP,	STORM, YAWN,	DOLE,	BLYTHE,
WALBURGA,	AGNES, *then*	JOY	PAINE
BOYLE,	JACOB *and*		
then JACOB	CYPRIAN		

Phlegmatic

YAWN (*entering through side door with* AGNES, *to* STORM) You are a true friend! (*Explains to him in dumb-show what has happened.*)

Choleric

BOYLE (*Entering with* WALBURGA *through side door, immediately turns to leave by middle door.*) At least I don't have to converse with that—

JACOB (*Enters through middle door.*) Does Mr. Boyle live here?

BOYLE I am he. What do you want?

JACOB My master, Mr. Storm.

BOYLE There he is. (*pointing to* NAPP)

JACOB (*looking at the sleeping man*) He?! Hahaha! That's ridiculous! I see I have come to the wrong place. (*Exits by middle door.*)

Phlegmatic

STORM (*listening to* YAWN'S *account*) Hell and damnation!

Choleric

BOYLE (*shaking* NAPP) Hi there! Sir, wake up! Up! (NAPP *awakens. Explanations follow in dumb-show.*)

Phlegmatic

JACOB (*Enters through middle door with* CYPRIAN, *who attempts to deny him entry.*) I don't care what you say, it is his voice!

CYPRIAN But this is not Mr. Storm!

STORM Of course I am.

JACOB I ought to know my own master.

YAWN (*surprised*) Storm, Mr. Storm?

Choleric

BOYLE (*undeceived by* NAPP'S *words*) You are Mr. Napp? (*Explanations follow in dumb-show.*)

Phlegmatic

STORM Of course!

YAWN Then you are not my friend Napp? (*Explanations follow in dumb-show.*)

Choleric

NAPP Next door, you say? No matter, certain things remain unaltered. (*with a tender glance to* WALBURGA) I know what I must do. (*Exits through middle door.*)

(*Converses with* AGNES *concerning what has occurred.*)

Phlegmatic

STORM What a devilish mixup! Nevertheless, this coincidence has brought together two hearts that nothing now can sunder. I was to marry there next door, but that will be cancelled, cancelled at once! (*Exits through middle door.*)

(*Converses with* IRENE *concerning what has occurred.*)

Sanguine

BLYTHE (*reluctantly entering through side door, followed by* PAINE, *to whom he speaks*) No, no, don't take offense, but you repel me, my dear Joy!

PAINE (*astonished*) Dear Joy? You mock me, sir, my name is Paine.

BLYTHE (*astonished*) What? (*Explanations follow in dumb-show.*)

Melancholy

JOY (*to* DOLE, *who enters by side door*) Don't be angry with me!

DOLE That was too much, our bond of friendship is broken, Mr. Paine.

JOY (*astonished*) What? Mr. Paine? (*Explanations follow in dumb-show.*)

Scene 21

Choleric	Phlegmatic	Melancholy	Sanguine
STORM, BOYLE, WALBURGA	YAWN, AGNES, *then* NAPP	DOLE, JOY	BLYTHE, PAINE

Choleric

STORM (*rushing in through middle door*) Do you recognize your Storm?

BOYLE It's he! Into my arms! (*They embrace vehemently.*)

Phlegmatic

NAPP (*Enters slowly through middle door.*) Friend Yawn!

YAWN What do I see here?

NAPP I am the real one, old Napp is here!

YAWN Rush into my arms!

(*Both men move slowly towards one another and embrace very lethargically.*)

Melancholy

JOY (*Enlightened as regards the misunderstanding, laughs loudly.*) Hahahaha! I beg your pardon!

Sanguine

PAINE (*Enlightened as regards the misunderstanding, says with grim astonishment.*) Hideous error! Doubly dreadful, should you deny me your daughter's hand! But you won't do that! She loves me!

BLYTHE Listen—

PAINE No, not a word, until I have relinquished my claim next door! (*Exits through middle door.*)

BLYTHE (*calling after him*) Permit me—!

Melancholy

JOY By the way, I have come to an understanding with your daughter, there's nothing you can do about that! Everything next door will be declared null and void! A fiancée by mistake—how charming! (*Hurries out laughing through middle door.*)

DOLE (*calling after him*) Sir!

Scene 22

Choleric	Phlegmatic	Melancholy	Sanguine
BOYLE, WALBURGA, STORM	YAWN, AGNES, NAPP	DOLE, PAINE	BLYTHE, JOY

Choleric

STORM (*to* BOYLE) You do not yet know the consequences of this misunderstanding; possibly you will find them unpleasant. But I cannot help that. I fell in love with Mr. Yawn's daughter when I took her for your daughter, and in spite of everything she is to be my wife; with your daughter, therefore, it's all over.

BOYLE (*indignantly*) How? What?

Phlegmatic

NAPP (*as a result of the foregoing pantomime*) I am sorry, but my mind is made up; I'm such an impetuous fellow.

Melancholy

PAINE (*entering middle door suppressing his tears*) Your friend Paine stands before you.

DOLE Is it possible? (*The two men fling themselves weeping into one another's arms.*)

(*Conversation ensues regarding the misunderstanding which has occurred, at the end of which* PAINE *relinquishes the hand of Dole's daughter.*)

Sanguine

JOY (*entering by middle door*) Blythe!

BLYTHE It is he! Joy! Comrade! (*They embrace joyfully.*)

255

(*Conversation ensues regarding the misunderstanding which has occurred, at the end of which* JOY *relinquishes the hand of Blythe's daughter.*)

Choleric

STORM (*to* BOYLE) Should you demand satisfaction, I shall be at your service. At the moment I am in a hurry to fetch a notary.[4] (*Exits by middle door.*)

Phlegmatic

NAPP I must run quickly for a notary. (*Exits by middle door.*)

Sanguine

BLYTHE What's this? You're going to jilt my daughter?

JOY I am sorry if you are angry, but it cannot be helped.

Phlegmatic

YAWN (*to* AGNES) Daughter, it seems to me he has spurned you.

Melancholy

DOLE (*deeply moved*) You reject the hand of my daughter? Ye gods, must I suffer this humiliation too?

PAINE Fate will have it so. (*Exits by middle door.*)

(DOLE *collapses in the chair, his head on the arm.*)

Phlegmatic

AGNES What harm has been done? I still have Mr. Storm.

YAWN (*somewhat vexed*) Yes, but I don't like him, this Storm!

Sanguine

BLYTHE And the weeping willow over there?

JOY Friend, *de gustibus*—in a word, everything must be put right today! Adieu, friend, goodbye! (*Exits by middle door.*)

Choleric

BOYLE (*in heated conversation with* WALBURGA) And I won't have that sloth!

WALBURGA Then who am I to marry?

Scene 23

Choleric	Phlegmatic	Melancholy	Sanguine
BOYLE,	YAWN, AGNES,	DOLE, IRENE,	BLYTHE, *then*
WALBURGA,	*then* ROBERT	*then* FELIX,	SLIPPY, GUIDO,
then EDMUND		HUTZIBUTZ	ISABELLA, MARIE,
			MRS. KORBHEIM

Sanguine

SLIPPY (*entering by side door*) I'd like to know what Master Guido is always whispering to Mrs. Korbheim about.

BLYTHE Ah, we'll put a stop to that! I know how! (*Speaks softly with* SLIPPY.)

Choleric

EDMUND (*Enters through middle door carrying the cap which Slippy wore when disguised as a braggart soldier.*) Mr. Boyle, your opponent has been vanquished!

BOYLE (*overjoyed*) Can it be?

EDMUND Here is the giant's cap, which I took from him as a token of victory. (*Hands it to him.*)

Sanguine

SLIPPY (*as a result of the conversation*) You don't want Paine and Joy doesn't want your daughter; under the circumstances, that is the wisest thing to do. (*Calls through the side door.*) Mr. Dole!

Choleric

BOYLE Then you—?

EDMUND Shot him through the right shoulder.

Sanguine

(GUIDO *enters through side door.*)

BLYTHE (*to* GUIDO) I must tell you straight from the shoulder—

ISABELLA (*entering by side door, to* GUIDO) Mr. Dole, you are to come to Mrs. Korbheim.

BLYTHE You be quiet!

Choleric

BOYLE This noble deed deserves a noble reward. Walburga! (*Leads his daughter to* EDMUND.)

Sanguine

BLYTHE (*to* GUIDO) What are you up to with Mrs. Korbheim? These gallantries and courtesies are not appropriate in a fiancé.

GUIDO Fiancé?

BLYTHE Especially my daughter's!

(MARIE *enters with* MRS. KORBHEIM *through side door.*)

Choleric

WALBURGA (*with heartfelt thanks*) Dad—!

BOYLE Don't thank me, you'll take him because I desire it, not because you do. I'll teach you to be obedient! (*Exits by side door.*)

Sanguine

GUIDO Is it possible? But you wanted—

BLYTHE (*observing* MARIE) Enough said, there you have her! (*Leads him to* MARIE.) You carry on your conversation there, and (*turning with a gallant flourish to* MRS. KORBHEIM) I'll carry on mine here.

Melancholy

(FELIX *opens the middle door, sees* DOLE, *who sits motionless in the chair. Signals to two* PORTERS, *who follow him carrying a large picture. They enter quietly,* FELIX *takes the easel and carries it quietly over to* DOLE, *placing the new picture upon it with care. The porters depart at once.*)

Phlegmatic

(ROBERT *enters by middle door with two porters carrying a large, handsome chaise longue. The porters place the chair downstage.*)

YAWN Is this a vision or a fantasy?

Melancholy

DOLE (*Turns by chance and catches sight of the new picture, which is a life-sized portrait of his wife.*) Do my senses deceive me? It is she! She who can never be forgotten! Is it magic or reality! To what do I owe this bliss?

FELIX (*coming forward*) To love!

IRENE (*entering by side door*) What is the matter, Father?

Phlegmatic

ROBERT (*to* YAWN) Permit me to replace the demolished chair with this one.

YAWN Oh, oh, this is too much for my heart! (*Settles comfortably in the new chair.*) Ah, I sit much, but never before have I sat like this.

Melancholy

DOLE How could this be?

FELIX On the back of the minature of your daughter, which she gave me at our parting, there was a portrait of your spouse. In my spare time I made use of my talent as a painter to create this picture, in hopes that in this way I might win my way into your heart. Have I hoped in vain—?

DOLE (*overcome by emotion*) No, no, you are my son! (*Leads* IRENE *into his arms.*)

(HUTZIBUTZ *enters by side door and looks at the picture.*)

Phlegmatic

YAWN How can I ever repay you? Ask anything, anything!

ROBERT You know my only wish is for the hand of your daughter.

YAWN Take it, but it is far too little for such a pleasure! (*Nestles comfortably in the chair.*)

(ROBERT *embraces* AGNES.)

Choleric

(BOYLE *returns through side door.*)

Melancholy

HUTZIBUTZ Not bad, but compared with this one—! (*Holds the blackened picture up beside the other.*)

DOLE Out of the sanctuary, profane fellow!

HUTZIBUTZ It this any way to treat a budding artist?

DOLE Begone!

HUTZIBUTZ (*Exits by middle door.*)

Scene 24

Choleric	Phlegmatic	Melancholy	Sanguine
As before; **NAPP** (*with notary*)	As before; **STORM** (*with notary*)	As before; **JOY** (*with notary*)	As before; **PAINE** (*with notary*)

Choleric

NAPP Here, I have brought the notary!

BOYLE But not for yourself, for here (*pointing to* EDMUND) is the bridegroom!

NAPP Don't say that!

WALBURGA (*apologetically*) Prior claims—

NAPP I've been swindled!

Phlegmatic

STORM Here, I have brought the notary!

YAWN But not for yourself, for here (*pointing to* ROBERT) stands the bridegroom!

STORM Damn and blast!

AGNES (*apologetically*) Prior claims—

STORM I have been hornswoggled!

together

Melancholy

JOY Here, I have brought the notary!

DOLE But not for yourself, for here (*pointing to* FELIX) is the bridegroom!

JOY What kind of funny business is this?

IRENE (*apologetically*) Prior claims—

JOY I've fallen between two chairs! (*Laughing and shaking his head, exits by middle door.*)

Sanguine

PAINE Here, I have brought the notary!

BLYTHE But not for yourself, for here (*pointing to* GUIDO) stands the bridegroom!

PAINE What a dreadful turn of affairs!

MARIE (*apologetically*) Prior claims—

PAINE Doubly dreadful turn of affairs! (*Exits by middle door, wringing his hands.*)

together

Phlegmatic

STORM Revenge! Bloody revenge! (*Exits in a fury by middle door.*)

Choleric

NAPP H'm! H'm! (*Exits slowly by middle door.*)

Sanguine

MARIE (*to* SLIPPY) Here is your reward. (*Gives him a purseful of ducats.*)

SLIPPY (*takes it*) I kiss your hand, but the sweeter reward stands here! (*pointing to* ISABELLA)

HUTZIBUTZ (*Entering simultaneously by middle door, steps between them.*) Too late! She's already spoken for!

ISABELLA (*to* SLIPPY, *who has begun to realize he has been deceived*) There's no more need for the trickster now that the trick has worked!

SLIPPY (*the scales falling from his eyes*) What do I see—?

HUTZIBUTZ A fox foxed, if you'll take a look in the mirror!

SLIPPY That's not nice. (*to himself*) But you'll pay for this. If I don't bring all these marriages to divorce within six weeks, my name isn't Slippy and I'll retire as an intriguer forever. (*Exits by middle door.*)

BLYTHE (*to* MRS. KORBHEIM, *pointing to* MARIE *and* GUIDO) If only the two weren't so different! Well, no matter.

Melancholy

FELIX

Four temperaments determine how one thinks,
And lend each feeling its distinctive hue,
Yet simple love all earthly creatures links,
And brings them all together, two by two.

Choleric, Phlegmatic, Melancholy, Sanguine

FULL CHORUS

In life things which seem to lie widely apart
Love combines as a single delight in the heart.

AMID UNIVERSAL MERRIMENT THE CURTAIN FALLS

---

1. The idiom "to lead one around by the nose" means the same thing in both German and English.

2. The rattling of keys in a theater was an expression of disapproval.

3. A popular drink made with tea, milk, egg yolks, and orange syrup.

4. Notaries in Nestroy's time handled a wide variety of legal matters, including the drawing up of marriage contracts and wills.

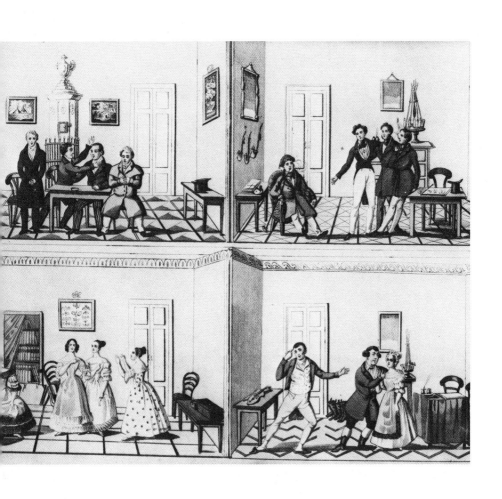

The House of Humors : Drawing by J. C. Schöller
(Bildarchiv of the Austrian National Library)